Data Processing

Volume 1   Principles and Practi...

GW00363535

The M & E Handbook Series

Data Processing

Volume 1 Principles and Practice

R G Anderson
FCMA, M Inst AM(Dip), FMS

Sixth edition

Pitman Publishing
128 Long Acre, London WC2E 9AN

© Longman Group UK Ltd 1987

First published in Great Britain 1974
Reprinted 1975 (twice), 1976
Second edition 1978
Third edition 1979
Reprinted 1981, 1982
Fourth edition 1983
Reprinted 1983
Fifth edition 1984
Reprinted 1986
Sixth edition (2 vols) 1987

British Library Cataloguing in Publication Data

Anderson, R.G.
    Data processing.——6th ed.——(M & E handbook
    series, ISSN 0265-8828)
    Vol. 1 : Principles and Practice
    1. Management——Data processing
    I. Title
    658′.05   HD30.2

    ISBN 0-7121-0696-0

Typeset by Avocet Marketing Services, Bicester, Oxon.
Printed and bound in Great Britain.

Contents

Part three   Checks, controls, security and processing techniques

Preface to the sixth edition

Since publication of the first edition of this M&E handbook, the subject has expanded from traditional data processing into the realms of information systems and related information technology. This has made it impossible for the subject to be covered in adequate detail in one volume and so it has been necessary to split the M&E handbook into two volumes.

This first volume deals with the fundamentals of data processing and covers the syllabuses of the following bodies:

The Chartered Association of Certified Accountants (ACCA) (Students taking Systems Analysis & Design should also read Volume 2.)

The Chartered Institute of Management Accountants (CIMA) (Students should also read Volume 2.)

The Institute of Chartered Accountants (ICA)

The Institute of Chartered Secretaries & Administrators (ICSA)

The Society of Company & Commercial Accountants (SCCA) (New syllabus—Information Technology)

The Association of Accounting Technicians (AAT) (Students taking Analysis of Systems & Design of Systems should also read Volume 2.)

The Institute of Data Processing Management (IDPM)

The Business and Technician Education Council (BTEC)

The Royal Society of Arts (RSA)

The City and Guilds of London Institute (CGLI)

The British Computer Society (BCS)

and many other bodies whose syllabuses concentrate on traditional data processing.

The content has been extensively revised and updated to take all recent developments into account.

Many subjects have been expanded. Data storage, for example, now includes inverted files, indexing methods and algorithmic address generation techniques. The latest developments in auditing computer systems and matters relating to optical discs and speech synthesis are also included. The section on distributed processing networks has been expanded to embrace ring, star and bus networks as well as close-coupled and value-added networks.

I have inserted new topics such as an appraisal of factors to consider when selecting a computer, practical examples of on-line operations relating to a building society and an insurance company, instructions on how a non-computer specialist can communicate with a computer and how on-line random files are updated. In addition, there is some material relating to multi-user and multi-tasking systems using windows. Matters relating to program maintenance and system modification requests are also dealt with.

The companion volume, Information Systems and Technology, covers management information systems and related information technology and is recommended to students preparing for professional examinations where a knowledge of systems concepts, systems behaviour, systems analysis and design, information systems, technology and management is required.

Acknowledgments. I gratefully acknowledge permission to quote from the past examination papers of The Chartered Institute of Management Accountants, The Association of Certified Accountants, the City and Guilds of London Institute and the Institute of Data Processing Management. The cooperation and assistance of the following organisations and persons, without whose help this book would not have been possible, are also gratefully acknowledged.

Apricot UK Limited: provision of photograph relating to the Apricot XEN computer.

Mr J K Atkin (author of *Basic Computer Science*): provision of information relating to bubble and holographic memory.

British Telecom: provision of information relating to Datel services, packet switching, System X and Kilostream.

Cadbury Limited: provision of details relating to the EAN bar code.

Compsoft Limited: details relating to their Data Management System.

Data Card (UK) Limited: provision of details and photographs relating to Data Key.

DVW Microelectronics Limited: provision of details and photograph of the Husky microcomputer.

IBM United Kingdom Limited: provision of information and various pamphlets and photographs relating to magnetic tape code, tape drives, 3081 computer, IBM 3290 Information Panel.

ICL: DNX-2000 digital PABX exchange and various other items.

Litton Business Systems Ltd: examples of Kimball tags.

MicroProducts Software Limited: details relating to accounting packages – BOS (Business Operating Software).

Midlands Electricity Board: supply of optical mark meter reading sheets and procedure chart.

Office Technology Ltd: details and photograph of the Information Management Processor.

Philips Data Systems: details and photograph of optical disc.

Quest Micropad Limited: details and photograph of Micropad.

Rank Xerox (UK) Limited: details and photographs of the Xerox 2700 distributed electronic printer, Xerox 9700 electronic printing system, diagram of mouse, details and diagram of Xerox 8000 Ethernet network system and the Star Information System together with diagrams of icons.

System C Limited: details relating to their program generator software.

Telford Management Services Ltd: details and photograph of TEL-time terminal system.

R G Anderson
February 1987

Part one
Profile of data processing and computing

1
Data processing and computing concepts

Data processing concepts

In the strict data processing context data may be defined as unprocessed information consisting of details relating to business transactions which are collected into homogeneous groups for input to a data/information processing system to produce a specific output, i.e. information.

The smallest unit of definable data is known as a 'data element', examples of which are name of customer, address of supplier, employee number, stock code and quantity in stock, etc. When data processing systems are designed data elements need to be specified precisely, including the name of the element, the number of characters it contains (size of the element), the type of character, whether alphabetic or numeric, and the range of values for validation purposes to ensure that data is correct before being processed. Data elements are also referred to as 'attributes' or 'fields'. (A data element is technically the logical definition of data whereas a field refers to the physical data within the element, e.g. the data element 'quantity in stock' is the name of the element which stores the actual quantity in stock.) Data elements or fields are grouped together to form a record relating to a specific entity. Other terms used to define a unit of data are 'data item' and 'variable'.

1. **Data processing defined.** Data processing is often a specialist activity performed by the administrative organisation for the

business and is concerned with the systematic recording, arranging, filing, processing and dissemination of facts relating to the physical events occurring in the business.

Before production can be commenced in the factory, raw materials and parts have to be procured, which involves the data processing system in the preparation of purchase orders. When supplies are received they have to be recorded on appropriate stock or job records, which again involves data processing. The accounts of suppliers have to be updated to show the value of the goods purchased from them and the remittances made to them.

When production is due to commence, materials and parts have to be issued to the production centres and suitability recorded on issue notes which are subsequently recorded on stock and job records. The issues are often priced and extended, which are also data processing operations.

Factory operatives are remunerated either for their attendance time, piecework or bonus earnings, and here the data processing system is concerned with wages calculation, preparation of payslips and payrolls and the collection and summarisation of data with regard to production orders or jobs.

On completion of production, the goods are despatched to customers, which involves the data processing system in the preparation of despatch documentation, invoices, sales ledger updating and the preparation of statements of account. Eventually, remittances are received from customers, which involves further data processing in respect of adjustments to the balances on customers' accounts.

The results of business operations for specific operation periods are summarised and presented to management in the form of operating reports, profit and loss statements and balance sheets. All of this, and more, is the province of data processing which, if effectively performed, may be classified as the information service of the business (*see* Figs. 1.1 and 1.2).

From this, it can be seen that data processing systems provide information and information provides the basis for managerial control of business operations to achieve corporate objectives as effectively as possible, which means making the most suitable decisions based on the information provided.

A management information system therefore embraces the data

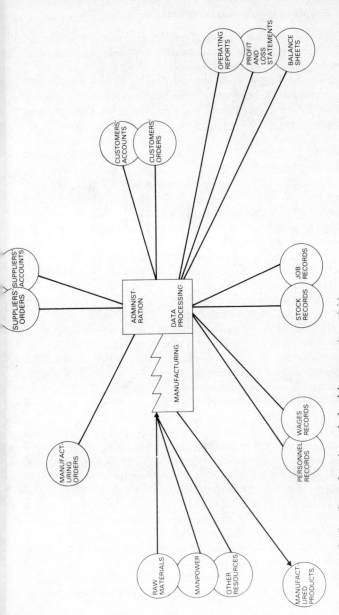

Figure 1.1 Outline of manufacturing and related data processing activities.

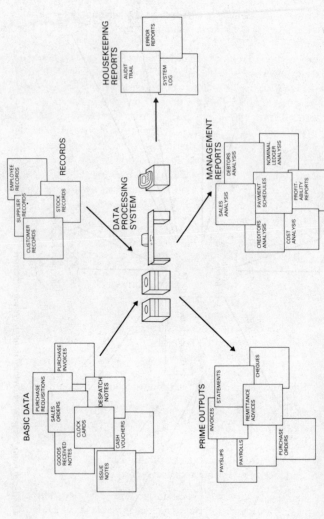

Figure 1.2 *The nature of data processing.*

BASIC DATA

- PURCHASE INVOICES
- PURCHASE REQUISITIONS
- SALES ORDERS
- DESPATCH NOTES
- GOODS RECEIVED NOTES
- CLOCK CARDS
- CASH VOUCHERS
- ISSUE NOTES

RECORDS

- EMPLOYEE RECORDS
- SUPPLIER RECORDS
- STOCK RECORDS
- CUSTOMER RECORDS

DATA PROCESSING SYSTEM

HOUSEKEEPING REPORTS

- AUDIT TRAIL
- ERROR REPORTS
- SYSTEM LOG

MANAGEMENT REPORTS

- SALES ANALYSIS
- DEBTORS ANALYSIS
- NOMINAL LEDGER ANALYSIS
- CREDITORS ANALYSIS
- PAYMENT SCHEDULES
- PROFITABILITY REPORTS
- COST ANALYSIS

PRIME OUTPUTS

- INVOICES
- STATEMENTS
- REMITTANCE ADVICES
- CHEQUES
- PAYSLIPS
- PAYROLLS
- PURCHASE ORDERS

processing systems, control systems (using information provided by the data processing system) and decision-making based on the facts indicated by the control systems.

2. **Processing operations.** In order to put data processing into its correct perspective, it is important to appreciate that although data processing activities are largely computerised there is very little actual 'computing' performed in most business applications. No doubt this is why the activity is called 'data processing' (*see* 1) and not 'computing'. Computing is a term restricted to performing 'number crunching', i.e. arithmetical calculations including adding, multiplying, subtracting and dividing as well as exponentiation (raising numbers to specified powers) etc. The primary operations for processing business data are summarised below.

(*a*) Capture and record data.

(*b*) Collect/transmit data.

(*c*) Control data throughout all stages of processing—prepare control totals.

(*d*) Prepare data in machine sensible form when relevant.

(*e*) Verify accuracy of data preparation.

(*f*) Input data to the computer.

(*g*) Validate data and generate control totals.

(*h*) Sort data to master file sequence.

(*i*) Compute value of variables.

(*j*) Update master files.

(*k*) Print list of transactions and control totals for accounting and audit trail purposes.

(*l*) Print schedules.

(*m*) Reinput data.

(*n*) Re-sort data for analysis purposes.

(*o*) Summarise data for management information.

(*p*) Produce analyses and statistical reports.

Examples of computing operations performed by a computer for a number of business applications include those shown in Table 1A.

It is the phenomenal speed of computers that makes them particularly well suited to pursuing activities that require instant solutions to complex dynamic problems. They are thus extensively used

Table 1A Computing examples

Application		Computations
Invoicing	Gross value	= Quantity sold × Price
	Discount	= Gross value × Discount rate
	Net value	= Gross value − Discount
	VAT	= Net value × VAT rate
	Invoice value	= Net value + VAT
Wages	Gross wages	= Standard hours × standard rate
		+
		Hours @ time and half × premium rate
		+
		Hours @ double time × premium rate
		or:
		Number of units produced × piece rate
		+
		Piecework supplement
	Net wages	= Gross wages − (income tax + standard deductions, etc.)
Stock control	New quantity in stock	= Old quantity in stock
		+
		Receipts
		+
		Returns to store
		−
		Issues
		−
		Returns to supplier
Electricity bill	Amount due	= Standing charge + Unit charge
	Unit charge	= (Present reading − Previous reading) × unit rate

in the control and monitoring of space vehicles; where they can respond to situations as they are occurring and in a fraction of a second make the corrections necessary to keep the vehicles on course. In addition, computers are ideal for high volume computing tasks such as the computation and analysis of statistical and mathematical data as well as scientific and engineering calculations.

The data processing model

3. Elements of a data processing system. A data processing system in its simplest form consists of three primary elements, i.e. input, processing and output. These elements apply whether the system is manual, mechanical or electronic. Data relating to business transactions such as items sold to customers, issues to production from the stores and hours worked by employees is input for processing. The data is subjected to processing operations in order to convert it into a more meaningful form prior to being output. The output, referred to as information, consists of documents such as invoices and payslips; schedules such as payrolls and sales summaries; and reports relating to customer credit standing and stock availability.

4. Characteristics of a data processing system. The characteristics of a data processing system may be contrasted with those of a factory manufacturing system; they are very similar although one processes raw facts and the other raw materials. The input to the factory system consists of raw materials for conversion into finished or partly finished products, whereas the finished product of a data processing system is information.

Two secondary, but nevertheless important, elements may be added to the primary elements of a data processing system. These are storage and control. Storage is concerned with filing documents and records relating to business transactions so that the state of affairs of specific business situations is readily available; e.g. amounts owing to customers, amounts owed by suppliers and the quantity of items in stock. Control relates to the monitoring by a supervisor to ensure that activities are conducted in the prescribed manner (*see* Fig. 1.3).

5. Elements of a computer system. A computer system also consists of the same five elements, viz. input, processing, output, storage and control. Special devices are used for input, such as terminal keyboards and bar code scanners. Processing is performed by the processor known as the central processing unit or CPU. After processing the data as prescribed by the stored program, the results are output to a specific type of output device which may be a line

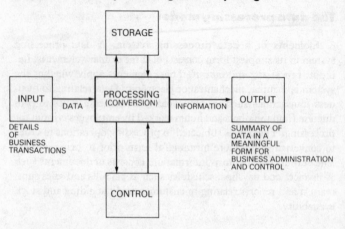

Figure 1.3 *Elements of a data processing system.*

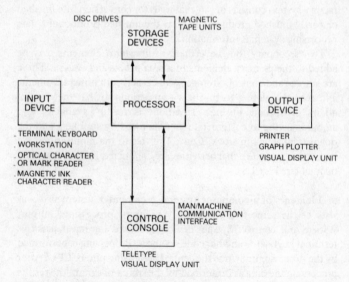

Figure 1.4 *Elements of a computer system.*

printer, video screen or plotter, or to backing storage—tape or disc (*see* Fig. 1.4).

Records are stored in master files consisting of tape or disc storage media. Control is effected by an internally stored program containing all the processing steps, known as instructions, which are executed to accomplish a specific task. A computer operator also controls processing activities by means of a console unit, which is an interface between the human element and the machine element, i.e. the computer system.

The processor consists of three elements (*see* 2:**16**), i.e the internal memory, the arithmetic/logic unit, usually abbreviated to ALU or AU, and the control unit. It may be said, therefore, that a computer consists of six elements, assuming the console to be an extension of the control element. These are input, internal storage, AU, control unit, output and backing storage.

6. Application processing. All applications, whether processed on a computer or performed manually, consist of primary activities such as those outlined in Table 1B below.

Table 1B   Relationship of input and output

Application	Input	Processing	Output
Payroll	Clock cards including hours worked and rates of pay	Computing gross to net wages, tax and standard deductions, updating payroll file	Payslips, payrolls, tax and deduction summaries
Stock control	Source documents indicating issues from store and receipts into store	Computing value of transactions, updating stock file	Stock list, reorder list
Sales	Sales orders indicating items required by customers	Computing value of items inc. VAT, updating customer file	Invoices, sales summaries, statements of account

(See Fig. 1.5)

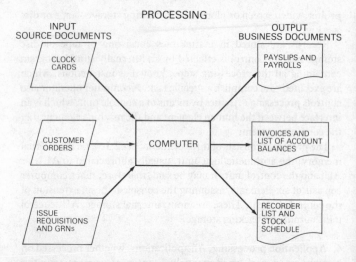

PROCESSING

INPUT
SOURCE DOCUMENTS

OUTPUT
BUSINESS DOCUMENTS

CLOCK
CARDS

CUSTOMER
ORDERS

COMPUTER

ISSUE
REQUISITIONS
AND GRNs

PAYSLIPS AND
PAYROLLS

INVOICES AND
LIST OF ACCOUNT
BALANCES

RECORDER
LIST AND
STOCK
SCHEDULE

Figure 1.5 *Relationship of input and output.*

The need for computer literacy in modern society

7. **Underlying philosophy.** Almost everyone will need to become familiar with data processing and computing (particularly micro-computing) to a greater or lesser extent, whether in the home, office, school, college or factory. The microcomputer is now widely accepted as a very efficient device for performing many types of operation, such as the display of business and other information from a Prestel database and for performing computations of varying types at high speed including professional, scientific, engineering and accounting calculations, as well as mathematical calculations for the classroom and word processing in typing and secretarial departments.

In business, the computer, whether a mainframe, mino or micro (*see* 2:5, **6**, and **12**), is recognised as a means of increasing administrative efficiency in payroll processing, sales invoicing, order processing, stock control and production planning. Insurance renewal notices and gas and electricity bills, for example, are usually printed by computer. This means that almost everyone will need to become what may be termed 'literate' in the computer context.

The nature of clerical work is changing as jobs are restructured to take advantage of the new technology. Many clerks are being provided with workstations, instead of pens and pads of forms, for dealing with customer orders being phoned in, so that the order details can be directly input to the computer for processing. This is known as an on-line order entry system. These new roles not only provide increased administrative efficiency but also increase the level of job enrichment as clerks become more interested and feel part of the new technology. Clerks do not need to become involved with the programming of computers as this is the prerogative of the systems staff. Package programs may be used for the various applications in most instances.

It is very interesting to obtain an understanding of how a computer functions and how it can be made to do what is required. Computer literacy requires some familiarisation with data processing and computer terminology, and students in particular are advised to consult a reference work such as the author's *A Concise Dictionary of Data Processing and Computer Terms*, published by Pitman Publishing. In addition, it is advisable and interesting to understand the nature of computer hardware, i.e. the machines and devices which make up a computer system and the nature of software, i.e. the programs without which a computer is inanimate.

8. Computing concepts. It is also advisable to obtain an appreciation of other computing concepts, such as the way in which characters are generated and stored in a computer. This knowledge is more for interest than operational necessity but does provide a greater understanding of computers. The stored program concept is of primary concern to the functioning of a computer.

Social aspects of computers

9. Primary problem. The primary problem stemming from the increasing use of computers in industry and commerce is the increasing level of unemployment as computer controlled manufacturing and administrative activities supersede the older technologies and working methods.

High unemployment causes many social problems and, as world demand for goods and services has declined, even fewer people are required to satisfy this demand, creating further redundancy in addition to that attributable directly to the implementation of computers.

High unemployment places an additional burden on the working population, as they are required to pay higher levels of taxation than would otherwise be required for the purpose of providing funds for the provision of unemployment pay and other social security payments.

Possibly the only remedy is a reduction in the world's population, reducing it to the level which is required to satisfy the world demand for goods and services and which the international economy can effectively cope with to provide a minimum standard of living for everyone.

How to overcome these problems is of paramount importance to the governments of the world. One remedy is the retraining of personnel in the new technologies: in the areas of computer-aided design, design of computers, design of systems and of programming techniques. This would reduce the level of unemployment caused by the technological factor.

Higher levels of productivity attained by automated processes and the use of robotics should reduce the cost of production. If such decreases are reflected in selling prices then demand, in theory, should increase thereby reducing the level of unemployment.

The retirement age could be lowered allowing the employed people to vacate their jobs earlier, thereby providing vacancies for the unemployed. This policy creates a financial burden on the government and the working population, as funds with which to finance early retirement pensions may create additional taxation unless monies for this purpose are redeployed from some other source.

10. Leisure time. The increasing amount of leisure time available to the population, owing to increasing unemployment and the shorter hours worked by the employed because of the introduction of new technology, has created a demand for more leisure facilities (at least for those who can afford them) thus providing some additional employment to offset the unemployment caused by the increasing use of computers (discussed in **9**).

11. Changing technology. Many people, particularly the older generation, cannot and do not want to change their ways of life, although changing technology tends to enforce this on the population. We are now approaching the era of supermarket shopping direct from the home by the use of home computers linked to Viewdata television sets; financial transactions occur between accounts filed electronically rather than between people, creating a cash-free society. Even the cheque, which itself replaced cash in many transactions, is on the way out. The transfer of documents by mail services is also on the wane as teletex services and electronic mail systems take over. Holidays may be booked and hotel accommodation and airline seats reserved directly by computer from the home.

12. Social unrest. Computerisation should lead to a more efficient society, on the other hand, it may also lead to social unrest as many people suffer from a lack of financial resources due to being made redundant. This can only be remedied in the long term by an enlightened world populace realising that technology marches on, the same as 'tide and time', and it is an irresistible force which must be accepted. Change must be seen as a challenge, not viewed apathetically, which must be taken up in the quest for a new and more interesting life style.

13. Benefits of using a computer in business. At one time, mainframes cost a fantastic amount of money and it was only the larger company that could justify their use both financially and from an administrative point of view, as it was necessary to have a computer due to the increasing volume of paperwork that had to be processed and the increasing cost of administrative staff. It was thought that computers would decrease costs, which no doubt they did in some instances, but in general other types of benefit were achieved. These are outlined below. Due to the high cost of mainframes it was often necessary to operate them round the clock as it were, that is on a multi-shift basis in order to achieve an acceptable pay-back period. No doubt this factor still applies in many instances. The cost of a microcomputer is very low, however, even for a complete business system, and its use quickly recoups its cost even when used only on an intermittent basis. The benefits obtained depend upon the type of computer and the use made of it. Prospective benefits depending upon individual circumstances may include some of those listed below:

(a) Improved customer relations due to fewer computational errors, more timely invoices and statements and speedier response to enquiries regarding the status of accounts and the availability of products.

(b) Improved cash flows due to improved sales accounting systems particularly those relating to credit control, invoicing and statement preparation.

(c) More effective control procedures including production control, sales control, cost control, budgetary control and credit control.

(d) Improved flow of information and information retrieval by means of on-line direct access enquiry systems.

(e) Greater control of raw material and other stocks allowing the investment in stock to be optimised and stock-out occasions to be minimised.

(f) Greater degree of systems integration on the basis that the output of one part of a system (sub-system) provides the input to a related sub-system which has the effect of eliminating duplication and delay.

(g) Simplification of problem solving by the use of problem solving software.

(h) Supply of information for improving managerial decisions.

Similar benefits to those outlined above may also be achieved by using a microcomputer in the business environment, but the benefits of using a personal micro are more likely to be from the enjoyment obtained from its use and from achieving skill in developing programs of various types.

Progress test 1

1. Specify the nature of data processing. (**1**)
2. List the primary operations relevant to processing business data. (**2**)

3. Specify the elements comprising a data processing system. (**3, 4**)

4. Specify the elements of a computer system. (**5**)

5. Indicate your views on the need for computer literacy in modern society. (**7, 8**)

6. Write an essay about the problems caused by increasing computerisation, suggesting how they might be solved. (**9–12**)(*C & G*)

7. What benefits would you expect a business to achieve from using a computer? (**13**)

2
Nature of computers

The computer defined

1. Definition of a computer. A computer consists of not one machine but a series of related machines. Normally, however, the generic term 'computer' is widely used to describe the central processing unit and the peripheral devices used for electronic data processing. The term will be used in this sense throughout the book.

A computer may be defined as a machine which accepts data from an input device, performs arithmetical and logical operations in accordance with a predefined program and finally transfers the processed data to an output device either for further processing or in final printed form, such as business documents, schedules and management control reports.

2. Purpose of computers. It is important to be aware of the purpose of computers, particularly microcomputers, in this modern technological age. They are primarily used in business for the processing of business data to maintain control of business operations and for the provision of information in a meaningful form for this purpose (*see* **1** and **3**).

Microcomputers are used in an information processing role, but may also be used for data processing activities in the smaller business. Many users employ them in a computing role for performing mathematical computations and statistical analysis. Many microcomputer installations are interconnected by a network, known as a Local Area Network (LAN), for the purpose of sharing resources such as high-speed storage, including a disc resident database and high speed printers.

Mainframe computers are used for large volume data processing commitments as they are capable of operating automatically at high speed. They print out invoices, payslips, payrolls, purchase orders, cheques and remittance advice slips in great volumes in a very short space of time according to the needs of individual systems.

Whichever type of computer is used for business data processing it is essential for information stored by the system to be as up to date as is necessary for effective control of business activities. This may require the implementation of real-time systems to control events as they happen. Information files must be updated as events occur so that they always represent the true status of the real life system. In other instances, pseudo real-time systems may be used as a matter of convenience rather than operational necessity. On-line systems enable direct enquiries to be made about such matters as stock availability and the credit status of customers. Instant responses are obtained from such enquiries and this improves administrative efficiency and customer relationships in many instances. On-line systems use direct entry keyboards for the input of data for processing, making the computer system more flexible and convenient to operate.

3. Mode of operation of a computer. Before computer processing can commence, the data must first be prepared in machine-sensible form. Data may be represented by patterns of magnetised spots (bits) on magnetic tape or disc. In addition, data may be input in the form of optical or magnetic characters.

Whichever mode of representing data is selected, it is necessary to have a special input device for the purpose of sensing the data and transferring it into the computer's internal memory for processing. The device may be a tape deck or disc drive, optical character reader or magnetic ink character reader, etc., depending upon the mode of input selected.

It is necessary to represent data for processing in a computer by binary coded characters which create pulse sequences (electrical flows) to allow data to flow through electronic circuits for processing. As the pulse sequences are represented by 'on' and 'off' electrical states this forms the basis of representing data in binary code. Binary is a two-state number system which is compatible with electrical flows which are also two-state, 'on' and 'off'. The two numbers of the binary number system are '1' and '0' and these are represented by an electrical 'pulse' and 'no pulse' signal respectively. Combinations of pulses, that is sequences of 'on' and 'off' states, are the basis of forming binary coded characters. Each character is formed by a series of binary digits referred to as 'bits', which is a contraction using the first and last letters of 'binary digits'. Characters consist of 8 bits known as a byte.

It is important to appreciate that descriptive data elements such as customer, supplier and employee names and addresses, etc. are processed in binary coded characters but data to be used in calculations, i.e. quantities and prices, must be processed in pure binary form.

The data is processed at electronic speed under the control of the computer's control unit and the internally stored program. All operations are performed automatically and the output is usually produced by an output device known as a line printer.

Master files are usually stored magnetically in the form of magnetic tapes or magnetic discs. Programs are stored on either magnetic tape or magnetic disc.

It is normal practice to have the input, output and storage devices attached to the central processing unit which controls their use. In this case, the devices are said to be 'on-line'. Off-line relates to the use of devices which are not connected to and are therefore not controlled by the processor, i.e. the main computer. An example of this is encoding data to magnetic tape by a stand-alone encoder or the use of a key-to-disc data preparation system.

A computer may be used for an infinite variety of tasks, including the preparation of payrolls, payslips, invoices, statements and purchase orders as well as updating master files containing historical records relating to employees, stocks, suppliers' accounts, customers' accounts, costs and production. They are also used for planning, problem-solving and presenting to management information on which to base decisions (*see* Fig. 2.1).

Spectrum of computers—mainframes, mini- and microcomputers

4. **Difficulty of classifying computers.** It is very difficult to classify

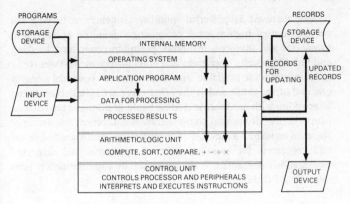

Figure 2.1 *Mode of operation of a computer.*

computers into specific types as there is a tendency for their operating characteristics to overlap, particularly in respect of storage capacity and speed of operation. It is useful, however, to be able to categorise them into mainframes, minis and micros for discussion and comparison purposes. It is often necessary to compare different models to assess their relative advantages and disadvantages in relation to their suitability for specific applications in a particular business.

5. Mainframe computer. Initially when computers came on the scene, the term mainframe referred to the main structure or framework of a central processing unit on which the arithmetic unit, main memory and control unit were mounted. The term now tends to be used in a number of ways, mainly to distinguish a large batch-processing/real-time computer from the smaller mini and microcomputers. The modern mainframe often supports a database accessible by distributed mini- or microcomputers.

A mainframe is the largest type of computer used for business and accounting applications in various environments including central and local government and other institutional bodies, such as professional organisations, universities and polytechnics. There is a tendency in the larger organisation to group together banks of mainframes to form supercomputers. As stated previously, mainframes are used as powerful 'number crunchers' satisfying the requirement of high volume processing, including holiday confirmations and invoices, insurance premium reminders, banking and building society operations and hotel management systems.

Mainframes are available with the features of powerful minis at one end of the range and at the other there are installations filling large rooms with hardware including banks of magnetic tape drives, printers, disc drives and communication equipment consisting of banks of modems in racks, device controllers, multiplexors, front-end processors for handling terminal operations and dispersed workstations connected to the processor by communication lines (*see* Fig. 2.7 and 2.8).

6. Minicomputer. This type of computer performs data processing activities in the same way as a mainframe but on a smaller scale. They are often used by medium sized businesses for stock control and invoicing, etc. The cost of minis is lower and generally suits the needs of the medium size business. Data is usually input by means of a keyboard. As the name implies, a minicomputer is small compared with a mainframe and may be called a scaled-down mainframe as the processor and peripherals are physically smaller. Minis have a memory capacity in the region of 2 Megabytes whereas the larger mainframe has a capacity in excess of eight Megabytes. In contrast, micros have a memory capacity in the region of 64–512K bytes (*see* **30**). A typical mini consists of the following.

(*a*) Processor 512K–4M bytes.

(*b*) Video screen (display terminal—up to 24 in some instances).

(*c*) Integrated disc unit (often incorporated in processor cabinet). Capacity in the region of 80 to 320 Megabytes.

(*d*) Cassette unit (often incorporated in processor cabinet).

(*e*) Printers with a speed in the region of 900 lpm.

(*f*) Tape drives.

Originally, minicomputers were developed for process control and system monitoring, etc. They were complicated to program and had minimal input/output capabilities as they were mainly concerned with 'number crunching' rather than handling large amounts of data relating to business transactions. However, they are now fully developed, powerful computers with a wide range of

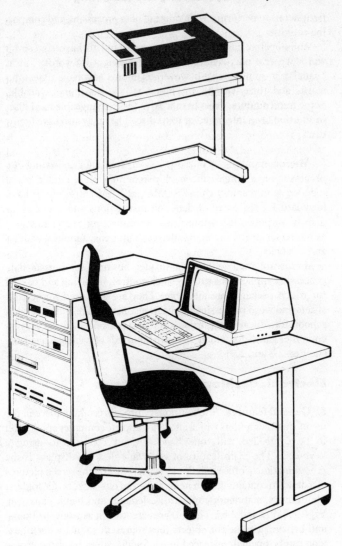

(Courtesy NCR Limited)

Figure 2.2 *Minicomputer configuration.*

peripherals to perform a wide range of data processing and computing activities.

Minis operate faster than micros and tend to have sixteen-bit words whereas micros have tended to have eight-bit words. This is changing to some extent, however, as micros now have sixteen-bit words and thirty-two-bit machines will be becoming available. Some minicomputers also have a drive for exchangeable hard discs in addition to an integrated or fixed disc. They may also have floppy discs.

7. Microcomputers. A micro is a small computer consisting of a processor on a single silicon chip mounted on a circuit board together with memory chips, ROMs and RAM chips, etc. It has a keyboard for the entry of data and instructions and a screen for display purposes. It has interfaces for connecting peripherals such as plotters, cassette units, disc drives, light pens, a mouse, paddles and joysticks.

Micros are used within the smaller business for normal data processing applications such as stock control, invoicing and payroll for which packages are available. They are also used for spreadsheets and word processing applications. Micros are widely used in schools for educational purposes and on a personal basis for playing computer games for which there are hundreds of packages available (*see* Fig. 2.3 and 2.9).

Electronic desktop display systems

8. General features. A revolutionary process is taking place in the use of small computers which allows a complete computer application to be controlled with one hand without recourse to using a keyboard. The main feature of electronic desktop displays is the representation of office functions by displaying on the screen pictures of a desktop containing such items as in- and out-baskets, file folders, file drawers, stationery cupboard, calculator and blank paper (*see* Figs. 2.4, 2.5 and 2.6). The pictures are known as icons (or Ikons) and behave just like the objects they represent so that a document icon can be opened, or placed into a folder icon in the same way as in a normal office operation. Other icons provide access to the shared resources of the network as shown by the printer, in-basket,

Figure 2.3 *Apricot XEN.*

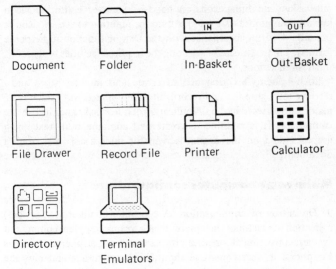

Figure 2.4 *Examples of icons. (Courtesy Rank Xerox (UK) Limited)*

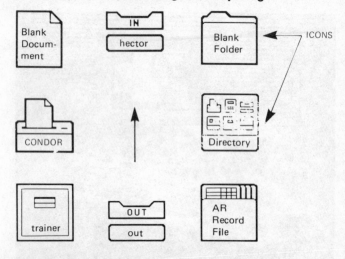

Figure 2.5 *Electronic desktop display indicating the nature of icons.*
(Courtesy Rank Xerox (UK) Limited)

out-basket and filing icons. A hand-held cursor control device known as a 'mouse' (*see* 4:**37**) is used for pointing to specific icons (*see* Fig. 4.19) in accordance with the task or function to be performed. This is a means of selecting the required facilities to achieve the desired actions.

Such systems are designed to create and modify, store and retrieve text, graphics and records in an automated way which is a major step forward in the simplification of office tasks and the use of computers. It is possible to create and combine both text and graphics data on the display screen for integration in a single document.

Mainframe computer configurations

9. Definition of configuration. A computer configuration is the collection of machines (hardware) which form a complete computer system; consisting of a central processor and its peripheral devices. Peripheral devices consist of input, backing storage and output devices which are normally connected to, and controlled by, the

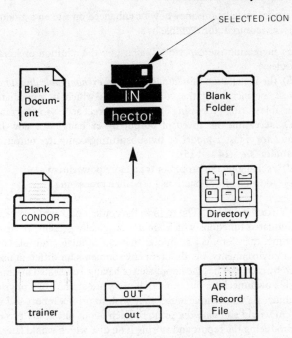

Figure 2.6 *Electronic desktop display showing selection of icon.*
(Courtesy Rank Xerox (UK) Limited)

processor. Modern computer technology is such that a wide range of peripheral devices and processors are available from which to build the computer configuration most suitable for the processing needs of a particular business. The choice of the most suitable configuration is established during the feasibility study.

A computer configuration is selected initially to suit both the current and the foreseeable future needs of the business with regard to the volume and type of data to be processed.

Eventually, it may be necessary to increase the processing power of the computer installation to contend with increasing volumes of data and the need for more management information. At one time, under these circumstances, it was necessary to change the existing computer for a more powerful model, but this is now unnecessary.

Computer installations may now be enhanced on site on a modular basis, as required, for example by:

(*a*) increasing the *capacity of storage* by the addition of storage modules;

(*b*) the installation of *additional fixed or exchangeable disc storage devices* for increasing the volume of data which is immediately accessible during processing or to obtain direct access to programs;

(*c*) increasing the speed of output by exchanging a slow line printer for a faster model or by substituting computer output by microfilm (*see* 5:**14** and **16**);

(*d*) exchanging the processor for a more powerful model;

(*e*) addition of workstations for on-line processing.

10. Virtual machine. The term in the context of computers refers to simulated functions which are not physically present. A virtual machine, therefore, is a computer that can simulate multiple computer environments, i.e. different environments for different users whereby each user has the impression of having a dedicated machine, i.e. his own machine but in fact all users are sharing one physical machine. As an example a user may wish to print a report and the system would simulate the printer which is not physically present by producing the report and storing it on disc which would later be output to the printer. Refer also to virtual storage (6:**29–30**) and mainframe operating systems (20:**11–13**).

11. Batch processing configuration. The older type of third generation computer configuration (which came into existence around 1964) typically consists of the following (*see* Fig. 2.7).

(*a*) *Input devices.*

(*i*) A card reader with a reading speed of 300 or 600 cards a minute. This device would only be used for transferring transaction data into the computer's working store.

(*ii*) A paper tape reader may be used (as an alternative, or in addition, to a card reader) capable of transferring 1,000 characters a second into the computer's working store.

Data may be captured in paper tape as a by-product of other accounting machine operations by means of a tape punching attachment.

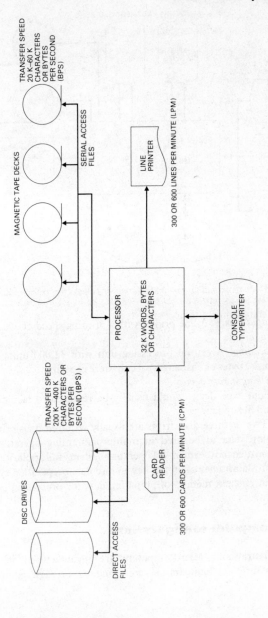

Figure 2.7 Older type of batch processing mainframe computer configuration.

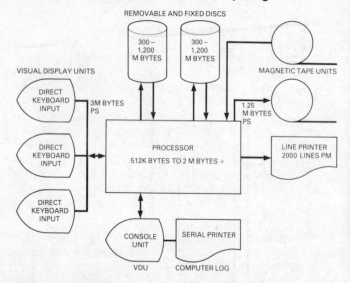

REMOVABLE AND FIXED DISCS

Figure 2.8 *Diagram outlining the main features of a typical modern mainframe computer.*

(b) *Output device.* A line printer with a printing speed of 300 or 600 lines a minute.

(c) *Processing.* A central processing unit with 32,000 units or more (words, bytes or characters) of core store capacity.

(d) *Backing storage devices.*

(i) Four tape decks would usually be required to facilitate sorting and file updating.

(ii) Two or three disc drives are usually required for storing master files, data to be used in multiprogramming operations required on demand, segments of operating systems and application programs. Mainframes often use key-to-disc data preparation systems as an efficient method of preparing data for processing (*see* 4:**6**).

Microcomputer configurations

12. Configurations. Microcomputers are manufactured in a number of different configurations according to the design requirements of a particular computer manufacturer. Basic configurations can be enhanced by add-on units such as printers and disc drives, as indicated above. Some are fully integrated units with a processor and memory, a visual display unit (VDU), a keyboard, built-in cassette units and/or disc drives.

A microcomputer for business use would require backing storage devices and a printer, but it is possible to purchase only the basic unit for personal computing, for playing computer games or for mathematical, statistical and financial calculations, thereby saving the expense of purchasing discs and a printer. It may be impractical however, even for personal computing, to load programs, especially lengthy ones, through the keyboard each time they are to be run, in which case it would be advantageous to have at least a cassette unit (*see* Fig. 2.9).

13. Elemental structure of a microcomputer. A microcomputer including optional peripherals and other add-on units may consist of the elements listed below:

(*a*) 8, 16 or 32-bit processor;
(*b*) internal memory 64K–256K+;
(*c*) backing storage—cassette, floppy disc, microfloppy discs, microdrive, silicon disc or hard disc;
(*d*) keyboard and screen (input and output);
(*e*) interface (for the connection of peripherals);
(*f*) bus (communication and control channels);
(*g*) printer and/or plotter (multicolour text and graphics);
(*h*) pulse generator (clock);
(*i*) light pens, mouse, paddles/joysticks (graphics and games);
(*j*) software (programs).

14. Microprocessor. The microprocessor is that part of a micro-computer which contains the circuitry for performing arithmetic and logic operations, usually contained on a single silicon chip. It also interprets and executes instructions. It is the equivalent of the central processing unit of a mainframe computer.

15. Silicon chip. A small piece of silicon containing a completely unpackaged semiconductor device, i.e. a transistor, diode or

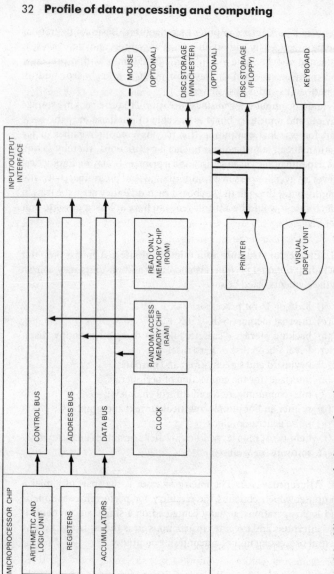

Figure 2.9 *Microcomputer business configuration.*

integrated circuit (IC). Due to technological developments it is now possible to have many thousands of transistors and diodes on a single chip of silicon with dimensions of not more than five mm square. This is largely due to the development of photolithographic techniques capable of forming transistors and their interconnecting circuits on a very small scale generating VLSI (Very Large Scale Integration). A silicon chip is produced by creating microscopic layers of metal and component material on a silicon wafer using successive photolithographic masks to obtain the required electronic components and the relevant microcircuits. A chip is encapsulated in a ceramic cover which has a number of connector pins for mounting on a printed circuit board (*see* Fig. 2.10). Chips are produced from a wafer which is a circular slice of semiconductor material cut from a single crystal of silicon. The slice is exposed to steam to form an oxide film on its surface. The slice is then treated by a photoengraving/diffusion/oxidisation process to form the circuits of the processor. The slice is then cut into many individual chips (*see* Fig. 2.11).

Figure 2.10 *Microprocessor chip.*

The central processing unit

16. General characteristics and compatibility of processors. The central processing unit or processor (often abbreviated to CPU) is the main unit within a computer system, and consists of three components: arithmetic/logic unit, control unit and internal working memory (*see* Fig. 2.12).

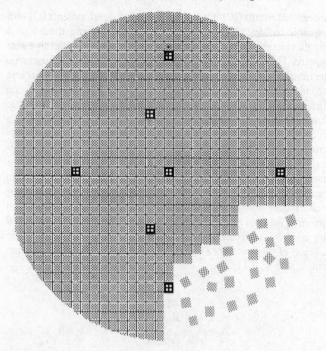

Figure 2.11 *Wafer.*

The processor accepts data for processing from an input device, carries out instructions specified by the program and outputs the results by means of an output device. Modern computers are often designed as a related family or series, whereby each processor in the series is compatible with every other. Compatibility is a design technique which enables any peripheral device to be connected to any processor in the series. The more powerful processors operate more efficiently, however, with the peripherals which are most suitable with regard to speed of operation. Program portability (transferability) is also a feature of computers within a series.

17. The power of processors. The power of processors increases progressively throughout the series, and may be distinguished by the following attributes:

CENTRAL PROCESSING UNIT (CPU)		
ARITHMETIC/LOGIC UNIT	INTERNAL WORKING STORAGE	CONTROL UNIT
ARITHMETIC: – ADDITION	ACCUMULATORS	INSTRUCTION REGISTER
– SUBTRACTION	SUPERVISOR PROGRAM	INSTRUCTION REGISTER
– DIVISION	APPLICATION PROGRAM	OPERATION DECODER
MULTIPLICATION	INPUT DATA	OPERATION DECODER
LOGIC: – COMPARING	WORKING STORAGE	ADDRESS REGISTER
– MATCHING	OUTPUT INFORMATION	ADDRESS REGISTER
– SORTING	CONSTANTS	INSTRUCTION COUNTER
DECISIONS	TABLES	INSTRUCTION COUNTER

Figure 2.12 *Major elements of a central processing unit.*

(a) store cycle time;

(b) storage capacity;

(c) number of data transfer channels;

(d) number of programs which may be interleaved for multi-programming operations;

(e) real-time processing capability;

(f) number of work stations which can be on-line for multi-user needs.

The control unit

18. Purpose and characteristics of a control unit. The overall control of a computer system is accomplished by the control unit, which is an integral part of the central processing unit.

The control unit coordinates the various parts of the computer system—the arithmetic/logic unit, internal working store and the peripheral units—to form a composite, integrated data processing system. In addition, the control unit also controls the transfer of data to, from and within the working store, as required by the program. The control unit also acts as a switching device to enable data pulses to flow along the appropriate channels.

A control unit, in respect of a single-address type of computer, consists of the following components:

(a) instruction register;
(b) decoder;
(c) address register;
(d) instruction counter.

The instruction register receives instructions from the internal working store in the sequence required for processing. The function or operation part of the instruction is then transferred to a decoder for translation of the operation to be executed, which causes the appropriate circuits to be connected for carrying out the operation in the arithmetic/logic unit.

The address register makes the required circuit connections to enable the data contained in a store location to be transferred to a specified accumulator via a register.

An instruction counter is used for recording the number of instructions executed, and is incremented by 1 after completing each instruction.

19. Cycle of operations. As both instructions and data are in binary form, there must be some means of enabling the computer to distinguish between them to avoid processing instructions as data. This is achieved by two distinct operation cycles known as 'instruction' and 'execution' cycles. The instruction cycle is concerned with connecting store locations to the adder to allow the transfer of data for processing. The execution cycle carries out the requirements of the instruction.

The arithmetic/logic unit

The arithmetic/logic unit performs arithmetic operations, data handling operations and logical functions. The unit consists of a 'mill' (adder/subtractor), electronic circuits, one or more 'working registers' to which operands may be transferred whilst being operated on and, in some computers, accumulators for storing the results of calculations.

20. Arithmetic operations. Although a computer performs all types of arithmetic operations—addition, subtraction, multiplication and division—it is important to appreciate that subtraction is performed by the addition of the 'complement' of the number to be subtracted to the other number involved in the calculation.

Multiplication is performed by combinations of 'shifts' to the left and addition. Division is performed by combinations of 'shifts' to the right and subtraction.

21. Logic operations and automatic decision making. Logic operations, as distinct from arithmetic operations, are concerned with comparing, selecting, matching, sorting and merging of data. When comparing data factors, the logical ability of the arithmetic/logic unit differentiates between positive and negative differences between the data factors and, in accordance with the results of the comparison, the alternative sequence of instructions to be executed is determined automatically. This is known as a 'conditional' transfer, and it provides the means for processing data on the 'exception' basis—that is, data requiring special processing according to the circumstances disclosed by the data. Conditional transfers of this type are appropriate when it is necessary to compare the credit limit of each customer with their account balance for the purpose of indicating by means of a special print-out, those customers whose balances exceed the credit limit for credit control. This is referred to as 'exception reporting'. In a stock control application the program may provide for the comparison of stock balances with reorder levels to indicate those items which require replenishment. This may be done either by printing out a reorder list or a purchase order directly. This may be referred to as 'automatic decision-making'.

Similarly, within a budgetary control application actual costs may be compared with budgeted costs and variance reports printed out, again on the basis of exception reporting. It is this important attribute of computers that makes them so useful as a tool of management.

Computer logic

22. Boolean algebra. The name is derived from the mathematician,

George Boole. The relevance of Boolean algebra to the logic of computers is based on two possible 'truth values' of a statement, i.e. true and false. These values are represented by the binary values 1 and 0 respectively, thus enabling Boolean principles to be applied to the logical circuitry of a computer. As a computer operates on the basis of electrical states, on or off, representing binary digits 1 and 0, circuits can be designed to facilitate Boolean operations by means of logic circuits (or gates).

23. Logic gate/logic circuit. These are synonymous terms for describing the logic circuits which have several inputs and one or two outputs depending upon the nature of the logic gate. Gates provide the foundations of all logic circuits which are etched on the surface of a silicon chip. Logic gates include: AND, NAND (Not AND), NOT, Inclusive OR, Exclusive OR and NOR. These are illustrated in Figure 2.13. Each logic gate has a truth table outlining its mode of operation which is based on Boolean algebra as indicated above.

24. Truth table. A truth table shows the outputs obtained from a logic circuit or gate as a consequence of specific inputs. Due to this relationship both truth tables and logic gates will be discussed together (*see* Fig. 2.13).

(*a*) *AND*. AND gates are sometimes referred to as 'coincidence gates' for reasons to be indicated. An AND gate gives an output of logical value 1 only when all of its inputs are logical value 1 (*see* Fig. 2.13). This facility could be used to find the carry digit when two binary digits are added together, as there is a carry of 1 only when the two digits to be added are both 1. Assume the content of an accumulator is 0001 1110 and the value of the operand to be added to the contents of the accumulator is 0100 1101. The result would be as follows:

contents of accumulator	0001 1110
value of operand	0100 1101
contents of accumulator after AND	0000 1100

(*b*) *NAND (Not AND)*. This gate produces an output of logical

LOGIC GATE
TRUTH TABLE

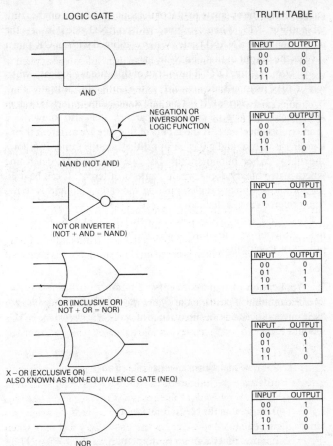

AND

INPUT	OUTPUT
0 0	0
0 1	0
1 0	0
1 1	1

NEGATION OR
INVERSION OF
LOGIC FUNCTION

NAND (NOT AND)

INPUT	OUTPUT
0 0	1
0 1	1
1 0	1
1 1	0

NOT OR INVERTER
(NOT + AND = NAND)

INPUT	OUTPUT
0	1
1	0

OR (INCLUSIVE OR)
NOT + OR = NOR

INPUT	OUTPUT
0 0	0
0 1	1
1 0	1
1 1	1

X – OR (EXCLUSIVE OR)
ALSO KNOWN AS NON-EQUIVALENCE GATE (NEQ)

INPUT	OUTPUT
0 0	0
0 1	1
1 0	1
1 1	0

NOR

INPUT	OUTPUT
0 0	1
0 1	0
1 0	0
1 1	0

Figure 2.13 *Logic gates and truth tables.*

value 1 when any or all of its inputs do *not* contain a logical 1 (*see* Fig.
2.13). By joining the two inputs together on a NAND gate it
becomes a NOT gate or an 'inverter' (*see* (*c*)). A NAND gate has the
same effect as an AND gate connected to a NOT gate (inverter).
Refer to relevant truth tables in Fig. 2.13 for AND and NAND. It
will be seen that the outputs are the complete opposite of each other.

(*c*) *NOT or INVERTER.* The logical value of the output of this gate is always the opposite to that of the input, as shown on the truth table in Fig. 2.13. When combined with an AND gate it inverts the output to that of a NAND gate. When combined with an OR gate it inverts the output to that of a NOR gate.

(*d*) *OR (inclusive OR)*. The output of this gate is a logical 1 when *any* or all of its inputs are logical 1, as the truth table indicates.

(*e*) *X-OR (exclusive OR)*. This gate is sometimes referred to as an anticoincidence gate or digital comparator. It is also known as a 'non-equivalence' gate. If the inputs of this gate are different then a logical 1 is output and a 0 is output if they are the same. It follows the rule of 'either' but not 'both'. The gate can be used to determine whether two binary digits are the same or different. It can be used for adding two binary digits ignoring the carry digit and is sometimes referred to as a 'half adder' for this reason.

(*f*) *NOR*. This has the same function as NOT OR. Its output has a value of logical 1 only when *all* its inputs have a value of 0 otherwise its output is 0.

25. Application of logic concepts. A number of business orientated examples will perhaps clarify the way in which truth tables are used in conjunction with the three principal logic elements, AND, OR and NOT.

		input	*output*
(*a*) AND			
(*i*)	It is true that a customer has placed an order	(**1**)	
	AND		
	It is true that the credit limit is not exceeded	(**1**)	
	It is true that the order is acceptable		(**1**)
(*ii*)	It is true that a customer has placed an order	(**1**)	
	AND		
	It is not true that the credit limit is not exceeded	(**0**)	
	It is not true that the order is accepted		(**0**)
(*b*) OR			
(*i*)	It is true that the level of stock has reached the reorder level (equal to)	(**1**)	

		input	output
	OR		

OR

It is true that the level of stock is below the
reorder level (less than) **(1)**

It is true that stock should be reordered **(1)**

(*ii*) It is true that the value of the order is less
than £50 **(1)**

OR

It is not true that the delivery distance is
greater than 20 miles **(0)**

It is true that delivery is to be charged **(1)**

(*iii*) It is true that the value of the order is
greater than £50 **(1)**

OR

It is not true that the delivery distance is
less than 20 miles **(0)**

It is true that delivery is not to be charged **(1)**

(*iv*) It is not true that the value of the order is
less than £50 **(0)**

OR

It is not true that the delivery distance is
greater than 20 miles **(0)**

It is not true that delivery is to be charged **(0)**

(*c*) NOT

(*i*) It is true we have excess stock **(1)**

It is not true that a purchase order is
required **(0)**

(*ii*) It is not true that we have excess stock **(0)**

It is true that a purchase order is required **(1)**

Internal storage

26. General outline. Developments in electronic and related
technology have affected the type of internal storage used in computers. Early computers had internal memories consisting of nickel
delay lines or magnetic drums. More recent computers have core
storage but this has tended to be replaced by semiconductor (MOS)
memory in later computers.

27. Summary of types of internal memory. The most usual types of memory in current use are:

(a) core storage;
(b) semiconductor memory (MOS):
  (i) RAM;
  (ii) ROM;
  (iii) PROM;
  (iv) EPROM;
(c) bubble memory;
(d) holographic (optical) memory;
(e) cache memory.

28. Purpose of internal memory. The internal memory of a computer is an integral element of the processing unit and may be referred to as the computer's working memory. It is used for storing software in the form of operating systems, application programs and utility routines, etc. In addition, the data input for processing is stored in the memory, as are the results of processing until they are output either to backing storage or to an output device such as a printer or VDU.

Data stored in the memory, as well as instructions, can be addressed and accessed very quickly and for this reason internal memory is often referred to as 'immediate access storage' (IAS). This attribute is ideal for having all programs and master files (consisting of business records and reference files) stored internally for immediate access when required. Unfortunately, however, internal storage, particularly core storage, has tended to be expensive and it has been necessary to use slower and less expensive types of storage for such purposes. Internal storage has to be complemented therefore by external storage, that is storage external to the processor, which is referred to as 'backing storage'. This is used for mass storage needs whereas internal storage is used for immediate access requirements.

Backing storage is less expensive, and has a higher storage capacity but a slower access time than internal storage. Programs, master files and reference files are stored in backing storage until required for processing, when they are transferred to the internal memory. All programs and data must be resident in the internal memory before processing is possible (see Chap. 7).

29. Units of storage. The units of storage in a computer system are usually expressed in bytes and/or words, which indicates the number of binary digits (bits) in a unit of storage. At one time computers had units of storage expressed in terms of characters consisting of six bits but these have tended to be replaced by the byte which consists of eight bits. Mainframes tend to have thirty-two-bit words equivalent to four bytes. The modern small computer tends to have a unit of storage in the form of a sixteen-bit word but others have an eight-bit processor.

30. Capacity of storage. Until recently medium scale mainframe computers had internal storage capacities, typically in the region of 32 to 48Kbytes, but even the small mini or micro now has a capacity which greatly exceeds this. Typical storage capacities may be summarised as follows:

(*a*) micros 64K–512K;
(*b*) minis in the region of 2Mbytes;
(*c*) modern mainframes 2Mbytes–8Mbytes +.

The abbreviation 'K' is used to denote 1,000 units of storage but it is actually 1,024 units of storage, i.e. 2^{10} which is an expansion of base 2, the base of the binary number system. 'K' should not be confused with 10^3 which is an expansion of base 10, the base of the decimal number system.

31. Core storage. This type of storage consists of small rings (cores) of ferromagnetic material which are threaded on wires by hand which made this type of storage very expensive to produce. Core storage consists of a number of adjacent core planes for storing bytes, one plane for each bit position in the byte.

The cores are magnetised to represent binary numbers—a zero is represented by negative polarity and a one by positive polarity. By means of combinations of negative and positive states in adjacent core planes it is possible to represent numeric, alphabetic and special characters each of which have their individual binary code.

32. Semiconductor memory. This type of memory has tended to supersede core storage in most computers, i.e. micros, minis and mainframes. The reason for this is attributable to four factors, viz.

it is smaller, has a higher capacity, is less costly and is faster with regard to access time.

Semiconductor memory is produced from silicon chips and is based on *m*etal *o*xide *s*emiconductor (MOS) technology. It is also referred to as '*m*etal *o*xide *s*emiconductor *f*ield *e*ffect *t*ransistor technology', i.e. MOSFET. Field *e*ffect *t*ransistor technology is abbreviated to FET.

There are two types of semiconductor memory:

(*a*) random access memory (RAM);
(*b*) read-only memory (ROM).

33. Random access memory (RAM). This type of memory is used for working storage requirements when running application programs. Its capacity can usually be increased on-site on many computers (large and small) by adding RAM chips to the circuit boards. This type of memory can be directly addressed in the same way as core storage to access specific data or instructions.

RAM is either 'static' or 'dynamic'. Static RAM remains unchanged until an electrical pulse is generated to change it. Dynamic RAM is volatile as it requires continual refreshing by electrical pulses. When the processor is switched off the contents are destroyed and the memory must be reloaded with the same program to restart the job. The same considerations apply for processing a job again at a later date—it is necessary to reload the program. To overcome the consequences of a power failure some computers have a memory support system using batteries to energise the memory when necessary to avoid loss of data.

34. Read only memory (ROM). The contents of ROM are physically fixed and cannot be accessed to alter them as can be done with RAM. The reason for this is that the writing circuit is disconnected during manufacture. Small computers use this type of internal memory for storing a BASIC interpreter which converts program statements in BASIC programming language into machine code. This is done during the running of a program. The contents of ROM are not destroyed when the computer is switched off as ROM is non-volatile because its contents have been burnt in during manufacture. Microprograms for input/output operations are stored on ROM chips. ROM also stores the operating system.

35. PROM. There are variations of ROM, e.g. PROM which stands for 'Programmable Read-Only Memory'. Whereas ordinary ROM is preprogrammed at the factory, PROM can be programmed by the user. A special device is required for putting the 'bit' pattern into a PROM chip; this is called a PROM programmer.

36. EPROM. This is a further variation of ROM, which stands for 'Erasable Programmable Read-Only Memory'. When data is recorded on this type of memory it is in effect the same as ordinary ROM in its behaviour but if the user requires to change the content of the chip an ultraviolet light is used to revert all the cells to '1s'. New data or programs can then be written on the chip.

37. Bubble memory. Bubbles may be described as cylindrical magnets which are formed from magnetic regions called 'domains' after the application of a critical bias value magnetic field. The bubbles are created on memory chips with capacities of typically 64K and 256K bytes. Rockwell has a bubble memory system with a megabyte of storage and a module with a capacity of one megabit.

Developments are taking place to reduce the size of the bubble or magnetic domain to less than two microns to enable one megabyte of memory to be stored on a chip not greater than about half a cubic inch (approximately 8,000 mm^3) in over-all size. Strings of bubbles allow streams of bits carried by the bubbles to become a series of electrical pulses providing output from the bubble memory. The ICL DNX – 2000 digital PABX system uses bubble memory so it seems that this type of memory is likely to be widely used in future.

38. Holographic (optical) memory. This is a ROM optical memory system whereby a pattern is recorded on a photosensitive plate by mixing laser light from a reference beam and laser light scattered from the object bearing the information to be recorded. The data in the hologram is effectively 'smeared' over the whole of the plate. A degree of redundancy is built into the system so that dust and scratches on the emulsion have little effect on the recorded information.

Data in the reconstructed image is arranged as an array of dots—one dot for each 'bit'. Information may be read out by directing a laser beam on to the hologram so that the reconstructed image falls onto a photodiode array on a silicon chip. At present the main limitation is that information on a holographic store is generally fixed and is presently of value for storing large amounts of fixed information such as machine instructions.

39. Cache memory. A highspeed memory capable of keeping up with the CPU. It acts as a buffer between the CPU and the slower main memory. As the CPU is not delayed by memory accesses the overall speed of processing is increased. Segments of program and data are transferred from disc backing storage into the cache buffer by the operating system. This type of memory is mainly applicable to the larger computer.

Selecting a suitable computer

40. Wide range of options. The selection of the most suitable computer configuration is a difficult task because of the wide range of options from which to choose. The optimum system is the one which will attain the required level of performance economically for both the current and foreseeable future needs of the business.

41. Modularity. Computer systems are available which can be structured or expanded on a modular basis to suit the information processing commitment of various organisations. Computers differ widely in size, speed, output capability and cost and it is necessary to select the most suitable combination of hardware, and indeed software, for the proposed applications. Computer systems should be selected with a defined migration path to allow for small systems initially and which can be built up by add-on memory modules, slow peripherals exchanged for faster ones and the addition of network facilities and additional terminals as required to allow for changes in the business environment.

42. Volume of transactions. The number of transactions to be processed is an important factor to consider in the choice of system. Relatively low volumes can be handled by a business microcomputer using keyboard data entry. This is a very slow method of data input, however, and larger volumes may necessitate the use of a small, medium or large mainframe using a key-to-disc method of data collection and validation.

43. Volume and length of records. Files containing many thousands of records of average length, in terms of characters (bytes), will require a large computer system with high backing storage capacity and high-speed data transfer capabilities. Applications consisting of 500–1,000 records may be suitable for processing by microcomputer as the capacity of floppy discs is limited compared to that of hard discs, i.e. Winchester discs. The larger business micros do have the option of adding Winchesters to the system for increasing the storage capacity and data transfer speed. If an application has many thousands of records to be processed then they would have to be recorded on several floppy discs which becomes very unwieldy as it is necessary to change discs to deal with specific records stored on them.

44. Total processing time: use of benchmarks. The total processing time for each application to be processed can be computed by multiplying the volume of transactions by the processing time for each process on each transaction. This may be established from benchmark timings which provide a basis for appraising the performance of different computers. The benchmarks provide timings for arithmetic computations, sorting routines, calling subroutines and handling arrays, etc. (*see* 16: **17, 18**).

45. Processor characteristics. Processors function at different speeds some of which, as an example, run at 2MHz or 5MHz. Depending upon the type of computer some have either 8-, 16- or 32-bit processors which indicates the size of numbers which can be processed at one time. In addition, the progression indicates that the more powerful processors have greater internal storage addressing capabilities because an 8-bit processor only has an address bus of sixteen channels which allows up to 64K bytes, i.e. 2^{16} which equals 65,536 bytes capacity. On the other hand, a 16-bit processor often has twenty 20 address channels which provides addressing facilities up to 2^{20}, i.e. 1,048,576 or one megabyte.

If integrated accounting packages and spreadsheets are to be implemented then a large internal memory capacity is essential in order to store the large number of instructions the programs contain. This may necessitate a minimum memory size of 256K *or even* 512K. The package specifications indicate the minimum memory size and other hardware requirements. If applications require frequent processing of large volumes of data then a fast processor is essential. For applications with relatively few computational needs but high volume printout requirements, a common feature of business systems, then high-speed printers are more relevant.

46. Operating system. The operating system adopted by a specific computer model should be evaluated because 'industry standards' have a vast amount of application packages already available whereas the less widely adopted operating systems have a scarcity of software. The reason for this is that software developers have an insufficiently wide market base to develop programs for. The cost of specific software is also likely to be higher in such circumstances as the development costs are spread over a smaller number of potential users. It is also necessary to consider if operating systems have multi-task or multi-user facilities as this may be an important factor in the choice of system.

47. Relative costs of hardware and software. In the early days of computers a major problem was the high cost of the hardware involved. The cost of hardware is now falling, mainly because of the great advances made in electronic technology which has reduced the size of computers whilst increasing their performance. As a result of this, attention is being increasingly focused on the costs and time involved in developing software. It is important to appreciate, therefore, that while hardware costs are falling the labour intensive task of producing software is increasing and it is necessary for an organisation to minimise the problems and costs involved in software development. Skilled programmers are employed who are conversant with structured programming techniques which allows program errors to be localised in one section of the program and so assists in program testing and maintenance. Structured programming also achieves standardisation in programming methodology allowing continuity of development if programmers leave and will also increase programming productivity.

The use of preprepared computer programs, known as application packages, will also assist in reducing the time and cost of development. Some manufacturers provide *bundled* software, i.e. the costs of software are included in the quoted cost of the system. This means it is essential to assess the total cost of any proposed computer system covering both hardware and software. It is, of course, necessary to assess the suitability of packages for the proposed systems to be run on the computer. Program generators can also be used for developing programs either by experienced programmers or by non-specialists in the operating departments.

48. Processing technique. Initially, it is necessary to determine the type of processing required whether batch, on-line interactive processing on a multi-user basis; on-line data input combined with batch processing; distributed processing to provide for the widely dispersed nature of the business or real-time control of critical operations. Having decided on the type of processing needed to achieve the information processing objectives it is necessary to determine the type of computer and its configuration to support the processing techniques required. Some of the hardware features for specific system needs have been outlined above (*see* **40–6**), but for situations when alternatives are feasible then it is necessary to compare the various costs of the different options. This subject is expanded in Volume 2.

49. Changing computers. It is sometimes necessary for a company to change its mainframe computer to that of another manufacturer. This may cause problems. If a company contemplates this change it is necessary to be aware that no compatibility will exist between the models. This will be due to differences in architecture, i.e. the design philosophy on which the computers are based and the fact they will probably have different operating systems and assembly codes. However small business computers are tending to become standardised to become IBM compatible. The transfer of a large batch system will entail some program recoding as the different operating systems will have different implementations of the high-level language in use. Even if this is COBOL which is a common language for use on any mainframe there will still be a need to recompile programs into the 'native' code of the particular computer.

The problems which are likely to occur include:

(*a*) disruption during the changeover period;

(*b*) the need to maintain the current system until the new system has proved to be satisfactory;

(*c*) prolonged system testing and comparison of the results of the two systems to detect errors;

(*d*) high overheads for running two systems in parallel;

(*e*) staffing problems due to excessive overtime;

(*f*) need to input transaction data twice—to each of the systems separately;

(*g*) need to reformat disc files;

(*h*) need to prepare new master files;

(*i*) time and cost of recompiling programs;

(*j*) need to prepare accommodation for the new system or arrange temporary space.

Progress test 2

1. What is a computer?   (**1**)

2. What is the primary purpose of computers in business?   (**2**)

3. Outline in simple terms the mode of operation of a computer.   (**3**)

4. Specify three basic types of computer.   (**4**)

5. What is the meaning of the term mainframe computer and what purpose does it serve in business applications?   (**5**)

6. How does a minicomputer differ from a mainframe?   (**6**)

7. What are the main features of a microcomputer?   (**7**)

8. Define the nature of electronic desktop display systems and specify their principal characteristics.   (**8**)

9. Define the term configuration.   (**9**)

10. What is meant by the term virtual machine?   (**10**)

11. Outline the structure of a typical third generation batch processing computer.   (**11**)

12. Outline the features of typical microcomputer configurations.   (**12, 13**)

13. What is a microprocessor?   (**14, 15**)

14. Specify the general characteristics of a central processing

unit and state how the power of processors is defined. (**16, 17**)

15. Briefly describe the functions of the control unit of a computer system. (**18, 19**)

16. What are the functions of the arithmetic/logic unit? (**20, 21**)

17. Define the features of Boolean algebra on which computer logic is based. (**22**)

18. What is a logic gate or logic circuit? (**23**)

19. What is a truth table? (**24**)

20. State the features, purpose and types of internal storage. (**26–39**)

21. What is meant by the terms:
    (*a*) RAM; (*b*) ROM; (*c*) PROM; (*d*) EPROM ? (**32–36**)

22. Outline the nature of (*a*) bubble memory; (*b*) holographic memory; (*c*) cache memory. (**37–39**)

23. What factors must be considered when selecting a suitable computer? (**40–48**)

24. In the early days of computers a major problem was the high cost of the hardware involved. With the falling cost of hardware attention is increasingly being focused on the costs and time involved in developing appropriate software. Discuss. (**47**)

25. What problems are likely to occur if a company considers changing its mainframe to that of another manufacturer? (**49**)

3

Organisation of a data processing department and a management services department

Organisation of a data processing department: by function or activity

1. Main sections and types of staff. The sectional organisation of a batch processing installation is shown in Fig. 3.1 and may be summarised as follows.

(*a*) Head of department—data processing manager:

    (*i*) responsible to: director of administration, managing director or company secretary according to specific requirements;

    (*ii*) immediate subordinates: chief systems analyst, chief programmer, operations manager and database administrator.

(*b*) Chief systems analyst responsible for activities of systems analysts.

(*c*) Chief programmer responsible for activities of programmers.

(*d*) Operations manager responsible for activities of chief computer operator and all operators, data preparation supervisor, tape and disc librarian and data control supervisor.

2. Principal duties of data processing manager. The duties of a data processing manager may be summarised in the following manner:

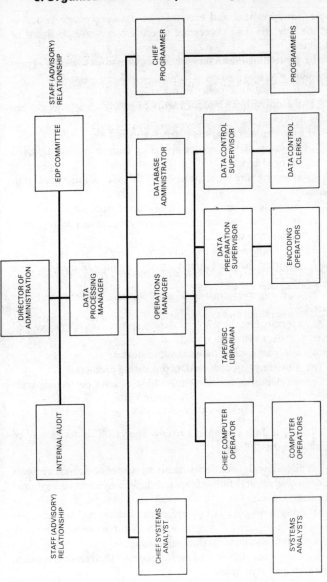

Figure 3.1 *Organisation chart: by function or activity.*

(*a*) interpretation and execution of data processing policy as defined by the data processing steering committee or Board of directors;

(*b*) controlling immediate subordinates in the attainment of project objectives;

(*c*) participation in policy formulation;

(*d*) liaison with user departments to ensure their interests are fully provided for;

(*e*) ensuring that company policy is adhered to;

(*f*) ensuring that computer operating instructions are updated when the need arises;

(*g*) assessing the effectiveness of the file maintenance procedures;

(*h*) assessing the suitability of file security procedures;

(*i*) ensure that program modifications are applied effectively;

(*j*) monitoring test runs;

(*k*) post implementation evaluation;

(*l*) ensuring that staff attend suitable training courses for their development;

(*m*) assessing performance of staff for salary awards and promotion;

(*n*) coordinating the whole of the data processing operations and ensuring that work flows smoothly;

(*o*) resolving conflict between subordinates;

(*p*) providing guidance on data processing problems;

(*q*) development and implementation of data processing standards.

3. Principal duties of chief systems analyst. The duties may be summarised as follows:

(*a*) liaison with user departments to ensure their requirements and problems are fully discussed before systems design and implementation;

(*b*) interpreting terms of reference before embarking upon systems investigations in order to establish the problem, areas of investigation and limits to the assignment;

(*c*) comparing the cost and performance of alternative processing methods and techniques;

(d) organising and coordinating the activities of systems analysts;

(e) reviewing performance of systems analysts;

(f) organising and reviewing systems documentation to ensure it complies with data processing standards;

(g) reviewing the progress of projects and reporting status to the data processing manager;

(h) presenting recommendations to data processing and user department management with regard to possible courses of action or design philosophy to achieve defined objectives;

(i) coordinating the implementation of new or modified systems;

(j) reviewing performance of implemented systems and assessing the need for amendments or additional training of staff;

(k) discussion of proposals with chief programmer.

4. Principal duties of chief programmer. These are summarised below:

(a) liaison with chief systems analyst to determine philosophy of proposed systems and establish the type of programming language to use—high level or assembly code (low level);

(b) review of systems specification to establish the details of systems requirements before discussing these with assigned programmers;

(c) defining test data requirements and monitoring test runs;

(d) reviewing programmers' performance;

(e) reporting status of program development to data processing manager.

5. Principal duties of operations manager. These are summarised as follows:

(a) control of all sections for which he is responsible, i.e. computer operations, data preparation and data control;

(b) development of operating schedules for all jobs to be run on the computer;

(c) ensuring that data is received on time from user departments;

(d) maintaining records on equipment utilisation;

(e) implementing standard procedures when appropriate to improve efficiency;

(f) controlling stocks of data processing supplies, tapes, stationery and discs, etc;

(g) maintaining a log of computer operations;

(h) report to data processing manager of situations such as hardware malfunctions, staffing problems and other operational matters.

6. The database administrator. As the whole concept of a database is to rationalise business systems by the integration of such systems it follows that the data needs of an organisation must be coordinated at a very high level. This is basically the responsibility of a database administrator who may not yet exist in many organisations. Nevertheless someone has no doubt been vested with such responsibilities, perhaps a senior member of the systems staff.

When data is common to two or more applications then programmers are not allowed the freedom they previously enjoyed to name data elements and subject them to processing independently of other application requirements. This is where the database administrator assumes command, as it were, because he must consider the data needs of the several applications under consideration for consolidation into a database.

He must first of all be conversant with business policy and strategy, particularly for the long term, as the very fabric of a business is dependent upon an efficient and effective management information system of which a database is a fundamental part—the roots of such a system in fact. He should play an active part in the planning of information systems particularly with regard to feasibility studies.

He should be an expert in all file management techniques and be able to advise management and system planners of the capabilities and shortcomings of various file management systems with regard to the application under review. It is essential that he liaise and consult with project teams with regard to the development of design specifications, program specifications, systems documentation and programs, etc. It is imperative that he monitor the implementation of a database ensuring that time and cost constraints are adhered to. It is of extreme importance that the administrator ensures that system objectives are achieved. Also of importance is that the initial preparation and maintenance of a data dictionary should be the responsibility of a database administrator, as this is essential for the

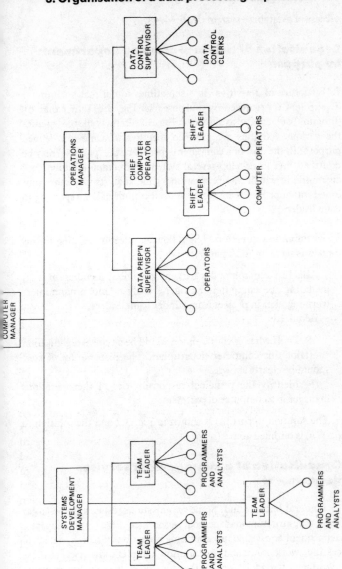

Figure 3.2 *Organisation chart: by purpose.*

success of a database system (*see* 6:**44–48**).

Organisation of a data processing department: by purpose

7. Structure of activities. It is sometimes found that a computer department is organised by 'purpose' (*see* Fig. 3.2) rather than by 'function' or 'activity' as shown on Fig. 3.1. In this type of structure the various activities are grouped together to achieve a defined purpose. In the case of a computer department the 'purpose' may be multifold, i.e. to develop several systems for computerisation concurrently, in which case programmers and analysts would be combined into a project team for each project undertaken reporting to team leaders.

8. Examination question. The following question relating to this topic was set in an ACA paper.

ABC Ltd's computer department contains 35 members of staff, including the computer manager. Analysts and programmers work together in project teams under team leaders.

Required:

(*a*) Draft what in your opinion would be a typical organisation chart for this computer department. The distribution of staff should be clearly shown.

(*b*) Identify the principal responsibilities of the operations manager in a computer department.

The solution to part (*a*) is shown in Fig. 3.2 and the solution to part (*b*) is outlined above (*see* 5).

Organisation of a management services department

9. General background. Some organisations, especially the larger ones, may structure management services (*see* Fig. 3.3) as a separate department or division incorporating operations research, data processing, work study and organisation and methods. Each of these disciplines would be under the control of a specialist manager reporting to a common superior, the manager of management ser-

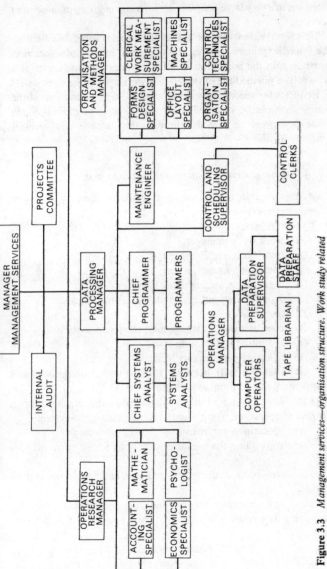

Figure 3.3 *Management services—organisation structure. Work study related to factory-based operations may also be incorporated.*

vices, or, in a very large combine, the director of group management services.

This form of structure recognises the importance of coordinating the interdisciplinary services at a high level in the organisation in order to gain the maximum benefit, for the corporate entity as a whole, by a planned use of skilled resources to optimise their use.

Requests for specific services from the different functions of the business would be channelled through a projects committee, in some instances, or directly through the management services manager in others.

10. Job specification—management services manager.

(*a*) Responsible to: managing director or director of group management services.

(*b*) Subordinates:

  (*i*)   work study manager;

  (*ii*) operations research manager;

  (*iii*) data processing manager;

  (*iv*) organisation and methods manager.

(*c*) Functional relationships: all departmental managers.

(*d*) Responsible for:

  (*i*)   coordinating all management services activities;

  (*ii*) recruiting and training staff;

  (*iii*) assessing performance of staff;

  (*iv*) ensuring staff keep up to date with management and problem solving techniques;

  (*v*)   investigating problems throughout the organisation in respect of operations, computing, data processing and systems;

  (*vi*) allocating assignments to relevant subordinates;

  (*vii*) controlling the use of resources and time spent on projects;

  (*viii*) resolving conflicts between staff and functional departments;

  (*ix*) optimising use of equipment, i.e. portable computers for capturing data relating to work study and operations research projects;

  (*x*)   making recommendations to the board and advising functional departments of relevant courses of action in prescribed circumstances;

(*xi*) monitoring performance of systems after new systems, methods or techniques have been implemented to ensure expected results are being achieved;

(*xii*) authorising further study as necessary to remedy adverse situations.

(*e*) Limitations on authority: no direct authority over functional department staff unless specially delegated for a defined purpose. Direct authority only over management services personnel; otherwise advisory only.

Progress test 3

1. Outline the main sections of a data processing department organised by function or activity.   (**1**, Fig. 3.1)

2. (*a*) Draft the organisation chart of a computer department of forty staff. Your chart should show clearly how the staff are distributed in the department and any assumptions made must be stated. (*b*) Give a concise outline of the principal duties of a systems analyst during the life of a systems project.   (**1–5** and Fig. 3.1 provide guidance for part (*a*) of this question and 15:**16** provides guidance for part (*b*)) (*ACA*)

3. Specify the principal duties of (*a*) a data processing manager; (*b*) a chief systems analyst; (*c*) a chief programmer; (*d*) an operations manager and (*e*) a database administrator.   (**2, 3, 4, 5, 6**)

4. What are the responsibilities of the person in charge of a computer room?   (**5**) (*C & G*)

5. State how you would organise a computer department by purpose.   (**7, 8** and Fig. 3.2)

6. Outline the nature of a management services department. (**9**)

7. Your company has an organisation and methods section with five staff and a computer department with a total of thirty-five staff (six systems analysts, eight programmers, fifteen staff engaged in data preparation and control and six operators). It has been decided to create a single management services department and to appoint a new manager. You are required to draft a job specification for the post of management services manager.   (**10**, Fig. 3.3) (*CIMA*)

Part two

Computer input, output, data storage and retrieval, databases and backing storage and media

4
Computer input

Computer input media and data capture methods and techniques

1. **General considerations.** There exist many different ways in which data can be collected or captured for processing by computer. The specific method or media chosen for input depends on the type of computer configuration installed, which to some extent is dependent upon the nature of business operations. Some businesses require real-time systems for their effective operation, in which case data is input to the computer by on-line terminal. Other businesses, with less critical information requirements, have batch processing configurations with data encoded on hard or floppy disc for input, in order to optimise the speed of inputting batches of data, for processing the payroll or for producing invoices, etc. In this instance, direct entry by means of the keyboard of a terminal device or workstation may not be suitable—being too slow for the volume of data to be processed. Large computers in the past tended to use either punched card or paper tape input but this has largely been phased out. The type of input selected also depends on the environment to which the data relates, which is why the 'shop floor' in the factory sometimes has factory terminals installed at strategic locations or portable computers, for the collection of data relating to factory orders and other requirements (*see* **24, 28** and **29**). Supermarket check-out points need some speedy method of capturing data relating to the items sold as customers come to the check-out point to pay for the goods. Bar code scanning is widely used in this situation for speeding up the flow of customers and minimising the

length of queue particularly at peak times.

It is unthinkable for banks to record every cheque transaction on a punched card with the many thousands of transactions which occur each day. Data would be punched into cards long after transactions had occurred and input bottlenecks would occur at an ever increasing velocity. For this reason, banks issue cheque books to customers with the cheques already encoded in magnetic ink characters.

2. Direct and indirect input. Input can broadly, but not precisely, be categorised, into two divisions: direct and indirect. The term 'direct' should be interpreted to mean that data is in a form suitable for processing without the need for data conversion. Some systems have what may be called direct input media, such as optical marks on source documents but convert them into magnetic tape media prior to input to the computer. A typical example is the way in which meter readings are processed by electricity boards. Consumers' electricity usage is captured by having the meter read and by recording the reading in optical marks on a meter reading sheet. These sheets are read by an optical mark reader which transfers the data to a tape deck for recording the meter readings on magnetic tape. The details on the tape are then input for processing (*see* **17**). In this instance, the optical method is 'indirect'. It would be 'direct' if the data was input into the computer without conversion. The same considerations apply to the use of Kimball tags as they are pre-punched ready for input to the computer when transactions occur but the data they contain is usually converted to cassette tape prior to being input for processing. Such conversions are performed electronically and automatically and do not involve time consuming and costly punching and verifying operations, as is necessary for punched cards and paper tape. It is for this reason that punched cards and paper tape are being phased out in favour of more cost effective and efficient media methods.

Microcomputers often have input direct from the keyboard for transaction data but this depends upon the nature and size of the micro, as some are equipped with devices for graphical input such as light pens, a mouse or paddles/joysticks. A 'mouse' is a small electronic device with one or two buttons on top and a ball bearing underneath which rolls on top of a desk. When the mouse is moved the cursor on the screen follows the direction of movement. This device allows the cursor to be moved to point at the required 'icon'. A click of a button selects this icon. This is a feature of electronic desktop display systems (*see* 2: **8**).

Table 4A summarises the various methods of input to a computer:

Table 4A   Methods of collecting and capturing data for computer input

Method/mode	Media	Data preparation/ data capture device	Input device
Punched	Prepunched tags (Kimball tags)	Tag punch	Tag reader
Magnetic	Magnetic tape (reel)	Encoder	Tape deck
	Magnetic tape (cassette) (Key-to-cassette)	Data entry terminal/ encoder	Cassette handler
	Floppy disc (key-to-diskette)	Encoding data station	Disc unit
	Exchangeable disc pack— exchangeable disc storage (EDS) (key-to-disc)	Key stations: VDU with keyboard	Magnetic disc data transferred to magnetic tape in some systems and input to computer is via a tape deck

Table 4A *continued*

Method/mode	Media	Data preparation/ data capture device	Input device
	Data transferred from punched cards to magnetic disc	Card reader/ disc drive Conversion by utility program Applicable for multi-programming operations	Disc drive
	Magnetically encoded characters: magnetic ink character recognition (MICR)	Characters printed when cheques are printed	Magnetic ink character reader/sorter
Handwritten, typed or printed optical characters	Documents prepared with optical characters: optical character recognition (OCR)	Hand, typewriter, line printer, cash register	Optical character reader
Handwritten optical marks	Documents prepared with optical marks: optical mark recognition (OMR)	Hand	Optical mark reader or Optical page reader
Handwritten normal characters	Pressure sensitive writing surface	Handprint data entry terminal	Handprint data entry terminal

Table 4A *continued*

Method/mode	Media	Data preparation/ data capture device	Input device
Electronic sensing	Plastic card/ keyboard	Bank cash point terminal	Bank cash point terminal
	Plastic badge— fixed data Prepunched card—fixed data Keyboard— variable data	Factory terminal	Factory terminal
	Graphical presentation of images on video screen	Light pen	Light pen/ computer
	Graphical input of images	Graphics tablet and stylus	Stylus/computer
Electronic scanning	Bar code/ optical characters printed on label	Retail terminal equipped with low-intensity laser scanner, light pens or slot scanners	Retail terminal or cassette handler
	Bar code labels	Portable computer equipped with bar code reading wand and keyboard	Portable computer
Audio	Human voice	Audio input unit	Audio input unit

Table 4A *continued*

Method/mode	Media	Data preparation/ data capture device	Input device
Analogue	Electronic signals	Sensor	Digitiser
Digital	Electronic signals	Terminal keyboard	Terminal
	Electronic signals	Terminal keyboard	Intelligent terminal
	Electronic signals	Terminal keyboard	Workstation
	Electronic signals	Paddles/ joysticks	Paddles/ joysticks/ computer
Electronic selection of icons	Electronic signals	Mouse	Mouse/ computer

Kimball tags

3. Retailing. Kimball tags are special types of price tag used in retailing which contain printed and punched or magnetically encoded information (*see* Fig. 4.1).

Tags are used to improve the control of merchandising by means of automated tag systems which provide automatic facilities for printing and punching information into tags. The tags are then attached to the appropriate merchandise ready for sale. When the merchandise is sold, the tags are removed and the information they contain is converted into magnetic tape for processing by electronic computer.

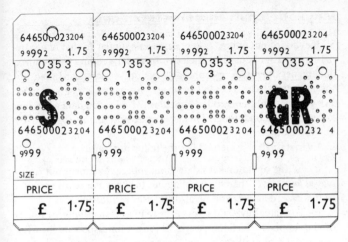

Figure 4.1 *Kimball tags. (Courtesy Litton Business Systems Limited)*

4. Data transmission. The information is then transmitted from remote locations by telephone line to a data centre where the information is received and converted into magnetic media for computer input. This method eliminates mailing delays and provides management reports much more quickly.

Machines are available which encode both printed and magnetic language on tags and labels. The magnetic language is easily and accurately read by means of a hand-held magnetic scanning device such as the Datapen reader. By means of the reader information can be automatically captured at the point of the transaction from the magnetically-encoded documents. The encoded documents stay on the merchandise and can be read more than once to record transfers, returns and other inventory data. Such documents have a large capacity for their size, and cannot easily be counterfeited or altered.

Such systems are aimed at capturing and processing data as economically and speedily as possible, in order to provide essential management information for forecasting and control of business operations.

Magnetic input: encoding techniques

5. Keyboard encoding. A keyboard very similar to that of a standard typewriter is used by the operator, who, reading from source documents depresses appropriate keys on the keyboard, causing the characters to be recorded on seven- or nine-track magnetic tape. For verification, the encoder compares the recorded data when it is keyed in a second time. This system is now being replaced by key-to-disc systems.

A variation of this method has the following features:

(*a*) As the operator keys data from source documents, *it is displayed on a CRT*, thereby enabling her to check her work visually. In this case, data preparation also includes verification.

(*b*) To enable keyboard errors to be reduced, *magnetic tape cassettes* can be supplied which have a special format for display on the CRT as a visual replica of the source document. The operator then keys in the information as if completing a form on a typewriter. As the data being keyed is displayed in the appropriate data boxes it enables the operator visually to check and correct the data as appropriate before depressing the 'send' key, which causes the data to be recorded on to magnetic tape.

(*c*) *Pooling is possible*, whereby a maximum of twelve operators can key into up to four tape drives.

6. Key-to-disc. Key-to-disc systems include a number of key stations (in the region of twelve to thirty-two) which enables that number of operators at one time to read data from source documents and encode the data onto magnetic disc. This is a more efficient method than punching data into cards and is more effective than the alternative method of encoding data to magnetic tape. This type of system is more than a data preparation system because in addition to encoding and verifying data, the system also provides for the validation of data fields, the generation or validation of check digits and the creation of batch totals, all under the control of a read-only program in the memory of the miniprocessor. Some systems are communications-oriented and transmit batches of data to a mainframe computer which may be located at a great distance away, such as another town.

After data has been encoded on disc, verified and validated, etc., records are written to magnetic tape ready for processing by a mainframe computer. The mainframe is then able to process the data which is free of errors and fully validated without having to carry out validation checks which saves valuable processing time.

Key stations may be located up to 300 metres from the processor, which enables them to be strategically sited near to data origination points in factory departments, stores or warehouses, etc.

The essential elements of a key-to-disc system include the key stations, miniprocessor, magnetic disc drive, magnetic tape deck and a supervisor's console for monitoring the status of the system.

When an operator keys in data, by means of a keyboard similar to that of a typewriter, it is automatically checked and invalid data generates a signal from the processor to the key station which causes the keyboard to lock, together with an audible or displayed warning. Error correction is facilitated by a VDU or panel display, which indicates the erroneous data by means of a cursor on the VDU or a light on the panel display.

Data is keyed into an entry buffer and when this is full the data is transferred to a defined area of the disc. When a key station is set to verify the appropriate record is retrieved from the disc and inserted into the key station's entry buffer so that it can be compared with the same record when keyed in for verification. Differences are displayed on the VDU for correction, either to the original record or the keyed in character by the verifier operator. Records are then moved to an output buffer on disc before being transferred to magnetic tape.

As with all magnetic file media, which can be accidentally erased or overwritten, security measures are necessary and in this instance data is retained on the disc until it has been processed successfully by the mainframe computer. Data is then erased from the disc to provide storage areas for the new batches of data (*see* Fig. 4.2).

7. Key-to-diskette. A data station is used for recording data on diskettes. As data is entered it is stored in a buffer on the data station and displayed on a screen for the purpose of correcting errors before being recorded on diskette. When data is received it

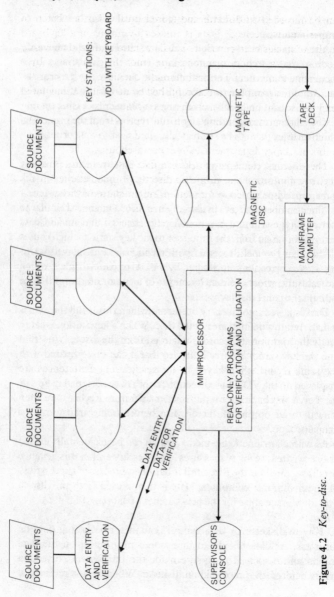

Figure 4.2 *Key-to-disc.*

can be recorded to diskette and stored until a further batch of similar data is received. Data is entered by means of a keyboard similar to an electric typewriter. The data station can be set to verify mode so that a second operator can re-enter the data from source documents to detect any errors before the data is input for processing. Input to a computer is accomplished by means of an integrated flexible disc unit built into a processor's cabinet or by a freestanding flexible disc unit depending upon the type of computer and the manufacturer.

8. Key-to-cassette. A key-to-cassette data entry terminal provides an efficient means of encoding data directly from source documents to magnetic tape stored in a cassette. Data is entered by a keyboard on the terminal and is displayed on a CRT screen. The lower portion of the screen is reserved for operator guidance messages, error warnings and system status displays.

When an error is detected the screen image begins pulsing to attract the operator's attention. When this occurs, the operator presses the keyboard release function key and a message describing the nature of the error is displayed.

Data may be entered and verified according to multi-level formats that are programmed to individual user needs. Within a level, fields are defined by number, name, length and field and data type. The terminal also provides facilities for check-digit generation and verification. During verification, source data is re-keyed for comparison with the original entry. If an error is discovered in the original data the operator has the option of correcting one character or of re-keying the entire field. Data recorded on cassette can be transmitted to another terminal or to a central processor over communication lines.

Magnetic ink characters

Magnetic ink is required for printing the characters, so that they may be interpreted for processing. The characters, in addition to being printed with an ink containing a ferromagnetic substance, are also designed in a special type font. As with OCR characters, they may be interpreted both by humans and by machines. Magnetic ink character recognition is accomplished by an input device known as a magnetic ink character reader/sorter. The technique of MICR is mainly used in banking to cope with the enormous task of sorting cheques and updating customers' accounts. It is a more effective method of input than punching a card for each cheque transaction.

There are two MICR fonts:

E13B;
CMC7.

9. E13B. This font was developed in the United States for the American Banks Association, and has been adopted by British banks.

Each character is made as unique as possible, in order to avoid misinterpretation.

Magnetic ink characters can be overwritten with ordinary ink without affecting their legibility for interpretation by the reader/sorter.

If any attempt is made to alter a magnetic ink character the subsequent mutilation is detected when the character is being interpreted by the reader/sorter.

The E13B repertoire consists of ten numeric characters, 0–9, and four symbols to signify the meaning of fields (*see* Fig. 4.3).

10. CMC7 (Caractère Magnétique Code). This font is the continental standard, and although the characters are encoded in

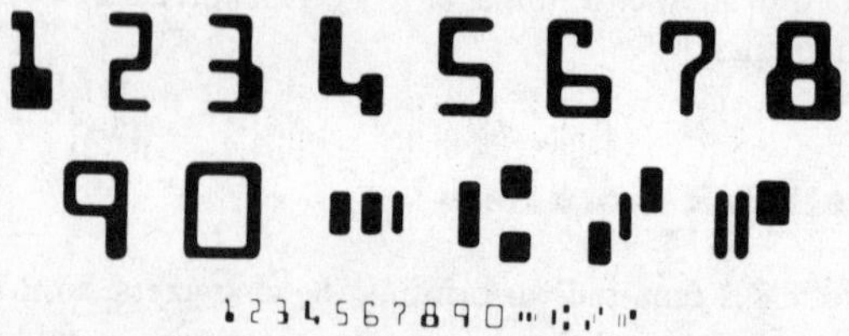

Figure 4.3 *MICR characters, E13B font. (Courtesy International Computers Limited)*

magnetic ink their structure is altogether different to E13B. The characters are formed from a 'gapped font' code, consisting of seven vertical bars.

Each character is identified by the format of the bars, which create a six-bit code. Each bar is separated by a gap; a wide gap equals 1 and a narrow gap equals 0. The MICR reader recognises each character by the variable distance between the vertical bars.

The CMC7 repertoire consists of ten numeric characters, 0–9, twenty-six alphabetic characters and five special symbols (*see* Fig. 4.4).

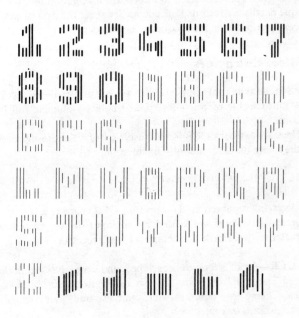

Figure 4.4 *MICR characters, CMC7 font. (Courtesy International Computers Limited)*

11. Magnetic ink character encoding. In respect of cheques magnetic ink characters may be encoded when the cheque is printed. The data pre-encoded would include:

(*a*) serial number of the cheque;
(*b*) bank branch number;
(*c*) customer's account number.

When a cheque is presented to a bank by a customer, the bank encodes the amount of the cheque. The encoding is carried out by a machine known as a MICR cheque encoder which has a manually operated keyboard. Alternatively, this may be performed by an encoding machine connected to a keyboard listing machine. When cheque details are recorded on a summary sheet the data is simultaneously encoded on the cheque by the encoder.

Optical characters

12. Special type font. Optical characters are designed in a special type font capable of being interpreted both by humans and by machine.

There are two basic OCR fonts in use, both of which are approved by the International Standards Organisation;

OCR—A;
OCR—B.

Special ink is not required for printing OCR characters.

Optical characters are sensed by an input device, an optical character reader, which transfers data to the processor.

13. OCR—A. This font was developed, and is widely used, in the United States. It comprises sixty-six different characters, alphabetical characters, numbers and symbols—and four standard character sizes (*see* Fig. 4.5).

14. OCR—B. This font is the result of the work carried out by the European Computer Manufacturers' Association (ECMA), and is widely used in Europe. It comprises 113 different characters and four standard character sizes (*see* Fig. 4.6).

ABCDEFGHIJKLM
NOPQRSTUVWXYZ
0123456789
•¬:;=+/$*"&|
'-{}%?⌠⅄⊣
ÜÑÄØÖÆ£¥

Figure 4.5 *Optical characters, OCR-A.*

15. OCR character encoding. The printing of characters on documents for optical reading is not so complex as printing magnetic ink characters, mainly because the font is not so intricate and the use of special ink is unnecessary. It is still necessary, however, to print the characters with a high degree of precision.

Encoding of characters may be performed in the following ways:

(*a*) *hand printing*, in accordance with specified rules for the formation of characters;

(*b*) by *typewriter* equipped with OCR font characters;

(*c*) *automatically*, by a line printer fitted with a print barrel embossed with OCR font characters;

(*d*) by cash registers *equipped with OCR font characters*.

ABCDEFGH abcdefgh
IJKLMNOP ijklmnop
QRSTUVWX qrstuvwx
YZ*+,-./ yz m åøæ
01234567 £$:;<%>?
89 [@!#&,]
(=) "´`^ ~ ˇ
ÄÖÅÑÜÆØ ↑≤≥×÷°¤

Figure 4.6 *Optical characters, OCR-B.*

Optical marks

16. Nature of optical marks. This method of collecting data utilises pre-printed source documents such as employee clock cards, confectionery order sheets and meter reading sheets as used by gas and electricity boards. It is a very speedy method of collecting data but care must be taken to ensure that marks are recorded, usually by hand, in the correct column otherwise invalid data will be processed causing error correction problems at a later date.

The documents are designed with predesignated column values and a mark is recorded in the appropriate column to indicate the number of hours worked on a specific job by an employee, etc. or to record the units consumed as indicated on a gas or electricity meter (*see* Figs. 4.7 and 4.8).

17. Example of OMR combined with OCR, demonstrating the use of turnaround documents. The Midlands Electricity Board

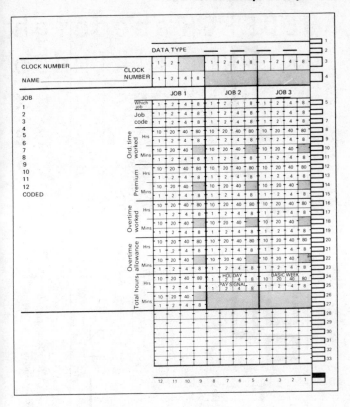

Figure 4.7 *Employee clock-card.*

produces meter reading sheets by computer which contain details printed in optical characters. The meter sheets are used by meter readers who record meter readings (electricity consumed by customers) by marks in pre-designated meter reading columns. The details are then transferred to magnetic tape by optical mark and optical character reading.

The magnetic tape file is then used to produce consumer bills with stubs. These are sent to the consumer who detaches the stub and returns it with the remittance. The stub is then read by an optical character reader and transferred to magnetic tape to provide

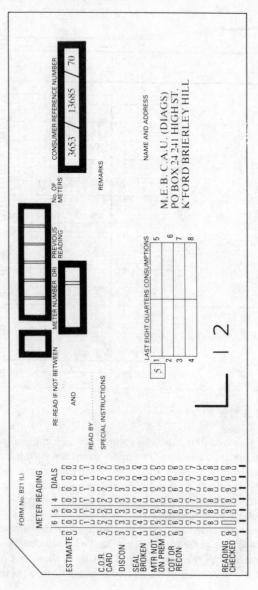

Figure 4.8 *Meter reading sheet: OMR and OCR: offpeak supply. (Courtesy Midlands Electricity Board)*

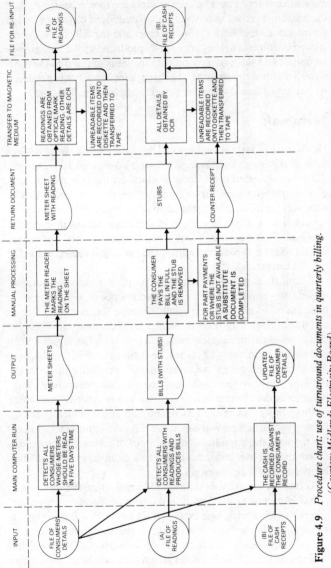

Figure 4.9 *Procedure chart: use of turnaround documents in quarterly billing. (Courtesy Midlands Electricity Board)*

a file of cash receipts. The cash receipts are then recorded against the consumer record to provide an updated file of consumer details on magnetic tape. Both the meter sheet and the bill stub are turn-around documents as they are initially produced by the computer as an output and subsequently become the basis of input to the computer for further processing. The computer has actually produced its own input data at an earlier output stage (*see* Fig. 4.9).

Terminals

18. Nature of terminals. First and foremost, terminals are devices for transmitting and/or receiving data over a communication channel. They are connected to a computer which controls the transmission of data over telephone lines. Clusters of terminals are controlled by a cluster controller, which attends to the requirements of individual terminals on a shared line basis, facilitating economy in the use of telephone lines especially if they are leased private lines. For further details relating to data transmission the reader is recommended to refer to Chapter 8.

Terminals may either be special purpose or general purpose, depending upon the operating environment, because some types of business require terminals specially designed for the nature of their activities. They may then be defined as dedicated terminals, i.e. dedicated to performing a specific task which applies to retail, bank and factory terminals. (These will be outlined later in this chapter.) Terminals operate in a conversational or interactive mode unless they are one-way terminals designed only for transmitting large volumes of data from a remote location to a centralised computing facility; this is referred to as remote job entry, which enables a factory to transmit payroll data to the central computer for computing payslips and payrolls. Conversational or interactive processing means that the user and the computer communicate with each other by means of specific dialogue.

Terminals are used in many and varied environments, e.g. a portable terminal can be used in the home or hotel room, or anywhere there is a telephone extension for connecting the terminal to a computer, for such purposes as: time sharing or teleshopping via the videotex system such as the Prestel Viewdata facility; for airline seat reservations, booking hotel accommodation or theatre tickets;

for the booking of holidays by tour operators; and for gas and electricity board consumer enquiry systems.

19. Summary of types of terminal. There exist many different types of terminal and the following summary will serve to identify them:

- (*a*) teletype;
- (*b*) visual display unit (VDU);
- (*c*) intelligent terminal;
- (*d*) factory terminal;
- (*e*) bank cash point terminal;
- (*f*) retail terminal;
- (*g*) bulk transmission/remote batch terminal;
- (*h*) handprint data entry terminal;
- (*i*) workstations;
- (*j*) branch terminal.

20. Purpose of terminals. It has already been indicated that the primary purpose of a terminal is the transmitting and/or receiving of data but a brief summary, prior to further study, of the different forms this may take should be beneficial.

(*a*) Transmission of data from one location to another or between computers in a local area network environment for text, data or electronic mail processing purposes.

(*b*) Access to a computer for time sharing facilities either for program development, problem solving or file processing.

(*c*) Random enquiry facilities for credit status enquiries, product availability, account status or hotel or airline seat availability.

(*d*) Real-time control of manufacturing processes and airline seat reservations.

(*e*) Point of sale data capture in supermarkets.

(*f*) Access to cash outside banking hours by means of cashpoint terminals.

(*g*) Processing business operations such as:
  - (*i*) on-line order entry;
  - (*ii*) on-line stock control;
  - (*iii*) on-line payroll processing.

(h) Collection of data relating to works orders.

(i) Transmission of handwritten data and signatures by hand-print data entry terminal.

(j) Console unit for controlling computer operations.

21. Teletype. This type of terminal is actually a teleprinter or telex machine as used in the telex system of British Telecom. It is now used for other data communication purposes due to the growth in data communications between computers. It is probably the best known keyboard/printer terminal which transmits data via a telephone line by depressing keys on the keyboard. In a telex system data is transmitted along a telegraph line. Each telex machine is connected through the telex network to other telex machines. However, we are interested in the use of the teletype as a terminal device for transmitting and receiving data in time sharing systems and as a control console for man/machine communications in the older mainframe installations.

A modem or acoustic coupler is required for connecting the terminal to the telephone line, as it is necessary to convert the digital signals transmitted by the terminal into analog signals required by the voice grade telephone lines. When the signals are received at the computer end of the line they are converted back into digital signals from analog signals prior to processing. This may change in the future with the advent of the Digital PABX telephone system which facilitates the digital transmission of both data and voice communications. Provision is made for prepunching paper tape for subsequent transmission of data at a faster speed than is possible by keyboard entry of data for direct transmission. Data can also be received on paper tape as well as being printed on the printing unit.

22. Visual display unit (VDU). The VDU (see Fig. 4.10), which is often referred to as a video unit or video terminal, is a general purpose terminal which can be used for a wide range of business applications including those itemised in **20** (a), (b), (c), (d), (g). It is more modern than the teletype and much quieter in operation, which is why the VDU is tending to replace it in most environments. In appearance a VDU is like a television set with a keyboard or even like a microcomputer. In fact a micro can function as an intelligent VDU. The screen is a cathode ray tube (CRT) which displays

Figure 4.10 *IBM 3290 Information Panel. (Courtesy IBM United Kingdom Limited)*

images such as graphs, diagrams, sprites and text. This is in contrast with the teletype which prints text and graphs on paper by means of the printing unit. If a copy is required of the screen image then this can be accomplished by copying the screen display to a printer connected to the VDU. A light pen may be used in conjunction with the VDU for graphical applications (*see* Fig. 4.11).

Data is displayed on the screen from incoming signals or direct from the keyboard as everything that is keyed in is displayed. The screen can be cleared by a function key without destroying the contents of the memory. Data can be corrected (edited) on the screen before transmitting it to another terminal or computer. Windows or split screens are available for displaying several different elements simultaneously; different document images for instance.

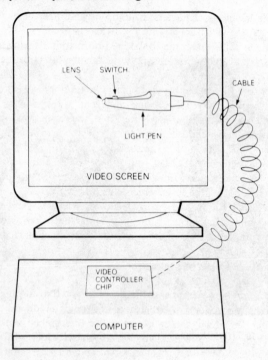

LENS   SWITCH

CABLE

LIGHT PEN

VIDEO SCREEN

VIDEO
CONTROLLER
CHIP

COMPUTER

Figure 4.11 *Video screen and light pen.*

A cursor, a moving bright spot on the surface of the screen, indicates the next position for entering characters. Sometimes, a winking cursor is used as a prompt for drawing attention to a specific section of the screen. Data is usually buffered allowing it to be transmitted in blocks of characters, instead of individual characters; this effectively increases the speed of transmission.

Other features which VDUs possess include character sets switchabie to other languages such as Spanish, German, French and English. Some models have screens which can be tilted and swivelled to suit the ergonomic needs of individuals. In addition they have switchable emulation facilities which allows one model to act as a different model. Various character resolutions are also available including characters made up of a number of bits in a matrix, among which are 8×10, 7×10 and 14×10.

Figure 4.10 illustrates the IBM 3290 Information Panel used for database/data communications applications and other similar tasks.

23. Intelligent terminals. Terminals with inbuilt processing capabilities are referred to as being intelligent, as they can perform tasks such as validating data before it is transmitted to a main computer. This is very useful because it relieves the main computer from this task allowing it to concentrate on high speed 'number crunching' activities. This of course generates a higher level of processing productivity. Intelligent terminals can be programmed to perform computing tasks which means that they are in effect computers which can be used on a stand-alone basis or can be part of a distributed network of terminals. Unintelligent terminals do not have built-in computing logic, only data transmission facilities.

Data collection systems

A data collection system is used for recording and transmitting data from remote locations to either a central point or directly to a computer. In general, data collection systems are applied where it is necessary speedily to collect data from dispersed locations within an organisation with a minimum of recording and in a form suitable for processing to obtain the desired information for the control of operations.

Applications include the recording of sales transactions at the point of sale and the recording of production data in respect of factory departments.

24. Factory terminal. The details which follow apply to the ICL Model 9603 factory terminal. It is a microprocessor-based terminal which allows data to be input via a keyboard, 10-column badge and 80-column punched card. It has a large, clear display for input instructions, error messages and replies to enquiries.

The prime types of data recorded include the completion of specific tasks, the movement of materials and components and attendance of personnel. Authorised personnel can retrieve up-to-date file information via the display. Typical enquiries include job status, next job details, component location or stock availability.

Variable information is entered via a 12-key numeric keyboard or a 42-key alpha-numeric keyboard. The keyboards are pressure sensitive. To simplify data entry, fixed information such as personnel or part numbers can be read in via a plastic badge.

The terminal has a card reader to accept standard or plastic 80-column punched cards. The terminal can hold up to 10 basic

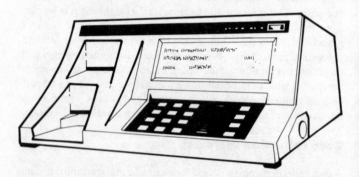

Figure 4.12 *ICL 9603 factory terminal. (Courtesy International Computers Limited)*

transaction programs which, together with guidance instructions, can be easily specified and amended by the user's own staff.

Initial program loading is directly from the 9600 System Controller, or via the card reader. A user identity check can be included in any program. The terminals can be located up to 7.6 wire km (4.7 miles) from the processor but this can be extended by a modem booster. The transmission speed is up to 4800 baud (bits per second) (*see* Fig. 4.12).

25. Article numbering and checkout scanning. Article numbering and checkout scanning is one of the most dynamic developments in retailing since self-service was introduced. It is being adopted by many supermarkets. The article numbering takes the form of an EAN (European Article Number) bar code (*see* Fig. 4.13) which is a series of bars and spaces of varying width to a predetermined structure and standard. A bar code is the machine-sensible version

Figure 4.13   *Example of a bar-code. (Courtesy Cadbury Limited)*

of a product's article number which is unique to each size, colour and pack of every item. Checkout scanning involves the scanning of the bar code on items sold by a low-intensity laser scanner and other electronic scanning devices such as light pens or slot scanners. The advantage to shoppers is more efficient checkout service, itemised till receipts identifying each item and its price, fewer items out of stock and possibly lower prices as a result of more efficient management of the supermarket.

26. Auto teller terminals. These terminals are for automating payments to bank customers and data collection. Many bank branches have facilities for providing customers with a cash withdrawal service outside normal banking hours. The availability of the service is determined by each bank. Each customer is provided with a plastic card which is placed in a special cash dispensing and recording machine (the auto teller terminal) installed through the wall of the bank. The customer keys in the personal number previously provided on the numeric keyboard of the terminal and enters the amount of money required on the same keyboard. The data is entered by the depression of a data entry key. The cash required is dispensed automatically (auto teller). The customer then removes the cash and the card from the terminal.

The transactions are recorded on the customer's statement, indicating which facility was used. A weekly withdrawal limit is given to each customer. The personal number ensures security because this is used in conjunction with the card. In the eventuality of the card being lost no one can use it without the personal number.

27. Remote batch terminals (distributed processing). Some remote batch terminals are designed as data communication systems for direct communication with a computer or as part of a comprehensive communications network forming a distributed processing system. Such terminals, at various remote locations, communicate with each other for the purpose of transmitting source data and printing documents from the transmitted data. They may also print documents from data prepared locally.

Portable computers and handprint data entry terminal

28. Portable computer for data capture. One particular model of computer, different from the normal microcomputer in appearance, is the HUSKY marketed by DVW Microelectronics Limited (*see* Fig. 4.14). It can be used for portable data capture or normal computer applications. It is used for the collection of routine data

Figure 4.14   *Husky microcomputer. (Courtesy DVW Microelectronics Limited)*

by non-computer personnel in such environments as the stores for the capture of part numbers, quantities and other data by means of a bar code reading wand, which reads bar coded labels on the bins containing the various stored items.

The machine can be interfaced for printing reports on most types of printer. Data can be transmitted to a central database for compilation if required or the data can be retained in the internal memory until the next period. It can also be used for electronic work study as its built-in calendar clock facilitates accurate timing of individual operations.

The features of the computer include a 40-key tactile keyboard; synchronous or asynchronous communication facilities; user programmability; a 128-character, 4-line LCD screen; a BASIC interpreter and a memory capacity of either 32K, 48K, 64K or 144K bytes.

29. TEL-time data collection terminal. TEL-time (*see* Fig. 4.15) is a system for the collection and analysis of work measurement data. The system uses portable data capture terminals which are programmable. They validate and store data entered by the observer ready for transfer to a microcomputer for analysis. The TEL-time is a flexible tool for use in work study and industrial engineering applications. It operates with the ACT Sirius and the IBM PC computers. The terminal is used to time each element and apply a performance rating. It is connected to a microcomputer and the study data is transferred to disc storage. The terminal and observer are then free to continue with the next study. The computer analyses the data and prints the standard reports included in the TEL-time package. The terminals can be either hand-held or used with a study board. Data can be communicated to the computer direct or by telephone line for remote operations. The terminal has a built-in display and may be used for any data capture/analysis applications.

30. Handprint data entry terminal. One such system is marketed by Quest CIL and is called Micropad Handprint data entry terminal (*see* Fig. 4.16). It is a local or remote terminal which enables handprinted data to be captured at the time of writing and the data is validated simultaneously. The device converts the handprinted

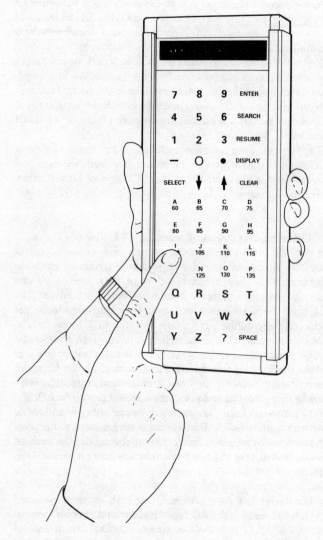

Figure 4.15 *Tel-time terminal. (Courtesy Telford Management Services Limited)*

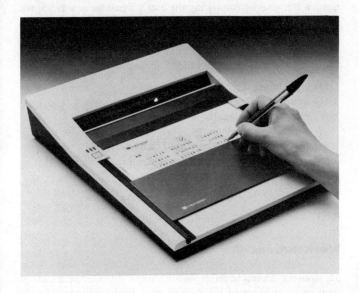

Figure 4.16 *Handprint data entry terminal. (Courtesy Quest Micropad Limited)*

alphanumeric characters into ASCII code and transmits this code to any host computer via a standard interface.

It comprises a pressure sensitive writing surface, an inbuilt microprocessor and an integral 40-character line display. Data and signatures are written using an ordinary ballpoint pen or pencil on documents designed by the user to suit their specific applications. This method of data capture may be used for entering customer order details, retail point of sale recording, payroll and file amendments, etc.

Available options allow the data to be transmitted immediately it is written or stored within Micropad and transmitted as a block of up to 512 characters, or validated locally within Micropad. Additional features include the ability to output alpha characters as upper or lower case and ASCII special and control characters. The Q-Sign option allows Micropad to function as a dynamic signature verification terminal by comparing the user's signature as it is written with the reference signature. This provides immediate authorisation for transactions.

Data is validated character by character and field by field before being transmitted. Standard validation checks include:

(*a*) alpha/numeric/special characters;
(*b*) left/right/full field justification;
(*c*) mandatory/optional field;
(*d*) logical data checks;
(*e*) maximum data field length: 32 characters;
(*f*) maximum number of fields per document: 50.

Special European character sets are available including Swedish/Finnish, Danish/Norwegian, and Spanish/Portuguese.

Workstations

31. General characteristics. Workstations provide the means of improving office productivity by using technologically based tools for creating records, amending records, processing and communicating information, inter-company transactions, electronic mail, electronic filing and word processing, etc.

The workstation consists of a video display unit (VDU), a keyboard, a microprocessor for text and image processing and also contains an internal memory. Workstations usually share printing and central storage resources when part of a network. Workstations may also have voice handling capabilities which enable voice messages to be stored and electronically mailed to other users on the network. Workstations may also be connected to mainframe computers for gaining access to a corporate database and to act as a data collection terminal (*see* Fig. 4.17).

32. Information Management Processor (IMP). This is an integrated office automation system available from Office Technology Limited (OTL) (which is part of Information Technology Limited (ITL)). It is a system aimed at improving the management of

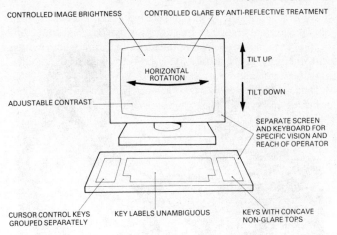

Figure 4.17 *Features of a workstation.*

information in work groups, i.e. secretary–manager relationships or groups of personnel whose work interacts and who need to share information. The system integrates text and voice handling, and word and data processing in the creation, storage and communication of information through electronic filing and electronic mail. The system provides each user with an integrated multi-functional personal workstation capable of handling all forms of information across a wide range of needs (*see* Fig. 4.18).

The system also aims at improving the productivity of office professionals and managers who originate and use information. The system's voice processing facilities enable these office principals, as they may be called, to create voice documents (or messages or annotation on existing documents) by speaking into the workstation's integrated handset and then SEND or FILE them just like text. The voice facility allows a 'casual' user to add easily and effectively annotations and commentaries to drafts and other documents. The office principal can also receive quickly comments on a document from a number of people. Voice messages can be registered in the 'IN-TRAY' facility, which enables a desk to be kept tidy and messages kept easily accessible, not buried under a mass of 'debris'.

Figure 4.18 *OTL Information Management Processor. (Courtesy Office Technology Limited)*

An office system controller provides shared information storage and distribution resources for the whole system. The system has two modes of workstation, one of which has facilities for handling text, data and graphics and the principal workstation, which, in addition to these, also has voice input and output facilities. Each workstation maintains its processing independence with its own 16-bit microprocessor and 256K bytes of memory. A daisy wheel printer is used with a range of typestyles and a printing speed of 40 cps.

The system is designed to meet the physical and psychological needs of the personnel using the facilities. Accordingly the display screen is designed to provide maximum visual comfort in order to minimise eyestrain and fatigue. It can be tilted and swivelled, independently of the keyboard, to the most comfortable position for the user. Documents are displayed on the screen in paper-like black-on-white and scroll smoothly up and down and side to side, where necessary, for extra-wide pages. The user is guided through the operation of the system with clearly marked keys, helpful menus and prompts; HELP facilities are also available.

The system's document processing package facilitates record processing applications such as directories, personnel records, inventories and customer and supplier lists. These records can be selected against a range of criteria, sorted or rearranged for a particular purpose. Powerful letter or list processing facilities are also provided on the system to produce personalised letters by merging variable information from customer lists into standard letters. The system can also handle pre-printed or user-defined forms.

The system provides an 'electronic' filing system on a high capacity, fast access filestore within the controller. The structure of the filing system is under the control of the user and can mimic the existing manual filing system in the way files are named, indexed, classified and accessed. Common information can be held in general files which are accessible to all members of a department. Personal files can be accessed only with knowledge of the individual user name and 'key' or password, thus upholding privacy and confidentiality. When a document is no longer required for current use it can be relegated to a 'wastebin' which is an extension of the electronic filing system. It can be retrieved in an 'uncrumpled state' when reference to it is necessary.

Speech synthesis and analog input

33. **Speech synthesis.** The recognition of speech is achieved using allophones, the basic speech sounds, by storing a digitised pattern in the form of a reference matrix. This is a pattern of signals unique for each vocabulary word; any English word can be constructed and spoken by this means. Words are recognised by a matching technique and the speech pattern of several speakers can be stored simultaneously. Having obtained a matrix pattern of the words the computer performs a search routine for the nearest match. When this is located it compares the bit count relationship with the memory pattern. The chosen word is then displayed. If a satisfactory match is not achieved it is necessary to repeat the word spoken.

It is possible to incorporate speech in BASIC programs to be run on microcomputers so that spoken words can be integrated in the normal program to be generated as output for games and other applications. Speech synthesisers have a built-in amplifier, volume control and speaker. The latest technology is based on sound discrimination over telephone lines which is speaker-independent. This requires improved discrimination of speech patterns which is accomplished by customised chip elements designed to distinguish the sounds that combine to create words. The systems are language-independent because of the technology used and their use is expected to increase at a fast rate over the next few years.

A new service which provides company information using voice technology has been launched by Dun and Bradstreet. The service called DunsVoice operates through a standard multi-frequency pushbutton telephone and is probably the first credit-control computer to speak with a friendly human voice. To make a credit enquiry the caller simply dials up the Dun and Bradstreet database which currently holds records on more than a million businesses in the UK alone.

34. Analog (digital) input. This type of input is applicable to process and machine control, data logging, patient monitoring systems and laboratory projects, etc. A sensor collects details relating to the status of the system being controlled in the form of analog signals which are converted to digital signals by a digitiser. Analog data is represented in a continuous form as contrasted with digital data which is in discrete form, i.e. finite values. Analog data is represented by physical variables such as voltage, resistance, temperature, pressure and rate of flow. As variations in these variables takes place they are input to the digitiser which is continuously scanned by the computer.

35. Light pen. A light pen is an electronic device in the form of a photo-diode on the end of a cable which is used in combination with a visual display unit or video screen. It is used to display, modify or detect images on the screen often in CAD (Computer Aided Design) applications. This is achieved by passing the light pen across the surface of the screen to trace the outline of the image to be displayed.

The computer can detect the position of the pen on the screen by counting the number of vertical and horizontal synchronisation pulses (*see* Fig. 4.11).

36. Graphics tablet. Sometimes referred to as a digitising tablet which is constructed from a sensitive semi-conducting material which can trace the movement of a stylus forming graphical shapes. The shapes are converted into digital signals which are input directly into the computer. A mouse may be used as an alternative to a graphics stylus for achieving the same purpose.

37. Mouse. This is a small device (*see* Fig. 4.19) which can be moved by hand in any direction across a graphics tablet by means of a ball-bearing on its underside and which has one or two buttons on its upper surface. It can be used to plot images in defined locations on a screen, to select icons (*see* Figs. 2.4–2.6) representing particular office facilities in electronic desk top systems, and in word processing applications to rearrange the text on screen and for modifying the font used.

In an electronic desk top application the cursor can be moved around the screen by moving the mouse in the direction required.

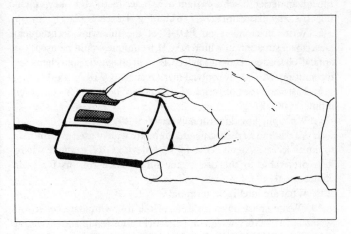

Figure 4.19 *The 'mouse'—hand-held cursor control device. (Courtesy Rank Xerox (UK) Limited)*

When the cursor is correctly positioned a push of the button on the mouse will select the corresponding office facility. In this way, a 'document' or 'folder' icon on the 'desk top' can be copied on to the 'out basket' icon for despatch to an electronic distribution list or sent for filing or printing by using the appropriate icons. With regard to electronic mail, documents on the screen can be selected for despatch to specific mail boxes stored in a file server. A small 'envelope' appears in the 'in-basket' on the screen of the receiver's workstation. This 'envelope' can then be opened by the receiver.

Progress test 4

1. Write short notes relating to computer input and data capture. (**1, 2**)

2. Specify the nature of Kimball tags. (**3**)

3. Specify methods of preparing magnetic media for computer input. (**5–8**)

4. (*a*) Describe, with the aid of a block diagram, a computer controlled keying system (key-to-disc or key-to-tape). (*b*) What are the advantages of such a system over older methods of keypunching? List any disadvantages. (**6 and Fig. 4.2**) (*C & G*)

5. Write brief notes on FOUR of the following techniques. Describe a situation in which EACH technique would be used: (*a*) optical character recognition (OCR); (*b*) magnetic ink character recognition (MICR); (*c*) optical mark readers (OMR). (**9–17**)

6. List the types of terminal which may be used for computer input. (**18, 19**)

7. What purpose do terminals serve? (**20**)

8. VDUs and keyboard printer units are widely used as terminals to multi-access systems. Give for each device ONE example where it is preferable to the use of the other. Give reasons for your choice. (**21, 22**)

9. What are intelligent terminals? (**23**)

10. Write short notes on each of the following data collection systems: (*a*) factory terminal; (*b*) article numbering and checkout scanning; (*c*) auto teller terminals; (*d*) remote batch terminals. (**24–27**)

11. Define the nature of the following methods of capturing data: (*a*) portable computer; (*b*) handprint data entry terminal. (**28–30**)

12. Workstations provide the means for improving office productivity. Discuss. (**31, 32**)

13. Computer input may be achieved by speech synthesis and analog signals. Indicate the nature and use of these methods. (**33, 34**)

14. Define the nature of a light pen, graphics tablet and a mouse. (**35–37**)

5

Computer output

Printed

1. Types of computer output. The various types of output from a computer system may be chosen from the following list according to specific requirements:

(a) printed;
(b) visual display;
(c) COM (Computer Output on Microfilm);
(d) graphical;
(e) magnetically encoded.

2. Printed output. Most systems require printed output in the form of payrolls and invoices and management information, etc. and according to the type of computer in use a large range of printers and printing systems are available. These include:

(a) line printers;
(b) matrix printers;
(c) band printers;
(d) visual record printers;
(e) laser printers;
(f) teletype;
(g) page printing system;
(h) portable printer/printing terminal;
(i) distributed electronic printer;
(j) electronic printing system.

3. Hard copy. A printer is very useful, in fact imperative, in a business computer system for obtaining printed documents in the form of cheques, invoices and labels, etc. For normal computing purposes it is very useful to have a record of programs and these can be printed out from memory when required. Similarly, when a program is run, especially for complicated tabulations, it is useful to have the results printed out. This is in distinction to displaying results of calculations on the screen in a transitory manner which is adequate for some types of calculations.

Types of printer

4. **Character printers.** Character printers print one character at a time in the same way as a typewriter except that they have facilities for printing from left to right and right to left. The dot matrix printer prints characters by a print head consisting of a matrix of pins which form the shape of the characters. The typical printing speed is in the region of 120/150 cps (characters per second) which is largely attributable to the bi-directional printing facility. The fairly high speed is accomplished because the printer is designed to print 'on the fly', i.e. whilst in motion, with the print-head moving at a uniform horizontal velocity and also bi-directionally as mentioned above.

Daisy wheel printers have a set of characters embossed on the tips of individual stalks radiating from the central hub of the wheel forming the appearance of a daisy. The wheel rotates until the correct character is positioned in front of a hammer which strikes the stalk or petal against a carbon ribbon to produce an image of the character. The daisy wheel printer is slower than the dot matrix printer mainly because the daisy wheel is momentarily stationary for each character to be positioned which slows down the speed of operation. This type of printer prints at a typical speed of 40/50 cps. The print quality, however, is superior to that of the dot matrix printer and produces 'letter quality print' which is of importance when considering a printer for word processing.

5. **Line printers.** Line printers are so called because they print a complete line after a complete revolution of the print barrel in respect of a barrel printer and after one revolution of the chain in respect of a chain printer. Line printers operate at various speeds

according to the model, e.g. typical speeds are 200, 300, 600, 720, 1,500, 2,000 and 3,000 lpm (lines per minute). The barrel type printer has character sets embossed around the print barrel. When a line is to be printed the barrel rotates so that all the As are printed followed by the Bs and so on. A chain printer has characters embossed on a chain which rotates so that every character passes the print position. A hammer prints the required character.

6. Thermal printers. This type of printer uses thermal electro-sensitive paper which has a thin coating of aluminium over a black or blue inked surface. By passing an electrical current through a needle onto the paper a spark is formed which removes a small area of aluminium exposing the black or blue undersurface in the shape of specific characters.

General features of printers

7. Features of printers. Small printers normally have speed defined in terms of characters per second whereas large fast printers, often classed as line printers or even page printers, have speed defined in terms of lines per minute or even lines per second. When selecting a printer it is necessary to determine the width of the carriage required in relation to the size of documents to be printed out such as payrolls which are very wide and require a corresponding size of carriage to accommodate them. It is also necessary to consider the number of characters per inch, i.e. the print density, as more characters can be printed on a line with a density of 15 characters per inch than ten per inch. The more characters on each line the fewer are the carriage returns for a given volume of printed matter which increases the speed of output. Printers are available with a wide range of features. It is such features that must be taken into account when assessing the most suitable computer configuration for specific needs. Some of the features are:

  (*a*) speed;
  (*b*) column width, e.g. 80 or 136 characters;
  (*c*) tractor or friction feed;
  (*d*) two-colour printing;
  (*e*) parallel or serial interface;
  (*f*) pin addressable graphics (printing of images);

(g) bi-directional printing;

(h) condensed and double-width printing;

(i) alternative character sets;

(j) plain or thermal paper;

(k) cut sheets or continuous stationery;

(l) single or multi-part sets;

(m) varying character pitches;

(n) price;

(o) baud rate.

Electronic (laser) printers

8. General considerations of laser printers. Laser printers function in a similar manner to xerographic copiers whereby the laser beam is scanned onto a photo-sensitive drum creating a reversed image of a page. The latent image is then cascaded with a carbon toner and transferred onto the paper. Lasers are quieter than all impact printers which is a major consideration when selecting a printer. They are also faster than impact and non-impact printers with facilities for dealing with text and graphics which is not a good feature of matrix and ink-jets. Daisy wheel printers cannot deal with graphics at all as they are restricted to the characters on the petals whereas lasers are faster printers producing images on paper from thousands of tiny dots. More details are provided below. Lasers were initially very expensive, costing in the region of £20,000 to £100,000 but they are now available at prices from £1,400–£3,000 upwards.

9. Distributed electronic printer. An example of this type of machine is the Rank Xerox 2700 printer (*see* Fig. 5.1) which is designed to operate anywhere; in the office, data centre or at a remote location. It is a small, quiet, multi-font laser printer designed for distributed printing in a general purpose data processing environment or as a printer on a small business computer. It can also be used in a network environment. It accepts digital input through communication lines or directly through parallel interfaces (either the standard Centronics or Dataproducts).

The machine produces high quality output on standard cut-sheet bond paper and provides the full International ISO 6937 character

Figure 5.1 *The Xerox 2700 distributed electronic printer. (Courtesy Rank Xerox (UK) Limited)*

set, which encompasses the Teletex character set. A high-resolution laser prints 90 000 spots per square inch. It can handle text applications such as letters and memos in addition to standard data processing outputs. It incorporates facilities to change font cartridges, and additional typefaces can be received from the host computer. An organisation's logos and executive signatures can be digitised and stored for use as required.

Typefaces can be changed within a single line to enable individual words or phrases to be emphasised. Simple forms or bar charts can be created through character substitution or by drawing rules. It can print up to twelve pages per minute. The heart of the system is a microprocessor and image generator.

10. Electronic printing system. The Xerox 9700 printing system (*see* Figs. 5.2 and 5.3) combines computer, laser and xerographic technologies. The system consists of a number of subsystems which are outlined below.

(*a*) *Input subsystem.* This provides data for the system via 9-track magnetic tape either 1 600 or 6 250 bits (bytes, in effect) per inch for off-line operation via a tape drive. An on-line interface allows the system to be directly connected to a host computer, or input can be obtained from an 850/860 word processor.

(*b*) *Control subsystem.* The system controller contains a 50 mega-byte disc for input buffering and user file storage. The controller performs all the data handling, formatting and input buffering tasks. Operator control of the system is facilitated by means of a keyboard/display console which is used for initiating and monitoring jobs. It consists of a minicomputer and control electronics.

(*c*) *Imaging subsystem.* The image generator provides electronic control for the blue laser beam. It accesses the font memory in the controller to create character images and forms. It accepts the formatted page of data including forms and logos; and utilises a scanning laser beam to generate lines of modulated light for the continuously moving photoreceptor of the Xerographic subsystem.

(*d*) *Xerographic subsystem.* This incorporates all the normal functions of a xerographic printer including paper handling and development of the latent image on the output page.

(*e*) *Output subsystem.* A two bin output stacker provides the capability for paper stacking, report collating and sample prints in the sample print tray. Reports are separated by offsetting each copy set approximately 12mm from the previous one. When the active bin has been filled, if the second bin is full, the system will stop printing.

Printing is performed from the system disc enabling multiple copies to be printed without retransmission of data when on-line to

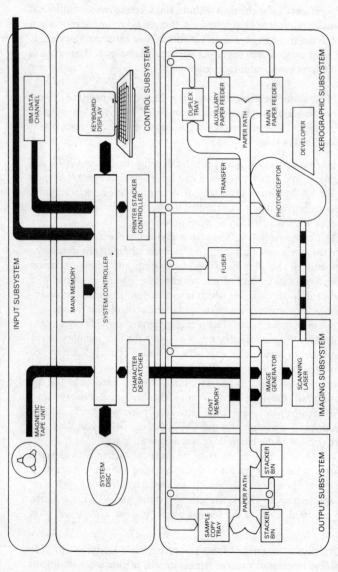

Figure 5.2 Outline of Xerox 9700 electronic printing system. (Courtesy Rank Xerox (UK) Limited)

a data channel. For off-line operation the operator can mount and feed a new tape while the system finishes the printing of the previous job. This system prints 2 pages per second or 120 pages per minute on plain paper. Unlimited font styles in sizes from 4 point to 24 point. Spacing is continuously variable from 3 to 18 lines per inch and from 4 to 30 characters per inch.

Magnetically encoded

11. Magnetically encoded output. Output in this form is usually for the purpose of storing records and the media used for this purpose include floppy discs, exchangeable and fixed discs and magnetic tape.

Visual display unit and graph plotter

12. Visual display unit (VDU). A VDU is a dual purpose device which has already been discussed in detail (*see* 4:22). It can be used as an input device for data, such as in an order-entry system, by means of the keyboard as well as being an output device for displaying text and graphical characters.

13. Graph plotter. In addition to the recently developed printer/plotter extensively used on microcomputers, a dedicated graph plotter is used for the output of graphical information on large and small computers. A plotter provides a permanent hard copy of the graphical output as opposed to a VDU, which displays graphical output in a transitory manner on the video screen as it disappears when the machine is switched off. The output can be multicoloured.

Computer output on microfilm (COM)

14. Nature of COM. Computer output by microfilm is an alternative to printed output, which is relatively slow even for the faster type of printer compared with the speed with which COM can be produced. COM not only produces output faster but also reduces stationery costs and the space needed for storing computer printouts. It is also an information retrieval system.

COM may be defined as a method which stems the tide of the 'paperwork explosion' which has long been a feature of computerised batch processing systems. Hard copy output is not always required consequently, if all computer output is committed to paper, a problem soon arises, not only deciding *who* should have *what* reports but *where* they are all going to be stored *just in case they may be needed*. Copies of computer output can be stored on microfilm or microfiche at much reduced size compared to the size of computer stationery pages. This makes storage of output less of a problem particularly when it is supported by an effective information retrieval system.

15. Hardware and software requirements. A typical COM system is minicomputer controlled and produces alphanumeric or graphical output on imaged, cut and processed dry silver microfiche, either direct by means of a COM recorder connected directly to the host processor or via COM formatted magnetic tapes for off-line mode. Disc drives are used for storage of parameters and job details. Software provides facilities for forms drawing and outputting. Reduction ratios are typically $24 \times$, $42 \times$ and $48 \times$. Images can be stored either on film or 105mm microfiche. The COM system adds an index to each image for reference and retrieval purposes. Microfiche is more popular than roll film as images are more easily accessed by simply moving the microfiche under the viewer to the desired image. This facilitates the location of component parts for a particular unit so that it can be located in the stores of a spares organisation, for instance. Related images can be stored on the same microfiche. Fiche are more easily stored than rolls of film and fiche readers are less expensive than roll film readers, are capable of a much higher quality of image reproduction and are also less complex.

16. Information retrieval. Information stored as images on film or microfiche can be accessed for retrieval purposes by a microfilm or fiche viewer. If a hard copy is required then this is facilitated by a 'demand' printer.

Computer graphics

17. Graphics defined. Graphics may be defined as pictures in the widest sense including graphs, diagrams, charts and moving images on a video screen of a microcomputer, VDU or workstation. There exists three broad categories of graphics, i.e. block graphics, pixel and high resolution graphics (to which may be added sprite graphics). Graphics are widely used on home computers for playing computer games, for which there exists a profusion of programs available off the shelf ready to load from cassette or key in from programs published in computer magazines of which there are also a great many.

From a business point of view, graphical presentation of information is often more useful and has a higher impact than detailed printed reports. Images can be displayed on a screen and printed out on such devices as graph plotters, printer/plotters and on normal computer printers, as it is possible to print a copy of the display on the screen with some computers. Graphical presentation also embraces the display of forms and documents on a screen to enable basic office tasks to be performed in a similar way but using electronic technology. In addition, some computers have electronic desk top facilities which display files and documents on a screen for a variety of purposes (*see* Fig. 5.3).

18. Vector graphics. This is a technique, rather than a type of graphics, as it is a means of displaying graphical images using line drawings on a video screen. If the input is by keyboard then statements containing PLOT or DRAW commands define the plotting coordinates. The same results are achieved by the use of a light pen applied directly to the surface of the screen or by using a graphics tablet as an alternative to a light pen.

Pixel and high resolution graphics

19. Pixel graphics. The screen of a microcomputer or VDU is divided into small squares called pixels, i.e. picture elements or picture cells. The pattern of pixels which are activated make up the image displayed on the screen. The quality of the image depends on the number of pixels on the screen: the higher the number, the higher the resolution. Some micros have picture elements consisting of a 6×2 matrix of phosphor dots. Each pixel is stored in RAM in binary code and can be input by keyboard or from backing storage.

Pixel graphics fall in between block graphics and high resolution

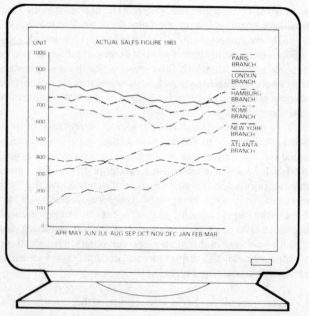

(Courtesy Sharp Electronics (UK) Limited)

Figure 5.3 *Sharp MZ-3541 Business Computer displaying graphics. (Courtesy Sharp Electronics (UK) Limited)*

graphics. They give the user some control over each picture element as each can be called up individually and located in specified positions on the video screen. A pixel is the smallest pattern of dots that can be accessed for display.

20. High resolution graphics. Resolution is defined in terms of pixels which can be displayed on the video screen, the greater the number, the greater the sharpness of the image. The less expensive microcomputers with HRG capability have low definition compared to the more expensive business micros.

Applesoft, for use on the Apple computer, has special commands which allows shapes to be drawn in high resolution graphics. Before they can be used however a 'shape' must be defined by a 'shape definition'. This consists of a sequence of plotting vectors which are stored in the internal memory. One or more shape definitions with their index make up a 'shape table' which can be created from the keyboard and saved for future use on disc or cassette. The shape definition is constructed in enlarged form on the screen by the plotting commands. The shape is formed by setting specific squares on the screen by cursor controls.

Block and sprite graphics

21. Block graphics. Some microcomputers have a display code containing a range of characters, including graphic shapes, specific to that machine. They may be displayed on the video screen by POKE statements. In addition to a display code some micros have a set of ASCII characters which can be displayed by a PRINT CHR$ (X) statement where CHR$ indicates that ASCII is being used and 'X' is the code number of the specific character to be displayed. Graphic characters available direct from the keyboard can be displayed by a PRINT statement.

Block graphics allow displays to be generated without unnecessary complexity but do not provide any control over the individual dots making up the image. The 'block' characters can be made to move on the screen by the use of vector graphic techniques, using SET and RESET and by modifying the display address on the screen in conjunction with a statement for clearing the screen of the previous display. The relocation of the graphic character simulates movement.

22. Sprite graphics. Sprites are user definable graphical shapes used in computer games. Originally developed by Texas Instruments, sprite graphics are available on several home computers including the Commodore 64. Atari users know sprites as PMGs, i.e. Player Missile Graphics.

Sprites can be moved across the surface of the screen while the background remains static. This is accomplished by means of several screen planes. Conventional graphics pictures are built up on a single screen but with sprite graphics the computer has several planes or layers (the Sord M5 having thirty-two separate planes) each of which can have its own pictures which generates a three dimensional effect. The Commodore 64 has software available for defining sprites which consist of 24×21 pixel shapes which can be manipulated by a series of POKE commands.

Turtle graphics

23. Turtle. A turtle, in the context of computers, is a mechanical device (a robot) which is connected to a computer by a cable. The turtle has two wheels and a pen and operates under the control of the computer using the LOGO programming language to draw lines on a sheet of paper to form squares, triangles, circles and other shapes. An alternative version of the turtle is a triangle of light on the video screen—the required shapes being formed by means of movement of the triangle.

24. Turtle graphics. Young children at school are often taught to use a computer by using a mechanical turtle (older children use the alternative version of the turtle in conjunction with a video screen and the LOGO language). The command FORWARD 20 causes the turtle to move forward 20 steps drawing a line behind it. The command RIGHT 90 causes the turtle to make a right angle and BACKWARD 10 causes the turtle to move 10 steps backwards. Various combinations of similar commands enables different shapes to be drawn. The turtle can also be instructed to remember the commands.

A square would be drawn by means of the following commands.

```
FORWARD 20
RIGHT  90
FORWARD 20
RIGHT  90
FORWARD 20
RIGHT  90
FORWARD 20
RIGHT  90
```

The same result can be achieved more simply by a BOX command:

```
TO BOX
REPEAT 4 [FORWARD 20 RIGHT 90]
END
```

25. Computer aided design (CAD). A technique for the development of graphical designs of various types using a computer equipped with sophisticated software and a light pen in conjunction with a video screen. These resources enable the initial design to be displayed on the screen and subsequently modified if necessary. The image on the screen can be rotated to obtain a three-dimensional view in order to assess its features from various aspects. The technique allows standard shapes to be stored on disc and accessed when required for incorporation in other designs. It saves considerable time in the design activity and improves quality as designs can be speedily checked to ensure compatibility with specifications. Errors can be corrected by light pen. The technique is widely used for the design of aircraft, cars and computers as well as a wide range of other products. *See* also Volume 2.

Progress test 5

1. Summarise the different methods of producing computer output. (**1**)

2. Summarise the different ways of obtaining printed output. (**2**)

3. Define the term 'hard copy'. (**3**)

4. List the main features of a dot matrix and a daisy wheel printer. (**4**)

5. Outline the features of: (*a*) thermal printer (*b*) line printer. (**5, 6**)

6. Specify the manner of determining the speed of printers. (**7**)

7. Printers are available with a wide range of features. List the features which you would take into account when selecting a printer. (**7, 8**)

8. Outline the features of an electronic printer. (**9, 10**)

9. Outline the nature of a visual display unit and a graph plotter. (**12, 13**)

10. The data processing manager of a large computer installation is concerned about the high volume of printout from the installation's two printers and the subsequent paper storage problems in the user departments. As a consequence he is considering the use of 'computer output on microfilm', COM (microfilm or microfiche). Explain what is meant by COM and the difference between microfilm and

microfiche. Give the advantages and disadvantages of the systems. (**14–16**)

11. What are computer graphics? (**17**)

12. Define the meaning of the following terms: (*a*) vector graphics (*b*) pixel graphics (*c*) high resolution graphics (*d*) block graphics (*e*) sprite graphics (*f*) turtle graphics. (**18–24**)

13. Define the meaning of CAD and specify its purpose. (**25**)

6

Data storage and retrieval: basic concepts

Data storage—file concepts

1. Data and data storage concepts. After data is processed it often needs to be stored for future use either for reference purposes, as in the case of customers' and suppliers' names and addresses for correspondence purposes, or for obtaining details of product descriptions and prices for processing customers' orders. Data is also stored to provide a running account of the status of an entity such as the amount outstanding on customers' and suppliers' accounts; the quantity of items in the stores and the value of work-in-process on the various jobs and contracts, etc.

At this juncture it is important to appreciate that although the output from an information processing system is classed as 'information' it is often referred to as being 'data' as in the case of data files or a database. The terms 'attribute' and 'data field' are meant to be interpreted as being the same thing, i.e. a unit of data such as a clock number, part number, quantity or price, etc. Such terms are used in the same context and this has been stated to avoid any possible confusion. Combinations of related data fields (data elements or attributes) constitute records. Sets of records stored together constitute a 'file'. Files are discussed in later sections.

2. Methods of storage. Data in a clerical system may be stored in loose-leaf ledgers, trays with visible card indexes in filing cabinets or containers of ledger cards. In a computer system data is stored in magnetic files which includes various types of magnetic disc and magnetic tape. However data is stored, it must be capable of being retrieved easily and quickly. To ensure this it needs to be organised into effective file structures known as 'file organisation' (*see* **11–20**).

The location of data needs to be known in order to access it and interpret it. It is also necessary to determine how data will be organised, as a set of related fields constitutes a set of related data elements which need to be grouped together. Data relationships is a major consideration in the structuring of databases. It is not necessary to store related data items together as they can be stored in separate locations and linked together, to be explained later, for retrieval. This is known as 'path dependency' because it is interpreted according to the path by which it is reached rather than its location. This is also a feature of some databases.

Storage and retrieval—use of pointers

3. Optimisation of storage and retrieval. To achieve effective storage and retrieval of data the two factors can be dealt with as separate activities. Data can be saved initially on to disc or tape files to achieve high-speed input of data to storage. The file can then be organised to facilitate the data retrieval method to be employed during processing activities.

4. Pointers. The linking up of data elements is achieved by 'pointers' which identify other related data elements. As an example a set of related data elements for a personnel record is constituted as follows:

(a)	*Surname*	Smith
(b)	*Christian name*	James
(c)	*Relative pointer*	120
(d)	*Absolute pointer*	20812C
(e)	*Marital status*	Married
(f)	*Status*	Accounts clerk
(g)	*Department*	Accounting

The relative pointer, 120, specifies that Smith's record is the 120th record on the payroll file. Provided a start address, i.e. the beginning of the file and length of each record is known, the 'absolute' address of a record can be computed by the file management system in the operating system.

'Absolute' pointers provide the fastest access to records. In this instance, the absolute pointer 20812C specifies the 'physical' address of associated data such as details relating to the career and training of James Smith. The address enables a record stored on a disc file to be accessed. Problems arise when data has to be relocated because it necessitates amendment of the pointers. Records are accessed more slowly using 'relative' pointers but they have the advantage of enabling records to be physically relocated on a disc file without needing to modify the pointers. As long as the operating system knows where the file commences the data can be accessed and retrieved. 'Symbolic' pointers, such as a name, although providing a logical link between data items also provide the slowest means of access compared with the other methods, as the symbolic pointer has to be converted into an actual address for retrieval purposes. If Smith's record contained an extra field such as INTERESTS then this could be used as a symbolic link to access details of his interests.

Fields

5. Key fields. A key field, also referred to as a 'record key', is used to identify a specific record unambiguously. Transaction data contains a key field which is matched with its record on the relevant master file for updating. Records on a reference file are also accessed by a key field. Key fields may consist of either an insurance policy number, employee number, catalogue number or product number, etc. Some key fields are made up of a 'faceted' code whereby each position in the code number has a specific meaning such as type of material, size, specification, stores location.

6. Types of key field. Key fields may be either 'unique' or 'generic'. Unique keys are used to refer to a single group of data fields comprising a complete record. If unique keys are used, which they usually are, then duplicate key fields cannot appear in the file as it will be impossible to specify a particular record uniquely. Generic keys identify several groups of data which have something in common. In respect of Smith's record, previously introduced, his surname can be used as a key to access all other records of people with the same name. Any field can be used as a generic key field.

7. Fixed-length fields and records. Records consisting of a fixed number of fields, of fixed length and always in the same sequence within a record are known as 'flat' records and they allow easier maintenance than non-flat records. Fixed-length implies that the number of character positions allocated to each field is constant for each specific record although particular fields will not all be of the same length. Some fields will not always require the full number of character positions as descriptive data varies in length. It becomes necessary to insert 'space' characters to the right in such cases so that each field has the fixed number of characters stipulated by the program.

8. Variable-length records: variable number of fields. When the number of fields in records varies they become variable-length records and are referred to as 'non-flat' records. This would occur if some records contained an additional fixed-length field to the normal number of fields in a record of a specific type. Records containing an additional field could have them stored in an overflow record associated by a pointer holding the relative address of the associated data. On the other hand, if the main record provides for the additional field which some records require then the file could have relative pointers addressing it. This avoids the complexity of processing variable-length records.

9. Variable-length records: variable-length fields. Variable-length records contain fields in which the number of characters varies according to the number of characters required which is attributable to the varying length of descriptive, prices, quantities, values and other similar data elements. This method of data storage recognises that all similar records do not always need the same number of character positions for the same field. Records which vary in length optimise storage capacity whatever the magnetic storage media used, as unnecessary character positions are not provided for. They do, however, require more complex programming. It is necessary to test for the end of one field and the beginning of the next since they do not occur in fixed positions as they do with fixed-length fields. This is achieved by an 'end of field marker', a 'bit' pattern which informs the software of the demarcation point between fields. A different bit pattern located at the end of the last field in a record informs the software that the end of a record has been reached.

10. Variable-length records: variable number of variable-length fields. Some systems require a variable number of variable-length fields. In such cases an index which identifies and separates the fields is located at the beginning of the record. The index identifies the type of field, its start position and length.

File organisation and retrieval of records

11. Methods of file organisation. The available methods include:

  (*a*) serial;
  (*b*) sequential;
  (*c*) indexed sequential;
  (*d*) direct;
  (*e*) inverted;
  (*f*) database:
    (*i*) hierarchical;
    (*ii*) relational;
    (*iii*) network.

12. Serial files. The records on the file are not in any specific order and this method of file organisation is therefore inefficient. If a file was recorded on magnetic tape it would be necessary to wind the tape backwards and forwards to locate a specific record as they are accessed in the sequence in which they are physically stored on the file media, i.e. serially. A full index would be necessary to access a specific record on disc. It is necessary to sort a serial transaction file into the sequential order of the master file before updating so that the file can be processed with a single pass (*see* Fig. 6.1).

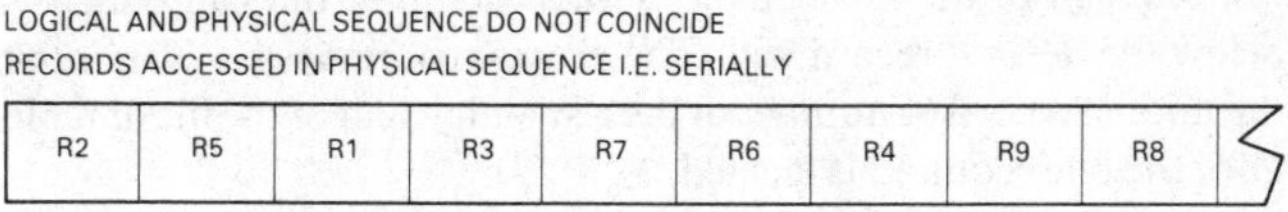

LOGICAL AND PHYSICAL SEQUENCE DO NOT COINCIDE
RECORDS ACCESSED IN PHYSICAL SEQUENCE I.E. SERIALLY

R2	R5	R1	R3	R7	R6	R4	R9	R8

Figure 6.1 *Serial organisation.*

13. Sequential files. With this method of file organisation, records are normally organised in ascending order of key field. When new records are added the sequence is maintained in respect of magnetic tape files by the insertion of records in the correct sequence on a new reel of tape. It is necessary to generate a completely new tape when applying file amendments including adjustments, deletions and additions because it is not possible to physically insert or delete them on the same tape.

On a disc file when records cannot be stored in the correct location on a track due to an overflow condition the logical sequence of records, not the physical one, can be maintained by using pointers and an overflow area. When the software reaches a pointer it retrieves the overflow record before dealing with the next in sequence. Serial and sequential access means the same thing in respect of files on magnetic tape when in sequence but this may not be the case with disc files as the records accessed serially may not be in a defined key sequence due to being displaced in an overflow area of the disc (*see* Fig. 6.2).

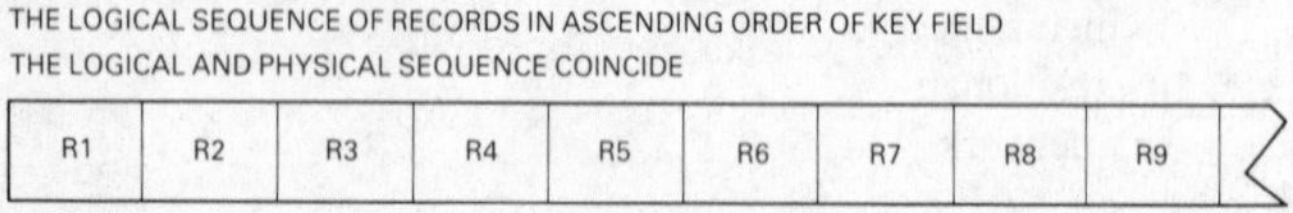

THE LOGICAL SEQUENCE OF RECORDS IN ASCENDING ORDER OF KEY FIELD
THE LOGICAL AND PHYSICAL SEQUENCE COINCIDE

R1	R2	R3	R4	R5	R6	R7	R8	R9

Figure 6.2 *Sequential organisation.*

It is possible to locate a record on a serially organised disc file without having to read each preceding record. This is achieved by the technique of 'binary chop', also referred to as 'binary search' and 'dichotomising search'. It is a speedy method of accessing specific records on a file or in a table. The method requires the various items on the file or in the table to be in a specific sequence; normally ascending order of key field.

The middle number or record key on a file or in a table is tested to determine whether it is above or below the one required. After the test one half of the file or table is discarded, i.e. the half which is below the desired record key. The process continues by examining the middle record or number of the remaining half of the file or table until the one required is located.

As an example of the functioning of 'binary chop', how many comparisons are necessary to discover the number or record key 20 in the following array of record keys?

1 4 6 14 15 17 19 20 22

The data contains nine record keys, the middle one being 15. The lower half of the record keys is below that required, i.e. 20, therefore it is discarded. This leaves record keys 17, 19, 20 and 22. The middle of which comes between 19 and 20 therefore the left-hand side of the set is discarded. The next test refers to record keys 20 and 22. As the first number is equal to that required no further examination is necessary. Three tests were required to find the required record key. Without the binary search technique the file would have been accessed serially, necessitating eight tests before record key 20 was reached on the file.

14. Indexed sequential. This method of file organisation is widely applied to the storage of records on magnetic disc. It allows a sequential file to be processed serially as the records are stored in ascending order of 'key' field. By means of a cylinder and track index however, it is possible to gain direct access to records for amendment, enquiry or updating. It provides for on-line order processing and on-line building society activities, stock control, on-line banking, holiday and theatre booking systems as well as airline seat reservation systems. Records can be deleted by physical erasing and amendments or updating of records by overwriting. When file activity is low this method is more suitable than sequential as it is only necessary to access those records affected by transactions. On occasions the recording tracks on a disc become overloaded and records are stored temporarily in an overflow area until the file is reorganised. To facilitate access to overflow records a cylinder/track index records the highest record key stored in the overflow area corresponding to each track indexed. The presence of the overflow address also indicates whether new records should be stored in the data area or the overflow area. It is important to maintain the sequence of records in the file and this is achieved by 'chaining' using link fields. By this technique a record which has been displaced into the overflow area has its new location recorded within the record which logically preceded it. The displaced record also has the location of the next record in logical sequence. This enables the sequential order of records to be traced.

A cylinder (*see* Fig. 6.3) is a hypothetical but highly practical notion comprising a set of data provided by each recording surface of the disc pack. It consists of the similar concentric tracks on all of the surfaces. Each track forms a ring or segment, in which records are stored in ascending order of key field, and to which are added the corresponding segments, i.e. the tracks of the other surfaces. The circular segments form a cylinder of records all of which can be accessed for a single positioning of the read/write heads. The cylinder is referred to as the 'seek' area. This is an efficient way of accessing records as the delay encountered by continuously repositioning the heads is eliminated. It is only necessary to reposition the heads for each new cylinder of records and for a disc pack consisting of ten recording surfaces the cylinder contains ten tracks of records. Each surface has its own read/write head which makes the cylinder concept a practical proposition. If each disc surface contains a hundred tracks then the disc pack has a hundred cylinders.

15. Random file organisation (directly organised). Individual records are not stored in any particular sequence of key fields, i.e. they are stored randomly. It is not possible to apply a general rule for retrieving records from this type of file and it is necessary to develop an index which indicates the location of each record or, alternatively, the application of an address generation system.

16. Inverted files. This type of organisation is useful when no single key can retrieve a record because a combination of keys is necessary. The record has to be searched using some combination of keys known as 'attributes'. Items possessing a specific feature are grouped together to form an inverted file. This reduces the time to retrieve records as it eliminates the need for serial searching. The keys and data are organised so that the keys (attributes) can be accessed one by one and only the relevant keys referenced. The organisation of an inverted file may be based on the structure outlined in Fig. 6.4.

Direct access methods

17. Full index. An index record contains the disc sector reference for every record in the file. The file is sorted initially into key

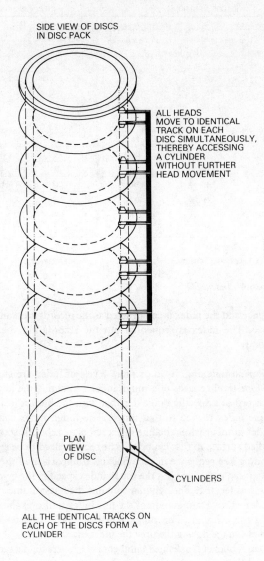

SIDE VIEW OF DISCS
IN DISC PACK

ALL HEADS
MOVE TO IDENTICAL
TRACK ON EACH
DISC SIMULTANEOUSLY,
THEREBY ACCESSING
A CYLINDER
WITHOUT FURTHER
HEAD MOVEMENT

PLAN
VIEW
OF DISC

CYLINDERS

ALL THE IDENTICAL TRACKS ON
EACH OF THE DISCS FORM A
CYLINDER

Figure 6.3 *Cylinder.*

BEFORE INVERSION

AFTER INVERSION

*PRODUCT	ATTRIBUTE 1 MAKE OF COMPUTER	ATTRIBUTE 2 TYPE OF PROCESSOR
1	A	Z8
2	A	Z12
3	B	Z8
4	B	Z9
5	B	Z12
6	C	Z8
7	C	Z9
8	C	Z14
9	D	Z8
10	D	Z12
11	D	Z15
12	D	Z18

ATTRIBUTE 1 MAKE OF COMPUTER	PRODUCT			
A	1	2		
B	3	4	5	
C	6	7	8	
D	9	10	11	12

ATTRIBUTE 2 TYPE OF PROCESSOR	PRODUCT			
Z8	1	3	6	9
Z9	4	7		
Z12	2	5	10	
Z14	8			
Z15	11			
Z18	12			

*ADRESS OR KEYFIELD OF RECORD

INVERTED KEYFIELD

Figure 6.4 *Inverted file.*

sequence and the index is constructed as the records are transferred to disc. The index is sequential but the records may be stored randomly.

18. Partial indexing. Two or more levels of index are stored on disc. One level consists of a rough index containing the key of the last record in a specific range together with the bucket location of the fine index related to that range. The rough index contains a cylinder number while the fine index refers to a specific sector on a specified surface in that cylinder. The records need to be stored in ascending key sequence in each bucket. Comparison of the key of the required record against the rough index specifies the cylinder in which it is located. The cylinder contains the relevant fine index as its first record. Examination of the fine index indicates the surface within the cylinder. The rough index is usually transferred into internal storage during the time the file is in use.

Note: A bucket is a defined number of characters for data transfers from/to disc to/from the processor. Some computers have discs with a bucket size of 512 characters which can be handled in ones or multiples to store records in bucket sizes of 512, 1,024, 2,048, or 4,096 character capacity.

19. Self-indexing. This type of organisation requires records to be stored in addresses that are related to their keys. File organisation is on the basis of:

(*a*) address = key;
(*b*) address = key + constant;
(*c*) address = (key + constant)/blocking factor.

There are many variations of this type of equation because of differing disc starting addresses, different blocking factors and the structure of keys.

If storage locations are available from location 400, each location holding one record, then the address of the record would be obtained in the following manner:

Record keys
120   Address = 120 + 399 = 519
141–180   Address = 141 + 399 = 540 − 579
190–300   Address = 190 + 399 = 589 − 699

Note: 399 is the 400th location as storage addresses commence at 0, therefore, 0−399=400. Some key sequences have too many gaps to be organised in this way as it is inefficient in the use of storage but when it is possible to link the address and key of a record directly, self-indexing files are feasible.

20. Algorithmic address generation. The basis of this method is a mathematical formula which is applied to the key of the required record which generates the bucket reference containing the record. The bucket is then searched to access the specific record. It is possible for the formula to generate the same address for different keys which will create an overflow situation necessitating several accesses to locate the desired record. Space is wasted too when records are deleted from a disc file as they will not be reassigned because of the nature of the algorithm. The formal manner of establishing a suitable algorithm is to examine the code number sequence in use or to be implemented. Code numbers should be numeric only. It is then necessary to establish a formula which will generate an even distribution of bucket addresses. Constants can be added to the formula to close large gaps in the sequence to avoid wasting storage space. It is essential to determine that the bucket address is acceptable to the type of disc drive in use.

Algorithms are computed in a number of ways:

(*a*) Random allocation of records is achieved by squaring the key, or part of it, and using some digits from the square, perhaps the centre digits, as an address. This technique can allocate more than one record to the same address and none to other addresses. The first record is stored in an address called a *home* record. If addresses can only hold a single record the subsequent records allocated to this address will have to be stored in overflow areas. These records are known as *synonyms*.

Example (*i*): Compute the address of the following keys by squaring the central two digits.

Keys	1111	1112	1113
Digits	11	11	11
Square	121	121	121

As can be seen all records are allocated to the same address and are therefore synonyms.

Example (*ii*): Compute the address of the same keys by squaring the last two digits.

Digits	11	12	13
Square	121	144	169

As can be seen gaps occur in the addresses of consecutive records.

(*b*) Divide the key by a prime number and use the remainder as an address. This method will generally provide a good distribution of records. Runs of keys produce remainders that do not generate synonyms as they each differ by 1. Constants can be added if necessary.

Example (*i*): Compute the address of the following record keys by dividing the keys by the prime number 13 and use the remainder as an address.

Keys:	1111	1112	1113
Remainder	6	7	8

As can be seen a good spread of records is achieved.

Example (ii): Using the same record keys compute the address using prime number 11 and use the remainder as an address.

Remainder   0   1   2

This also generates a good distribution of records.

File activities

21. File conversion and creation. When applications are to be transferred to a computer the master files must be converted from their present form, perhaps ledger cards, to a computer compatible form, i.e. magnetic media. In effect this means the conversion of records from a visible form, on ledger cards, to an invisible form as magnetic spots on magnetic tape or disc (*see* Fig. 6.5).

Before conversion, it is necessary to reconcile the balances and other data on existing records before encoding the details of each record onto floppy disc or magnetic tape. New code numbers for particular classes of records may be required particularly if they are to incorporate self-checking numbers with in-built check digits.

File conversion creates a high volume operation and suitable arrangements must be made for this commitment, especially as the records must also be verified to ensure they have been converted correctly.

During the file conversion run the new records are printed out and these must be manually reconciled with the old records to ensure there are no irregularities. All errors must be corrected. Most files are not static during the changeover period from the existing system to the computer system, as data is obtained from various sources within and without the organisation and data is for ever changing owing to the frequency of business transactions. Difficulties arise in the task of attempting to maintain files in phase during parallel running. During this stage it is necessary to update two sets of records, i.e. master files for reconciliation purposes to ensure the computer is producing accurate results.

22. File security. This important topic is dealt with in the chapter dealing with Checks and Controls in Computerised Systems (*see* Chap. 9).

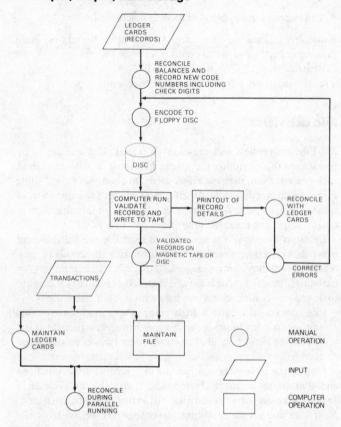

Figure 6.5 *File conversion and creation.*

23. File updating. An important feature of data processing is file updating and in this respect it is important to appreciate that all data and the records, to which the data relates, must be stored in the internal memory of the processor before any data processing operation or file updating is possible. Records are transferred by means of the appropriate backing storage device, which is normally either a tape deck or disc drive, depending upon the media used for storing master files—magnetic tapes or discs (*see* Figs. 6.6 and 6.7).

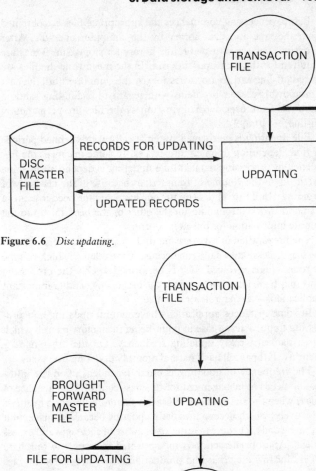

Figure 6.6 *Disc updating.*

Figure 6.7 *Magnetic tape updating.*

Before processing commences the appropriate files are obtained from the tape and disc library by the computer operator. After updating they are returned to the library for storage until they are required for the next updating run. In the meanwhile the files are stored off-line and are not accessible by the computer until the next run and this creates problems with regard to facilitating random enquiries from user departments unless the files are permanently on-line (*see* 10:**8, 9**).

File updating is performed systematically at pre-defined periods of time depending upon circumstances. In some instances the frequency of processing data and file updating is dependent to some extent upon the volume of transactions because of the necessity of avoiding a build-up of data on the one hand and the need to achieve a smooth work throughout on the other or the need for up to the minute information for business control.

The preparation of invoices and updating the sales ledger master file may necessitate a daily run because of the relatively high volume of transactions involved. If it is performed weekly the processing time may be so long as to preclude the processing of other important applications—the payroll for instance.

In some instances applications have natural updating and processing frequencies, a case in point being the factory payroll which has a natural weekly updating frequency. On the other hand a monthly staff payroll has a natural monthly updating frequency.

The frequency of updating is often dependent upon the information needs of management for business control. One instance of this is when the status of stocks is a key factor in running a business effectively, which necessitates daily updating because management require a daily schedule in order to be aware of shortages and excess stocks. Appropriate action is then effected in respect of purchase orders for raw materials and production orders in relation to sales orders.

24. File activity or 'hit' rate. The proportion of records updated or referenced on each updating run in relation to the total number of records on a master file is referred to as the 'hit' rate. This is a very important consideration in computer configuration deliberations regarding the type of storage media most suitable for specific applications, i.e. magnetic tape or magnetic disc.

In respect of magnetic tape files, it is necessary to access each record on the file serially, even though some of the records are not affected by current transactions. What is more, the whole of the file has to be rewritten on a new tape file. In this case, a file with a low 'hit' rate can increase processing time and would be better stored on magnetic disc, which has direct access capability. Direct access requires only those records affected by the transactions to be accessed for updating. In addition, records stored on disc do not have to be written to a different disc after updating since records are overwritten.

As a payroll has a high 'hit' rate, there is no advantage in storing it on magnetic disc, as every employee's record needs to be updated each pay period. Magnetic tape has a high storage capacity and is cheaper than magnetic discs. On the other hand, a stock file may contain records which are only affected by transactions occasionally, therefore the whole of the file does not change each time a computer run is made. In this case, processing time can be reduced by storing stock records on magnetic disc (*see* Figs. 6.6 and 6.7).

25. File amendments. File amendments include the addition of new records or the deletion of obsolete records from a master file, for example the addition of new starters and the deletion of terminations from the payroll or employee master file. Reference files may require amendment occasionally in respect of changes of names and addresses, product selling prices and wage rates, etc. (*see* Fig. 6.8).

From the following, illustrate and explain the effect of file amendments on a newly created carried forward master file on magnetic tape.

OLD MASTER FILE

	Record Number	Name	Credit Limit £	Balance due £
(1)	106075	Syson	5000	4275
(2)	106076	French	1000	450
(3)	106080	Bishop	2000	0000
(4)	106082	Osborne	4000	2500
(5)	106085	Corbett	8000	6350

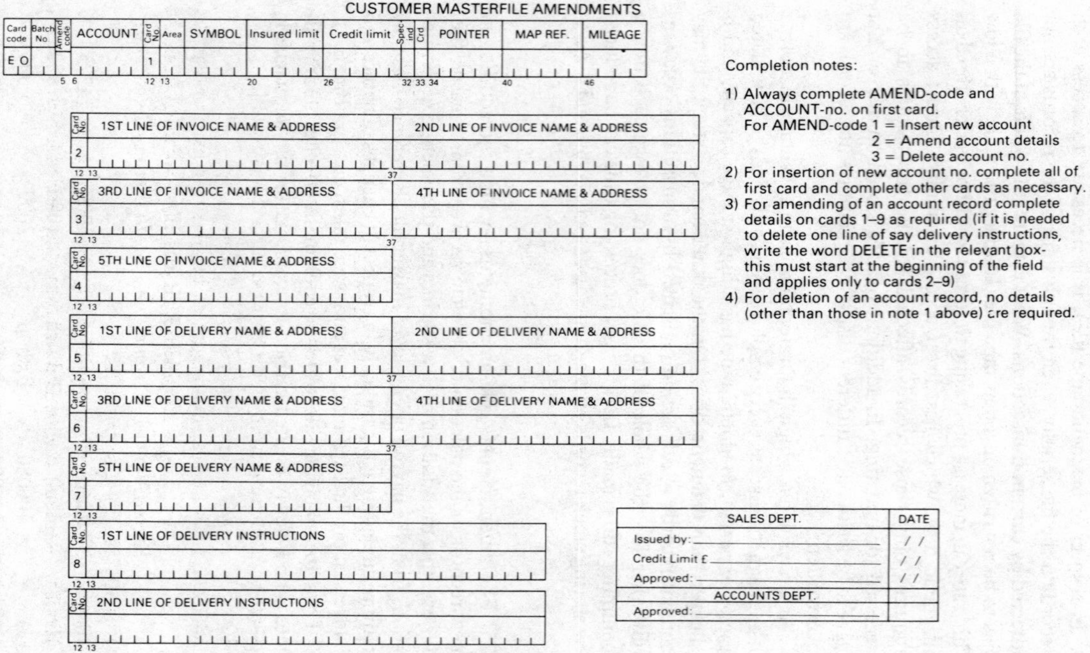
CUSTOMER MASTERFILE AMENDMENTS
Card code
Batch No.
Amend code
ACCOUNT
Card No
Area
SYMBOL
Insured limit
Credit limit
Spec ind
Crd
POINTER
MAP REF.
MILEAGE
E O
1
5 6
12 13
20
26
32 33 34
40
46
Completion notes:
1) Always complete AMEND-code and ACCOUNT-no. on first card.
For AMEND-code 1 = Insert new account
2 = Amend account details
3 = Delete account no.
2) For insertion of new account no. complete all of first card and complete other cards as necessary.
3) For amending of an account record complete details on cards 1–9 as required (if it is needed to delete one line of say delivery instructions, write the word DELETE in the relevant box-this must start at the beginning of the field and applies only to cards 2–9)
4) For deletion of an account record, no details (other than those in note 1 above) are required.
Card No
1ST LINE OF INVOICE NAME & ADDRESS
2ND LINE OF INVOICE NAME & ADDRESS
2
3RD LINE OF INVOICE NAME & ADDRESS
4TH LINE OF INVOICE NAME & ADDRESS
3
5TH LINE OF INVOICE NAME & ADDRESS
4
1ST LINE OF DELIVERY NAME & ADDRESS
2ND LINE OF DELIVERY NAME & ADDRESS
5
3RD LINE OF DELIVERY NAME & ADDRESS
4TH LINE OF DELIVERY NAME & ADDRESS
6
5TH LINE OF DELIVERY NAME & ADDRESS
7
1ST LINE OF DELIVERY INSTRUCTIONS
8
2ND LINE OF DELIVERY INSTRUCTIONS
12 13
37
SALES DEPT.
DATE
Issued by:
Credit Limit £
Approved:
ACCOUNTS DEPT.
Approved:
/ /

Figure 6.8 *Customer masterfile amendment form.*

AMENDMENT FILE

	Record number	Name	Transaction code	Credit Limit £	Balance due £
(A)	106076	French	1	7500	
(B)	106077	Green	3	4000	0000
(C)	106079	Ball	1	4250	
(D)	106080		2		
(E)	106082	Osborne	1	3000	

Transaction code: 1—Amendment
                      2—Deletion
                      3—Insertion

The solution to the question is outlined below:

The effect of applying the amendments to the file are shown as follows:

Record number	Name	Credit Limit £	Balance due £
106075	Syson	5000	4275
106076	French	7500	450
106077	Green	4000	0000
106082	Osborne	3000	2500
106085	Corbett	8000	6350

The following details provide an explanation of the amendments.

106075   Remains unchanged and is copied to the carried forward file

106076   Amendment to credit limit on carried forward file

106077   A new record to be added to the file

106079   Indicated as an amendment but does not exist on the file. The record is signalled as an error and excluded from the master file

106080   Deletion from the file

106082   Amendment to credit limit on carried forward file

106085   Remains unchanged and copied to carried forward file

Activities concerned with file amendments on magnetic tape include the reading in of a record to the processor's memory from the master file together with an amendment from the amendment file. The 'key' fields are compared to establish if there is a match. Appropriate action is then taken either to write the record unchanged on the new file if it is not affected by an amendment, or, if it is affected by an amendment, to adjust it in the memory before it is written to the new file. If the amendment is a deletion, then the record is omitted from the new file but if it is a new record then it is added to the new file. All this must be effected before the master file is updated by transaction data. It is essential that records are amended before being used in processing.

Relationship between master files, transaction files and reference files

26. Definition of a master file. A master file is a group of related records, e.g. stock file, customer file, employee file, supplier file. This type of file is periodically updated with current transaction data, in order to show the current status of each record in the file. Other types of master file contain reference information such as product prices, names and addresses and wage rates, etc. Such files may be used for general reference, or can form an integral part of data processing activities. Each record in a file is allocated an identification number or reference key and filed in ascending number order to facilitate ease of access or reference.

There are also several types of master file, and the type used is also dependent upon the processing method employed.

(*a*) Loose leaf ledger or binder.
(*b*) Container of ledger cards.
(*c*) Reel of magnetic tape or exchangeable disc packs.
(*d*) Floppy or fixed discs.
(*e*) Cassette tape.

27. Transaction file. A collection of data relating to business transactions is referred to as a transaction or changes file. This contains details relating to stock movements—stock transaction file, wages—wages transaction file, items required by customers—orders file, and so on. Such details are input for processing, including computing the value of stock movements, gross wages and the value of gross wages and the value of goods sold to customers. These values are then used as part of the information printed out on documents and schedules as well as being recorded on the relevant records in the appropriate master file to which they relate.

Transaction data may be collected for a period of time and processed in batches or may be processed as it arises on an interactive transaction processing basis. A file may not always be in evidence in such cases but if batches of transactions are dealt with as they arise then this process forms a transaction file dealt with on a transaction basis, i.e. on an individual rather than a batch basis.

28. Reference file. This is a file which contains reference information, i.e. information which is referred to during data processing operations, whether for random enquiries or for details required during batch processing. Such files contain details pertaining to product prices to be used for invoice computations, names and addresses of customers and suppliers to be used for the production of mail shots and for addressing documents such as invoices, statements and purchase orders, etc. Wage rates may also be recorded in this way.

If names and addresses are required predominantly for general mailing needs then the file may be structured separately, otherwise it may be integrated with the relevant master file, such as the customer or supplier file. If wage rates are reasonably stable then they may be incorporated in the payroll master file in respect of those employees paid on the basis of attended hours. The rates may otherwise be input as current wages data and omitted from the file completely.

Virtual storage

29. Concept of virtual storage. Some computers incorporate a storage management technique known as 'virtual storage'. The technique increases the apparent capacity of internal storage by an amount many times its actual capacity. Concurrent processing of several programs, that would otherwise exceed the main internal storage capacity, is made possible.

30. Mode of operation. Virtual storage uses magnetic discs which are used to store programs required for processing. This is instead of loading them to internal storage (main storage), which is the normal method employed.

In order that the main storage available is used in the most efficient manner, the technique splits the program into small segments called 'pages'. Only those pages which are required for processing are called into main storage at one time. The remainder of the program stays in virtual storage.

The addresses within a page refer to virtual storage locations and when transferred to main storage the addresses must refer to main storage locations before processing can be executed. It is necessary, therefore, to effect address translation, which is achieved by a hardware-assisted table look-up.

Other storage aspects

31. Volume. This term is often used to mean a unit of magnetic storage such as a set of exchangeable discs, i.e. a disc pack, or a reel of magnetic tape. Discs, hard and floppy, can be divided into multiple volumes each having a discrete entity, e.g. the sectors on a disc surface which effectively divide the surface of the disc into blocks. It is then necessary to specify the disc volume which stores the program required. This applies to Winchester discs in particular.

32. Formatting/soft and hard sectoring. A computer, by means of a DOS (disc operating system), keeps track of the location of records on a disc and can access any record by moving the head to the relevant track and then waiting for the sector (block) containing the required record to come into position. Two methods are used to indicate the location on a track where each sector starts:

(*a*) soft sectoring, whereby special signals are recorded on the disc surface and detected by the software; and

(*b*) hard sectoring whereby holes are punched through the disc around the central hole, one per sector.

These are referred to as formatted discs (*see* 7:**22**).

33. Archiving. The process of removing infrequently used files from the filestore. A filestore consists of files organised in a library under the control of an operating system. Archived files are omitted from the directory of current files and are normally stored on magnetic tape, reducing the number of discs required to be on-line. This effectively reduces operating costs and increases the efficiency of computer operations. Tape files can be converted to disc files when operational necessity requires it.

34. Logical and physical records. The records on a file are normally grouped by type whereby all similar records are stored on the same media. The individual records relating to a specific entity, e.g. account of customer X, the earnings and tax records of employee Y or the stock record of item Z, are logical records. The file media on which they are stored, i.e. the reel of tape or the specific disc pack is the physical storage media, therefore many logical records will be stored on a physical file (*see* Fig. 6.9).

The individual records are referenced, updated, amended and information is extracted from them according to the needs of the business. For effective file handling and processing a computer handles physical records, i.e. groups or blocks of logical records. A block may be 512 bytes (characters) in length and the number of records in the block is determined by the systems designer on the basis of the number of characters in each record and the size of the block.

This achieves efficiency in the transfer of data from the physical file to the processor as it is impractical to stop/start a tape deck after transferring single records as there would be more stop/start time

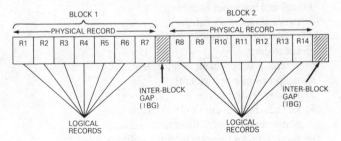

Figure 6.9 *Blocked records illustrating the relationship of physical and logical records.*

than data transfer time. A disc drive does not stop when transferring records but it does function on the basis of the 'block' as blocks of records are transferred from the disc drive to the processor, not single records. The block containing a specific record for processing needs is searched after being transferred to internal memory to locate the record required (*see* Fig. 6.10).

An 'inter-block gap' is used to allow the tape to slow down and stop after a block of data has been read or written, and to allow the tape to re-start and accelerate to the appropriate reading or writing speed for the next block of data to be input or output.

If data blocks are short, then the deceleration and acceleration of the tape between blocks can exceed the time actually taken in transferring data to and from the computer. In order to eliminate this unproductive time, the block size should be increased as much as the available internal storage locations will allow.

Logical records and files

The details which follow outline the contents of master files of various applications.

35. Payroll master file. Typical contents are summarised as follows:

   (*a*) clock number;
   (*b*) name;
   (*c*) tax code;
   (*d*) national insurance number;
   (*e*) national insurance category;
   (*f*) taxable gross to date;
   (*g*) tax to date;
   (*h*) taxable gross previous employment;
   (*i*) tax previous employment;
   (*j*) holiday credit to date;
   (*k*) sickness holiday credit weeks to date:
   (*l*) employee's National Insurance to date;
   (*m*) total National Insurance contributions to date;
   (*n*) fixed deductions:
      (*i*) charities;

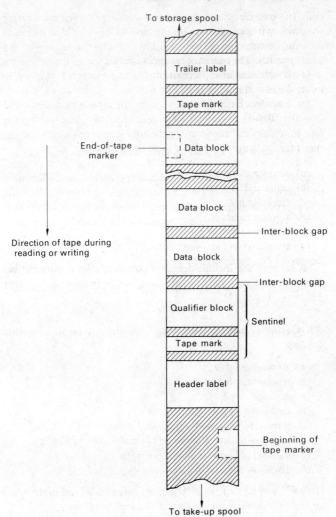

Figure 6.10 *Layout of a data file on magnetic tape. (Courtesy International Computers Limited)*

    (*ii*) overalls;
    (*iii*) savings;
    (*iv*) loans;
  (*o*) weekly salary amount (as appropriate);
  (*p*) hourly rate (as appropriate);
  (*q*) holiday credit flat rate;
  (*r*) employee bank details;
    (*see* 10:4–7).

36. Customer file. Typical contents of this file include:

  (*a*) account number;
  (*b*) name and address;
  (*c*) credit limit;
  (*d*) account balance;
  (*e*) category/discount rate;
  (*f*) age analysis of account balance.

This file may also include details of customer sales history but can be structured separately to suit the needs of processing as shown below (*see* Fig. 6.11).

37. Customer sales history file. This file may be structured as follows:

  (*a*) account number;
  (*b*) representative code;
  (*c*) customer type;
  (*d*) area code;
  (*e*) turnover this period—analysed by product;
  (*f*) turnover to date since week 1—analysed by product;
  (*g*) number of orders to date since week 1;
  (*h*) discount received to date.

This file may be structured to include cost of sales and profitability or this requirement may be stored on a separate file.

38. Product file. This file could be structured as follows:

  (*a*) product code;
  (*b*) product description;

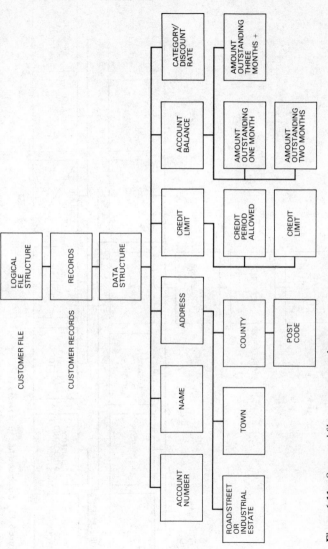

Figure 6.11 *Structured file: customer records.*

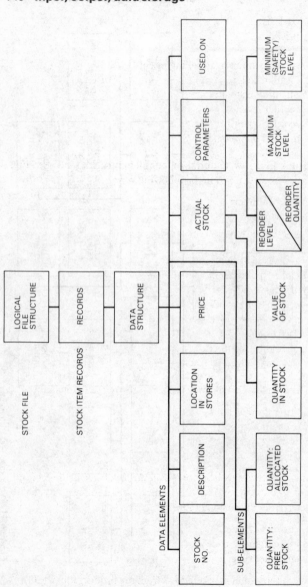

Figure 6.12 *Structured file: stock records.*

(c) pack size;

(d) price;

(e) VAT code;

(f) recommended retail selling price;

(g) location code;

(h) quantity in stock;

(i) reorder level;

(j) reorder quantity;

(k) ordered but outstanding.

39. Stock file: raw material or components. This file (*see* Fig. 6.12) may be structured in the following way:

(a) stock number;

(b) description;

(c) location in stores;

(d) price;

(e) actual stock;

(f) control parameters:
   (i) reorder level;
   (ii) maximum stock level;
   (iii) minimum stock level;

(g) used on;

(h) quantity: free stock;

(i) quantity: allocated stock.

40. Orders file. This file may be structured in the following way:

(a) order number;

(b) account number;

(c) product code;

(d) quantity.

The above details may be recorded on the orders file by direct input using a VDU in an on-line order entry system followed by details extracted from the customer file, viz.

(e) customer name;

(f) representative code;

(g) customer type.

Further information may be added from the product file (*see* **38**).

41. Plant register file. The contents of this file provide information for asset accounting requirements, giving details relating to specific items of plant and equipment.

   (*a*) General information:
      (*i*) type of asset;
      (*ii*) plant code;
      (*iii*) supplier;
      (*iv*) manufacturer;
      (*v*) rating (horsepower (hp) or kilowatt (kW) rating);
      (*vi*) floor area;
      (*vii*) date of installation;
    (*viii*) location;
      (*ix*) transfers.
   (*b*) Accounting information:
      (*i*) date of purchase;
      (*ii*) original cost;
      (*iii*) installation cost;
      (*iv*) depreciation class;
      (*v*) annual amount of depreciation;
      (*vi*) cumulative depreciation;
      (*vii*) written-down book value;
    (*viii*) maintenance costs;
      (*ix*) cost of additions;
      (*x*) disposal value.

42. Problem relating to files. The details which follow relate to a CIMA question set in a MISDP paper (students should note that currently magnetic media are used, not punched cards):

Selected data from purchase invoices are punched into cards as follows:

supplier account number; purchase invoice number; purchase order number; quantity supplied; part number and/or expense code; value of invoice.

The above data are processed on the company's computer, which has magnetic tape backing storage, to produce numerous accounting and stock control reports included among which are the following:

Remittance advices containing supplier's name and address and details of invoices being paid;

Credit transfers containing the company's own and payee's banking details and amount of transfer.

Supplier analysis giving total expenditure for current month and year to date per supplier within each purchase classification.

It will be noted that this purchase classification is a broad group of expense codes with sub-sections. For example,

purchase classification, Raw materials—100

includes numerous expense codes, such as:

Steel—110, Copper—130, Zinc—160, etc.

Expense code analysis giving total expenditure for each expense code for the current month and year to date.

You are required to describe what files you would recommend should be maintained to produce the outputs given above and, for each of the files recommended, to state details of its sequence and minimum content.

43. Solution to file problem. An outline solution to the question is given below:

Purchase ledger file. This file would contain financial details relating to the suppliers dealing with the company as follows:

(*a*) Supplier account number.
(*b*) Supplier's name and address.
(*c*) Account balance.
(*d*) Details of invoices:
    (*i*) purchase invoice number;
   (*ii*) value of invoice.
(*e*) Details of remittance relating to invoices being paid:
    (*i*) purchase invoice number;
   (*ii*) value of invoice or amount being paid on account.
(*f*) Company's own and payee's banking details.

Details of invoices to be paid would have to be input so that they may be extracted from the appropriate accounts to update the account balance and for the details to be printed on the remittance advice.

The total amount to be paid would be printed on the credit transfers together with the company's own and payee's banking details.

Supplier history file. The punched cards could be sorted to supplier within purchase classification key for updating the history file by classification key by customer for the purpose of producing a supplier analysis as follows:

Supplier account number:
  Purchase classification:
      Total expenditure   Steel—110—current month
                                         year to date
      Total expenditure   Copper—130—current month
                                         year to date
      Total expenditure   Zinc—160—current month
                                       year to date
      Grand total expenditure   —current month
                                       year to date

Purchase history file. This file would contain details of expenditure for each expense code for the current month and year to date for the purpose of producing an expense code analysis as follows:

Expense code—Steel   110—Total expenditure   current month
                                              year to date
        —Copper   130—Total expenditure   current month
                                              year to date
        —Zinc   160—Total expenditure   current month
                                             year to date
      Grand total expenditure   current month
                                              year to date

This file would be updated from details on the punched cards after they had been sorted to expense code. This information could be used for updating expense codes in the nominal ledger for the extraction of a trial balance and the preparation of final accounts.

Databases

44. Databases. The traditional approach to the computerised storage of data is to provide each application with its own functional files consisting of records relating to personnel, payroll, customers, suppliers, etc. Some files contain records with similar data, such as the personnel and payroll files, and this causes problems and creates inconsistency and unreliability if the common data is not updated at the same time. A database consists of a centralised store of data for use by all relevant applications. When data is updated its up-to-date status is available to all users who then use it with a greater degree of confidence. Transaction data is entered once only thereby eliminating duplicated processing activities and duplicated data storage.

45. Database variations. It is necessary to draw a distinction between database software used on mainframe computers such as IDMS and IMS and that relating to microcomputers which provide only conventional file handling facilities. The less complex databases are referred to as file managers, record handlers or flat-file databases. Some databases are menu driven but others have a database language. Others consist of pop-up database programs which are used in conjunction with application programs. These are resident in memory for the purpose of providing data to the main program on demand.

46. What does a database software package offer? A DBMS, i.e. database management system (data management software), consists of programs including a Data Description Language (DDL) and a Data Manipulation Language (DML). The software manages database activities including file amendments, file updating, deletion of obsolete records and the initiation of new records. The DBMS also allows the user to validate, sort, search and print records from the database as well as providing facilities for performing calculations and maintaining a dictionary. Some systems provide for the printing of standard letters and the merging of text with data such as names and addresses. Records can be displayed on the screen and browsed through making amendments as necessary. File security is also provided for by making copies of disc files, and passwords may be used for data protection purposes. Files are reorganised automatically to allow for overflow conditions on disc tracks. Fields may be removed from records and files may be merged or separated according to needs. The software allows the user to structure records according to needs and to print or display reports on a monitor screen.

A query language is used for obtaining facts or information from the database which speeds up data retrieval and analysis. When a user asks 'What is the sales performance of a specific branch?', it interprets the question as requiring to know both target and actual sales figures to compute the response to the request. It retrieves the data, calculates it and presents the report to the user in a format that is clear and concise. All selection and tracing data in the database, computations and formatting of reports is automatic.

47. Equipment required to run database software. Database software is usually designed to run on specific models of computer having specific operating systems. The processor must have adequate internal memory for storing the software, e.g. dBASE 111 plus of Ashton Tate specifies a minimum 256K bytes. It also specifies two 5¼″ 360K bytes minimum capacity floppy disc drives or one fixed disc drive and one floppy drive; monochrome or colour monitor and any printer with at least 80 columns. A keyboard is also required for the input of commands and data.

48. Use of a database. A database can be used for any number of purposes including:

(*a*) Processing of customers' orders from customer, product and order details stored in the database;
(*b*) Ad hoc reports requiring the retrieval of data by means of a query language;
(*c*) Storage and processing of personnel records;
(*d*) Storage and processing of student records;
(*e*) Mail shots;
(*f*) Printing lists and reports consisting of data from records with specific attributes, i.e. parameters;
(*g*) Storage and processing of supplier and customer accounts;
(*h*) Printing labels.

Further matters relating to databases are discussed in 3: **6** and Volume 2.

Electronic document storage and retrieval

49. Storage of unstructured documents and records. The storage of logical structured records, relating to specific aspects of business activities, such as purchases, sales, stocks, production and employees has always been a routine element of data processing activities. Such records are stored on master files on physical storage media, such as magnetic tape or discs which are accessed for amendment and updating as required during processing runs.

The question now arises of how best to store and retrieve the data of an unstructured nature found in such documents as:

(a) stock reports;
(b) standard price schedules;
(c) estimates and quotations;
(d) sales summaries;
(e) budget reports—income and expenditure by department;
(f) labour turnover reports;
(g) candidate assessment forms;
(h) minutes of meetings.

The types of document outlined above normally reside in office filing cabinets in the relevant secretary's office but this area of business activity has been overtaken by the new electronic technology as electronic filing and retrieval systems using floppy disc based microcomputers are now becoming very common.

50. Electronic filing and retrieval systems. These systems are often referred to by various descriptive titles. However, it is confusing as to whether the nature of the systems under consideration differs or if it is a matter of a shovel being called a spade. The terms which may be encountered include those listed below:

(a) electronic document storage and retrieval systems;
(b) text filing and retrieval systems;
(c) file management systems;
(d) electronic retrieval of free text documents.

51. Electronic retrieval of free text documents. Systems which store documents electronically and which enable complete documents or sections of documents to be retrieved are predominant as floppy disc based microcomputers are being used instead of normal office filing cabinets. This is a good thing because even in the most efficient filing system documents tend to go astray and it is often difficult to trace them as they can be classified under various titles. Such electronically stored documents can be retrieved by specifying words or phrases that occur within the text. The words can be located anywhere within the text, eliminating the need for keyfields. Such systems require the ability to capture and retain documents electronically and retrieve them from a partial description of their contents.

Retrieval technique in general utilises 'user friendly' language but more complex queries can be effected by using Boolean operators 'AND', 'OR' and 'NOT'. These can be applied when combining two factors, i.e. search terms which may be phrased as 'find all documents which include both the words male AND single' or, 'find all documents relating to personnel who have "O" level passes in Mathematics AND "A" level passes in English', or, 'find those records of employees who are male AND staff NOT in the pension scheme'.

Synonyms can be applied in a query to expand a search term when different words can have the same meaning or can be spelled differently. If the search term is 'computer' it may have the synonym 'electronic computer' or 'digital computer'. When applying the synonym facility the system automatically interprets the query as 'computer' OR 'electronic computer' OR 'digital computer'.

Truncation is applied for a root search whereby all subjects with a similar root are signalled by the system, very often by the asterisk sign, e.g. finance*, which could generate the following subjects— financial, financing, etc.

Masking may be applied when the user is not sure how a name should be spelled for searching purposes. This allows the middle characters of a word to be masked out, e.g. the name of a company Hindacem may be masked as Hind*cem if one is not certain whether it is Hindicem or Hinducem.

Note: The subject of databases is dealt with in Volume 2.

Progress test 6

1. What is the purpose of storing data? (**1**)
2. How does the method of storing data differ in a clerical system

to that of a computer system? (**2**)

3. In the context of data storage what is the nature and purpose of pointers? (**4**)

4. Define the terms 'relative pointer' and 'absolute pointer'. (**4**)

5. Define the term 'key field'. (**5**)

6. Define the meaning of 'unique' and 'generic' in the context of key fields. (**6**)

7. Records and fields can be fixed or variable-length. Discuss the significance of this statement. (**7–10**)

8. Specify the essential differences between serial and sequential files. (**12, 13**)

9. Define the term 'indexed sequential' in the context of organising records on magnetic disc and state the significance of the 'cylinder'. (**14**)

10. How can records be retrieved on a randomly organised file? (**15**)

11. Define the nature and purpose of an 'inverted file'. (**16**)

12. Define the following terms: (*a*) full indexing; (*b*) partial indexing; (*c*) self-indexing. (**17–19**)

13. The basis of the algorithmic method of address generation is a mathematical formula. Specify two typical formulae which may be adopted for this purpose. (**20**)

14. When applications are transferred to a computer the files must be converted to a computer-compatible form. Outline the procedure for file conversion. (**21** and Fig. 6.5)

15. An important data processing activity is file updating. State the nature of this activity distinguishing between the method of updating disc and magnetic tape files. (**23**)

16. Before deciding to store records on magnetic disc or tape it is necessary to consider file activity or the 'hit rate' as it is known. Define the meaning of this term and why it is important. (**24**)

17. File amendments are an essential requirement of a data processing system. Specify the nature of file amendments. (**25**)

18. What is a master file? (**26**)

19. Distinguish between a master file, transaction file and reference file. (**26–28**)

20. What is 'virtual' storage? (**29, 30**)

21. What is meant by the terms: (*a*) volume; (*b*) formatting/soft and hard sectoring; (*c*) archiving? (**31–33**)

22. Specify the difference between logical and physical records. (**34**)

23. List the contents of the following typical master files: (*a*) payroll file; (*b*) customer file; (*c*) customer history file; (*d*) product file; (*e*) stock file; (*f*) orders file; (*g*) plant register. (**35–41**)

24. What is a database? (**44–48**)

25. Outline the nature of electronic document storage and retrieval systems. (**49–51**)

7
Backing storage devices and media

The nature of backing storage

1. External storage. Normal office filing cabinets are used for non-computerised systems for the purpose of storing records until they are required for reference, amendment or updating. The filing cabinets are an extension to the information stored in the memory of personnel performing activities in the system, as it would be impossible for a person to store information in his/her memory relating to all aspects of office activities which they deal with.

Although a computer could retain all business information in its internal memory it would be rather impractical to do so as it would require millions of bytes of storage capacity such as semiconductor memory in the form of RAMs, i.e. random access memory. It is usual to provide the computer system with off-line storage, referred to as auxiliary storage, for the storage of master files and programs relating to specific applications until they are required and transferred into the internal memory. Computers generally employ magnetic storage of one type or another but new developments are taking place such as optical discs which record data by means of a laser.

2. Types of backing storage. By far the most common types of backing storage are magnetic discs and tapes but these are now available in many different varieties to facilitate the needs of various types and sizes of computer, the volume of records to be held in backing storage, and data transfer speed requirements. The different types are summarised as follows:

(a) magnetic tape (reels);

(b) magnetic tape (cassette);

(c) hard discs:

    (i) exchangeable disc storage (EDS);

    (ii) Winchester discs;

    (iii) data module;

    (iv) high capacity fixed discs;

(d) soft discs:

    (i) 8 inch (200mm) floppy discs;

    (ii) 5¼ inch (133mm) mini-floppy discs;

    (iii) 3 inch (76.2mm) and 3½ inch (88.9mm) microfloppy discs;

(e) integrated discs;

(f) microdrive/cartridges;

(g) personality module (used with discs);

(h) silicon discs;

(i) optical discs.

(j) tape streamers

Magnetic tape (reels)

3. General characteristics. Magnetic tape is widely used for backing storage, and is also used as a means of recording transaction data for input into the computer. Magnetic tape not only allows data to be entered into the computer at very high speeds, but also provides the facility for writing output data to tape at high speed. A further important feature is that it is a very compact means of storing programs and master files.

Magnetic tape in common use is ½ inch (12.70mm) wide and 2,400 feet (731.52m) long, and is stored on a reel. A tape deck is used for writing data to magnetic tape from the processor and reading data from tape to processor. This is accomplished by read/write heads (*see* Fig. 7.1).

4. Magnetic tape codes.

(a) Data are recorded as magnetised spots which are known as *binary digits* or 'bits'.

(b) Data is recorded in *parallel tracks* along the length of the tape,

Figure 7.1 *IBM 3420 magnetic tape drive. (Courtesy IBM United Kingdom Limited)*

the number of tracks may be seven but nine-track tape is now more widely used.

(*c*) The tracks *across the width of the tape* provide one column of data, i.e. one character which may be either numeric, alphabetic or special.

(*d*) A character is represented by a code consisting of a *unique 'bit' combination* of 0s and 1s. For example, a seven-track tape may use a code consisting of seven positions of binary notation divided into three divisions, as shown in Table 7A (*see also* Fig. 7.2).

(*e*) The parity bit check is for ensuring that each character has the correct number of bits (*see* **7** and **8**). The zone bits are used in combination with numeric bits to represent alphabetic or special characters. The numeric bits are assigned the first four binary values of 8, 4, 2 and 1, which are used for representing, in binary coded decimal form, the decimal numeric digits 0–9. Seven-track tape therefore consists of six data tracks and one parity track (*see* Fig. 7.2). Nine-track tape consists of eight data tracks and one parity track for recording bytes.

Figure 7.2 *Seven-track magnetic tape. (Courtesy International Business Machines Corporation)*

Table 7A   Structure of seven-track tape code

Position	Designation	Number of bit positions
1	Parity check	1
2 and 3	Zone	2
4, 5, 6 and 7	Numeric	4

5. General features of magnetic tape.

(a) It is possible to record 800, 1,600 and 6, 250 bpi (bits per inch), this is referred to as the packing density. However, the row of bits across the width of the tape forms a character or byte, which means that bits per inch may be translated as also meaning bytes per inch to avoid confusion in expressing data transfer speeds (these are defined in terms of bps, i.e. bytes per second). The speed at which data is transferred from the tape deck to the processor is dependent upon three factors: the packing density, the speed at which the tape moves past the read/write heads and the blocking factor. This is in the region of 45–200 inches per second (ips) depending upon the model of tape deck in use. Speeds for a packing density of 1, 600 bytes per inch (bpi) vary between 72K and 320K bytes per second. For a packing density of 6,250 bpi the speed increases to 1.25MB/s, i.e. Mega (million) bytes per second. This compares very favourably with the earlier disc drives which had a transfer speed of about 200KB/s. At the higher end of the speed range of 1.25MB/s (1.25 million bytes per second) this is equivalent in some instances to the speeds of modern disc drives which range from 600KB/s to 1.2MB/s. Typical speeds for older tape units are 60, 120 or 200K bytes per second for 9-track tape and 30K bytes per second for 7-track tape.

(b) The capacity of a standard reel of magnetic tape is in the region of 100 Megabytes for the higher packing density but this may fall to 20MB for tape with a low packing density.

(c) Characters are grouped into fields, examples of which are account numbers, names and addresses, quantity, price and value.

(d) Related fields constitute a record.

(e) Records on tape may be fixed or variable length.

(f) Records on tape are stored in blocks and the number of

records within a block may be fixed or variable.

(g) Reels of tape may be used repeatedly:

    (i) old data may be erased and the tape reused;

    (ii) old data may be overwritten by new data.

(h) The process of writing to a magnetic tape which already holds data destroys the data already recorded, therefore control procedures are necessary to ensure that current data is not overwritten in error.

(i) Data on magnetic tape can be *used repeatedly*, because the process of reading tape is non-destructive.

(j) As records held on magnetic tape (especially master files) are normally *in sequence with regard to a particular field* (account number or part number, for instance) the records are stored sequentially and accessed serially (*see* Fig. 6.1).

6. Uses of magnetic tape. Magnetic tape may be used for a number of different purposes, but in general it is used as a media for input, storage, output and for backup copies of files or the complete contents of discs. Specific uses of magnetic tape are indicated below.

(a) *Input for processing.* Transaction data may be encoded directly to magnetic tape, but historically data was first punched into cards and input to the computer in random order; then validated and written to magnetic tape for further processing to take advantage of magnetic tape transfer speeds and flexibility.

(b) *Storage of master files.* Magnetic tape provides a compact means of storing records which are either subjected to updating or used for reference purposes.

(c) *Storage of programs.* Computer programs are often stored on magnetic tape, as it provides a fast media for their transfer to the internal memory of the computer in readiness for processing.

(d) *Storage of intermediate processing results.* Very often the output from one run is recorded on magnetic tape, which becomes the input for the next run.

(e) *Output for conversion.* The output from a powerful computer may be in the form of magnetic tape, which is subsequently converted to printed output by off-line operations to avoid holding up the processor by slow printing speeds.

Parity checking of magnetic tape characters

7. Odd or even parity. When data is being written to magnetic tape, in the form of magnetised spots (bits), an additional magnetised spot is written to each row of spots (representing characters) when necessary to conform to the mode of parity used—'odd' or 'even'.

When using parity mode the number of bits representing a character will have a parity bit recorded if they come to an even number, in order to make them add up to an odd number.

When using even parity, the number of bits representing a character will have a parity bit recorded if they come to an odd number in order to make them an even number.

8. Purpose of parity checking. Parity checking is used to ensure that data (in the form of characters) has the correct number of bits written on tape. Parity is automatically checked after being recorded by a read-after-write parity check.

When data is being read into the computer from tape, the parity is again checked and the parity bit is then discarded, as it is not stored in the internal memory. If parity checks indicate invalid characters (incorrect number of bits) then the data are subjected to either re-reading or re-writing and if, after several attempts, the parity check fails, an error is indicated in the data.

Advantages and disadvantages of magnetic tape

9. Advantages of magnetic tape.

(a) It is perhaps the most widely used form of backing storage, because it is *relatively inexpensive* and has a *large data storage capacity*.

(b) It is capable of *transferring* data to and from internal storage at *very high speed*.

(c) Data held on magnetic tape can be *sorted by the computer* into the sequence required for updating master files.

(d) Transaction data can be *recorded directly on to magnetic tape* by means of magnetic tape encoding machines.

(e) Old data may be erased and the *tape used repeatedly*.

(f) Records held on magnetic tape do not *take up much storage space* as compared with records held on punched cards.

10. Disadvantages of magnetic tape.

(a) It is only possible to *access records serially*, which necessitates the reading of all records until the one required is reached.

(b) Input data relating to transactions must always be sorted into the *sequence of the master file* before updating can commence. This is unnecessary with random access devices such as disc drives.

(c) Data can be *accidentally erased or overwritten* unless stringent control procedures are used.

(d) Updated information cannot be *written back to the same location* on the same tape. It must be written to a different tape, thus necessitating an additional tape deck. With random access devices it is possible to write updated information to the same storage location by the process of overwriting.

(e) *Visual reading of records* is not possible.

(f) *Stringent environmental control* is necessary to eliminate dust and static electricity from the atmosphere, which otherwise could adversely affect the quality of data recorded on the tape, thereby affecting the capacity to read the data accurately.

Cassette tape

11. General outline. This type of storage provides for serial access to records or programs which are stored sequentially, one after the other, along the length of tape in the same way that music tracks are stored on musiccassettes in an audio system. It is necessary to read all the records to reach the one required, which takes a considerable time compared with the time required for magnetic discs. The same considerations apply to programs—lengthy programs seem to take hours to load and, what is more, all programs which precede the one required must be accessed first.

12. Important rules. A number of rules must be observed to ensure that tapes are used efficiently; these may be summarised as follows:

(*a*) Recorder and recording head must be kept clean.

(*b*) Tapes should be stored in a plastic box in a clean environment: no excessive dust and free from damp.

(*c*) Tapes should be kept away from electric or magnetic fields otherwise data or programs may be erased or distorted (corrupted).

(*d*) Tapes should not be placed on top of the cassette recorder (handler) as it contains an electric motor.

Tape streamers are tape drives used in association with micro and minicomputers for back-up purposes. When files are updated on a Winchester hard disc, for instance, they are copied to a tape streamer at very high speed. This avoids the cost of using expensive hard discs for back-up purposes and eliminates the need to handle many floppy discs with their relatively low capacity (*see* **14**).

Magnetic discs: Winchester and exchangeable

13. Hard discs: general characteristics. Winchester and exchangeable disc packs are 'hard discs' as they are made from a rigid light alloy coated on both sides with a layer of magnetisable oxide. The discs rotate at very high speed on the drive and access to records is made as the disc rotates. Data is stored on the disc surfaces along concentric tracks. These tracks are divided into sectors similar to blocks on a magnetic tape. A track index locates specific records directly without having to search the file as with magnetic tape. Data on the discs is stored in binary code and data is written to the disc from data stored in the processor's internal memory. Similarly, data is read from the disc and transferred to the processor's memory for reference or processing purposes.

Read/write heads do not come in contact with the disc surface but float above it on a cushion of air. Thus hard discs do not suffer from so much wear as floppy discs and are therefore suitable for frequent usage. A disc cartridge is another type of hard disc used on some minicomputer systems. Other systems use very large-capacity fixed discs for storing large volumes of data which is frequently referred to. Such discs are sealed within the disc drive and cannot be interchanged as with EDS. An IBM 3380 fixed disc has a transfer rate of 3.0MB per second (Megabytes, i.e. million bytes, per second) and a capacity of 630MB and the 3344 model has a transfer rate of 885MB and a capacity of 280MB (*see* 24).

14. Winchester discs. This type of disc is a hard disc and they are being used to complement floppy discs or replace them in some instances on some models of microcomputer. They have a much greater storage capacity, typically 5, 10 and 20MB compared with the capacity of floppies which is in the region of 250K–1MB. This type of disc is rigid and sealed in a case. It rotates at a much faster speed than a floppy which allows data to be transferred much faster. As an example of this, floppy discs typically rotate at between 200 and 360 rpm but hard discs rotate in the region of 3,600 rpm. The Winchester's data transfer speed is, therefore, much higher—around 800K bytes per second compared with 100K bytes per second for floppy discs.

Portable computers such as the Panasonic PL-H7100 now have built-in hard disc drives with 10MB of storage capacity complementing floppy disc storage. The discs are 5.25 inches in diameter—the same physical size as some floppy discs.

There now exist exchangeable hard discs which are inserted in a disc drive in the same way as a floppy disc.

Security measures need to be taken with Winchester discs for the same reason as any other discs. Moreover, due to the high volumes of data stored on such a disc an economical media needs to be used for back-up purposes. Copies of the files are normally stored on magnetic tape using a high-speed tape spooler (*see* 12).

15. Exchangeable disc storage. This type of disc is known as EDS, an abbreviation for exchangeable disc storage. Such discs are widely used in batch processing environments as they are very flexible and can be exchanged in accordance with the programs and files needed for a specific application. A number of discs—from six to twelve—form a disc pack which is stored in a plastic container. The capacity varies accordingly between 60 and 300MB which in terms of storage capacity for records of 100 characters gives 600,000—3,000,000 records. Some computers can handle four disc drives by means of a disc controller others have banks of drives, perhaps no more than four drives for each controller which gives a capacity of 1,200MB or 1.2GB, i.e. gigabytes (a thousand million). The read/write heads are an integral part of the disc drive and are located in pairs for each disc surface as shown in Fig. 7.3. There are disc modules however, in which the read/write heads are part of the disc module and not the drive itself (*see* Figs. 7.3 to 7.5).

Floppy discs

16. Applications. This type of disc is widely used on micro-computers for storing data and programs and is also used for storing text for word processing application and for storing transaction data for input to a mainframe computer. They are known as floppy discs (floppies) or diskettes, because they are made from a soft pliable material.

17. General features. Diskettes are available in three sizes 8, 5.25 and 3.5 inches diameter. The first discs (disks is an alternative spelling) were 8 inches in diameter. Later discs were 5.25 inches and the current popular size in wide use is 3.5 inches diameter. The size is determined by the computer specification of particular man-ufacturers. The 3.5 inch discs are housed in a rigid plastic casing with a sliding shutter which automatically closes when they are removed from the disc drive. The rigid casing allows the disc to be carried around with little risk of damage. The capacity of discs varies but the 3.5 inch Sony disc, as an example, is double-sided with a capacity of 720K bytes. These discs are more robust than the larger ones which are stored in a cardboard cover and have an aperture allowing access to the recording tracks by a read/write head—either for reading or writing data to, or from, the tracks. The surface of a disc is magnetised which allows data to be recorded magnetically in the form of ASCII code, i.e. a binary code whereby each character is stored as a group of 1 or 0 bits or in pure binary form.

A variety of discs is available, apart from differences in size. Some are single- or double-sided, single- or double-density or

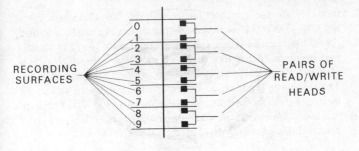

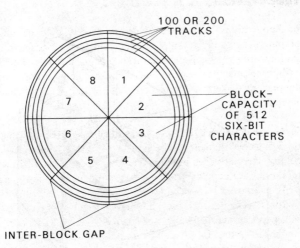

Figure 7.3 *Exchangeable discs.*

single-sided, quad-density. Double-density and double-sided features increase the data storage capacity.

Discs provide direct access or random access to specific records, documents, text or programs by the use of an index which indicates their location on the disc tracks without having to read through the disc tracks until the desired record or program, etc. is found as is the case with magnetic tape files. This is accomplished by means of a disc directory which is outlined below.

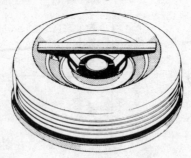

Figure 7.4 *Exchangeable disc pack.*

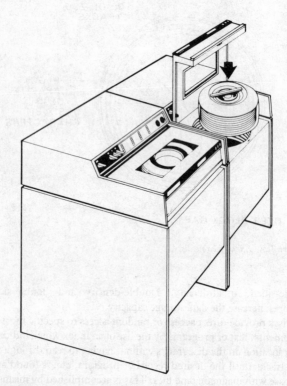

Figure 7.5 *Exchangeable disc drive.*

18. Tracks, sectors and blocks. Data is recorded on the surface of a disc in a series of concentric tracks—not one continuous track as on a phonograph record—but a hypothetical track(s) consisting of a stream of binary digits (BITS) representing characters. A sector is a section of a track which is used for storing text, data or programs. A sector usually consists of 256 bytes which are transferred to and from the processor at one time. Each sector has a sector header which tells the computer that information is to follow which is stored in a sector data area. A sector gap, like an inter-block gap on magnetic tape, separates each sector. During disc operations a cyclic redundancy check, a field comprising several bytes, is read and a number of calculations are carried out. If the result differs from a pre-computed value it signifies that a read/write error has occurred. Each sector has a file control block containing details such as drive code, file name and file type which are used by the operating system and disc controller.

19. Disc operating system. Control of the location of records, files or programs stored on disc is maintained by the computer in conjunction with a disc operating system or DOS for short. Often the first three tracks on a disc are used for storing DOS. The operating system works out where to locate files and programs and maintains a directory of the files or programs on the disc. Disc directories are usually situated on tracks in the centre of the disc. The operating system also controls the copying of files from one disc to another for file security purposes. DOS begins storing text, data or a program wherever it can find an unused sector. When a sector is filled, DOS searches for a free sector and continues recording the data or program at that location. As a file is stored on disc a track/sector list is compiled by means of a pair of bytes assigned to each file, one byte with the track reference and the other with the sector location. These bytes are called the track/sector pair. A link pair of bytes contain the location of the next portion of the track/sector list.

20. Disc security. A number of rules are worth remembering for ensuring the safety and security of discs. These are listed below.

(a) Maintain backup copies of programs and important, lengthy text or data files to avoid having to laboriously re-enter them by the keyboard in the event of loss or corruption.

(*b*) Never use the original master program disc during processing as it can be very costly to replace if the disc drive or disc is damaged or corrupted. For security, construct a backup copy and put the original in a place of safety. If the surface of the copy disc is damaged due to the disc drive malfunctioning then it is possible to replace it by making another copy from the original.

The frequency of generating backup copies depends, to some extent, on how often files are updated. If this is a daily process then making backup copies could be done weekly—if this degree of risk is acceptable. Daily backup, however, would offer greater security. If updating is a weekly routine then the updated file should be copied immediately.

Many computers automatically generate backup copies of files.

(*c*) The latest 3.5 inch discs are provided with a sliding tab in a groove located on the reverse side, lower, left-hand corner. When the tab is moved downwards to uncover the hole in the disc casing it 'write-protects' the disc. This can be verified by looking through the disc casing—if you can see daylight then it is write-protected. The computer can still read the information but accidental overwriting is prevented. It is necessary to purposely adjust the position of the tab in the groove to enable writing to take place on the disc. This will be necessary before a file can be updated by writing new data to the disc and overwriting previously recorded data. Overwriting is destructive as it destroys the previous contents of the disc at a specific location which is why it is essential to make backup copies. The larger discs have a notch near the bottom left-hand corner which prevents accidental overwriting when covered by sellotape.

21. General rules for handling discs.

(*a*) Avoid touching the recording surface of a disc.

(*b*) Ensure the disc is placed in the disc drive the correct way round.

(*c*) Do not bend the disc.

(*d*) Do not expose disc to dust as this can corrupt data on the tracks.

(*e*) Do not remove a disc from the drive while the disc light is glowing.

(*f*) Never leave discs in the disc drive while the computer is switched on or off as the disc can be corrupted.

(*g*) Do not place discs near magnetic fields such as on the top of the computer or hi-fi unit or even near a telephone when in use.

22. Formatting discs. A new disc must be formatted by a special program before information or programs can be written to it. The program writes identifying data onto the tracks for reference by the disc operating system. Formatting is done by either of two techniques according to the particular model of computer. Some adopt 'soft sectoring' which is a sector-identification technique whereby the sectors on a disc are identified by coded signals recorded on the disc tracks. 'Hard sectoring' is a technique which identifies sectors on a disc by means of holes punched through the disc around the central hole marking the beginning of each sector.

Disc formatting is often accomplished by selecting a 'disc icon' on the screen of the monitor. The blank disc is then inserted into the disc drive after removing the system disc. It is then necessary to indicate by locating the cursor on the screen over the relevant prompt: SINGLE OR DOUBLE-SIDED DISC. Formatting is then performed automatically after the cursor has been located over SELECT TO START and pressing the Enter key (*see* also **6:32**).

Data module and fixed discs

23. Data module. This is a multi-platter disc unit with in-built read/write heads housed in a transparent plastic case. This differs from standard disc systems whereby read/write heads are part of the disc drive. The data module is more expensive than the standard disc pack but the drive is correspondingly less expensive. Disc surfaces are kept cleaner and if a head crash occurs the consequences are localised compared with standard disc packs, where head crashes can be more drastic. Up to 140MB can be stored on a dual-spindle unit with a transfer speed up to 885K bytes per second.

24. High capacity fixed disc units. The IBM 3380 is a fixed disc storage unit for large computer systems. Each unit consists of two spindles (drives) each with a capacity of 1,260MB, a total of 2,520MB, i.e. 2.52 gigabytes (billion bytes). The data transfer speed is 3MB/s (megabytes per second) with an average access time of 16ms.

This type of storage allows current data to be continuously on-line which improves the effectiveness of data processing operations (*see* 13).

Silicon, integrated and optical discs

25. Silicon disc. This is a method of using a RAM card as if it were a disc. This allows much faster access to information than with an actual disc, as it is unnecessary to position read/write heads over tracks and sectors and for information to be transferred from backing storage to internal memory. This type of storage is volatile.

26. Optical disc. Optical data discs are rotating storage devices which use lasers to read and write data from and to disc. They are read-only devices, but erasable systems are expected to become available. Information is held on a metallic layer that is sandwiched in a protective transparent envelope made from glass or plastic. The information is stored on the disc by a laser beam which burns a hole in the metallic layer or raises a small blister. Information is read by a beam bounced off each hole or blister onto a light-sensitive device which interprets or reads the beam's angle of refraction. The use of this technique is also expected to expand greatly because of its vast storage capacity. To appreciate the storage capacity of optical discs a few comparisons will be made. If a filing cabinet in an office contains in the region of 10,000 A4 documents of 2,000 characters (bytes) each, then this is equivalent to 20,000,000 bytes. An optical disc of one gigabyte capacity i.e. 1,000,000,000 bytes (one billion) has the capability of storing 500,000 of such A4 pages. This would require: 2 000 floppy discs each of 500 000 bytes capacity; fifty 20MB Winchester discs or fifty reels of magnetic tape of 20MB capacity. Moreover, Winchester discs are fixed, which can be rather expensive if vast amounts of data need to be stored and accessed as each disc requires its own drive. Optical disc devices are expensive but the costs must be related to the amount of data they are capable of storing compared with that of fixed discs for an equivalent

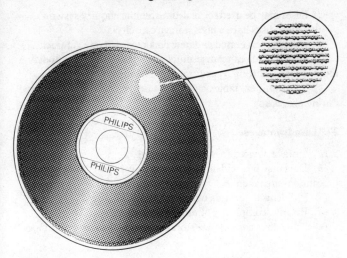

Figure 7.6 *Philips (optical) disc. (Courtesy Philips Organisation)*

capacity. From a security point of view data on an optical disc cannot be erased accidentally as is the case with magnetic discs.

27. Integrated discs. Some modern small computers have integrated discs stored in the same cabinet as the processor and memory. The discs are mounted in a pull-out unit and a single spindle unit holds one fixed two-surface disc and one removable two-surface disc. Each disc has a capacity of approximately 4.9 million bytes and a transfer speed in the region of 312 kilobytes per second (*see* Fig. 2.2).

Advantages and disadvantages of direct access storage

28. Advantages.

(*a*) Any item of data can be directly addressed depending upon the method of the file organisation used.

(*b*) High data transfer speed.

(*c*) Data can be input in random order (without the need for sorting).

(d) Discs may be used for real-time remote enquiry systems.

(e) Latest discs have a high storage capacity.

(f) Data may be erased and new data recorded on data tracks.

(g) Different discs or disc units are not required for updating records as the existing records may be amended by overwriting.

(h) Sub-routines, tables and rates may be called in as required during processing.

29. Disadvantages.

(a) Storage devices are rather expensive.

(b) Data may be accidentally erased or overwritten unless special precautions are taken.

(c) Problems of locating overflow records on discs.

(d) Relative complexity of programming.

(e) Some discs have a lower storage capacity than magnetic tape.

Progress test 7

1. Why is it necessary to have backing storage? (**1**)

2. Summarise the types of backing storage available which are used on micros, minis and mainframes. (**2**)

3. Outline the general characteristics of magnetic tape. (**3–10**)

4. Discuss the factors which determine the time it will take to update a magnetic tape master file containing 50,000 records with a transaction file, also on magnetic tape, containing 5,000 records. (**5**) (*C & G*)

5. Specify the uses of magnetic tape and state the purpose of parity checking. (**6–8**)

6. State the advantages and disadvantages of using magnetic tape as a file media. (**9, 10**)

7. Describe the characteristics of cassette tape. (**11, 12**)

8. Define the following terms in respect of hard discs: (a) exchangeable disc storage (EDS); (b) Winchester discs; (c) floppy discs; (d) data module; (e) fixed discs. (**13–24**)

9. Increasingly, the choice of backing storage for computer systems, particularly at the micro or mini level, is between 'floppy discs', 'Winchester-type discs' or some combination of the two. You are required to describe: (a) the characteristics and facilities

offered by these disc systems and give advantages and disadvantages of each; (*b*) the concepts of 'hard sectoring' and 'soft sectoring' as applied to disc backing storage.   (**14, 16–22** and 6:**32**) (*CIMA*)

10. What differences are there likely to be between a disc storage unit attached to a large mainframe computer and one attached to a microcomputer? The answer should include diagrams and give approximate details of physical size, transfer rates and data capacities.   (**13–24**)

11. Specify the nature of the following types of disc: (*a*) silicon disc; (*b*) optical disc; (*c*) integrated disc.   (**25–27**)

12. Specify the advantages and disadvantages of direct access storage.   (**28, 29**)

8
Data transmission

Basic concepts

1. **General aspects of data transmission.** Data transmission is the movement of information in coded form comprising binary digits (bits) over some kind of electrical transmission system (*see* Table 8A). Communication between business units by means of data transmission facilities using either telephone or telegraph lines is increasing. The reason for the increasing use of data transmission rather than voice communication and the normal mail service is due to the expanding use being made of computers in business organisations, especially those with dispersed operating units. This is particularly so with regard to businesses with a centralised computer installation used for processing the data of the various operating units in order to achieve economy in data processing activities and efficient control of business operations.

Instead of despatching data for processing by normal mail services or an internal messenger service, it is much faster to send it by data transmission facilities. The processed data may then be retransmitted to the originating unit and converted into printed form locally if suitable facilities are available, or, if not, it may be sent through the normal mail service or internal messenger service. Data transmission may be either on-line or off-line, and it is now proposed to outline the characteristics of both communication techniques.

Before proceeding, it is important to appreciate the difference between telephone lines and telegraph lines. The former are referred to as 'voice-grade' lines, which allow data to be transmitted at higher speed than telegraph lines allow (*see* 5).

2. On-line data transmission. On-line data transmission indicates that the communication lines are connected directly to the computer either by means of a multiplexor or an interface unit (*see* Fig. 8.1). The interface unit scans the communication lines frequently to detect those ready to send or receive data. When a line is ready to transfer data the scanning ceases and the channel number of the line is signalled to the CPU; if the processor is in a position to accept data, transmission begins.

3. Off-line data transmission. This type of data transmission indicates that the communication lines are not connected directly to the computer. Key-to-disc systems are often used for off-line preparation and transmission of data as remote job-entry systems.

Communication equipment

4. Multiplexor. A multiplexor is a device which enables a number of data channels to be accommodated on a single communication line, for the purpose of transferring data to and from the computer.

A multiplexor receives data from a number of terminals in the communication system which transmit and receive data at low speed. The multiplexor batches terminal messages and transmits them at high speed to the computer. A number of terminals may share a multiplexor located at a regional office as in time sharing operations. All transmissions are then communicated to the computer by a single communication line via a multiplexor at the central location. This arrangement economises in the number of lines required and reduces the cost of leasing telephone lines.

Multiplexors are used as an alternative to polling which requires dedicated software and more complex terminals (*see* Fig. 8.1).

5. Modem. The term 'modem' is derived from 'modulator' and 'demodulator' and is an item of equipment connected to each terminal in a communications complex using telephone lines. As telephone lines use analog signals and data terminals transmit signals in digital form a modem is necessary for converting digital signals to analog signals and vice versa. Telecom modems are designed to a standard

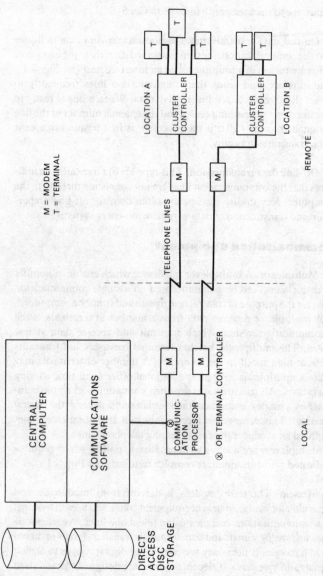

M = MODEM
T = TERMINAL

⊗ OR TERMINAL CONTROLLER

Figure 8.1 *On-line data transmission—clusters of terminals*

interface as recommended by the Consultative Committee International Telephones and Telegraphs (CCITT). Modems are included in the Datel service provided by British Telecom.

6. Front-end communications processors. These are programmable devices which control the functions of communications systems. They support the operations of a mainframe computer by performing functions which it would otherwise be required to perform itself. The functions include code conversions, editing and verification of data, terminal recognition and control of transmission lines. The mainframe computer is then able to devote its time to data processing rather than data transmission (*see* Fig. 8.1).

Facsimile document transmission is an electronic mail service which transmits copies of documents electronically to worldwide locations. It uses a public electronic carrier—the telephone which is used to make the initial connection with the recipient. The operator dials the recipient's number, waits for the signal and then feeds in the page of text, diagram or document to be transmitted. Standard telephone charges apply when transmitting. The line can be used to discuss the document by pressing a 'talk' button. There are three groups of machine available which use the telephone to make the connection but a fourth group works on a store and forward basis whereby the details are stored temporarily and released for transmission when a transmission path becomes available at a later time. Transmissions to different time zones can be 'stored and forwarded' to the destination during normal daytime.

The use of the service is gaining momentum with demand increasing greatly and 1.5 million machines installed worldwide. Some machines can transmit at 9,600 bps which allows a typical page to be transmitted in 30 seconds or less.

Encoding data for transmission and error checking

7. Coding. Data for transmission is encoded in binary code. A number of different codes exist but there is a tendency towards international standardisation of such codes by using, for example, the International Alphabet Code No. 5 (IA5). The code emanated from a standard developed by the American Standards Association which is known as American Standard Code for Information Interchange (ASCII).

Some codes are based on a 6-, 7- or 8-bit code structure. ASCII is a 7-bit code which generates 128 different characters due to that number of combinations of seven bits, i.e. 2^7. Thirty-two of the codes are reserved for special control functions. A further code widely used by IBM is the Extended Binary Coded Decimal Interchange code or EBCDIC. It is an 8-bit code which can generate 256 characters from the different combinations of the eight bits.

The codes are designed for transmission of digital information by telegraphic or data transmission facilities which also provide codes for special functions including transmission control, format effectors, information separators and device control.

8. Error checking. In most data transmission systems redundancy checking is often used for the detection of errors which are then corrected by retransmission of the blocks containing errors. Redundancy checking detects errors by computing additional bits from the data which are added to blocks of data. The receiving terminal then performs checks by comparing bit patterns in the data blocks, which identifies bits which have been lost or corrupted during transmission. Blocks containing errors are then automatically retransmitted. Parity checking can also be applied whereby an additional bit is added to the frame of bits forming a character before transmission. Parity checking can be either even or odd parity. This requires the count of 1 bits to be either even or odd according to the mode of parity selected. Errors may also be detected by retransmitting signals received back to the transmitting terminal on a separate channel. The signals are then compared with the original transmission, differences indicating the presence of transmission errors.

9. Speed of data transmission. Although the speed of data transmission is usually expressed in terms of bits/s, i.e. bits per second, a term used to define the speed of transmission in terms of the number of pulses which can be transmitted in a second is the baud. If data is transmitted serially one bit at a time then 100 baud is equivalent to 100 bits per second. If, however, the data consists of two-bit groups then 100 baud is equivalent to a baud rate of 200 bits per second. Typical baud rates are 110, 300, 600, 1,200, 2,400 and 4,800.

Telecom Datel services

10. Definition of Datel. Telecom consider data transmission facilities of such importance to commercial, business and industrial undertakings as to merit the provision of a separate group of communications services known as 'Datel Services'. Datel is a word derived from (Da)ta (tel)ecommunications and the services available are indicated below. It is important to appreciate that it is necessary to obtain permission from Telecom to connect any communications equipment to Telecom services.

Datel services are summarised in Table 8A.

Table 8A   Datel services at a glance

Service	Signal path	Transmission Speed – bits per second	Operating Mode	Remarks
Datel 200	Public Telephone Network	300	Asynchronous	300 bit/s may not always be attainable with older equipment
	Private Circuit	300	Asynchronous	
Datel 600	Public Telephone Network	600	Asynchronous	Speeds of up to 1200 bit/s are also possible
	Private Circuit	1200	Asynchronous	4-wire private circuits are required for duplex working
Datel 1200 Duplex	Public Telephone Network	1200	Synchronous or Asynchronous	
Datel 2412	Public Telephone Network	2400	Synchronous	Over some connexions it may be necessary to switch to 1200 bit/s

Table 8A   *continued*

Service	Signal path	Transmission Speed – bits per second	Operating Mode	Remarks
	Private Circuit	2400	Synchronous	A 4-wire private circuit is required
Datel 4800	Public Telephone Network	4800/2400	Synchronous	Over some connexions it may be necessary to switch to 2400 bit/s
	Private Circuit	4800/2400	Synchronous	A 4-wire private circuit is required
Datel 4832	Private Circuit	4800/3200	Synchronous	A 4-wire private circuit is required
	Public Telephone Network (Standby)	4800/3200	Synchronous	PSTN only operation is not available
Datel 9600	Private Circuit	9600/7200/4800	Synchronous	A 4-wire private circuit is required
	Public Telephone Network	9600/7200/4800	Synchronous	
Datel 48K	Wideband Circuit	40.8K 48K 50K	Synchronous	

(Courtesy British Telecom)

11. International Datel services. International Datel 200, 600 and 2,400 services provide for the transmission of data over the PSTN to most of Europe, the USA and many other countries. The transmission of data internationally can be arranged over privately leased circuits, whether or not the International Datel Service is available to the country concerned.

12. Datel Network Control Systems (DNCS). DNCS are available for use with most Datel Services. Specially equipped racks, housed in an attractive cabinet, provide the termination points for the circuits and hold the modems, control units and other necessary equipment. The systems are modular; as the user's needs increase, more 'building bricks' are added to it. Where a customer uses more than one Datel Service, DNCS may contain a mixture of these different services.

13. Multipoint circuits for data transmission. In addition to point to point circuits, data may also be transmitted over a multipoint circuit. This allows from two to twelve terminals to be connected to a central station and allows the transmission of data from the central station to any terminal and from terminals to the central station. Direct communication between terminals is not possible.

14. KiloStream and MegaStream. These are digital private circuit services which transmit text, data, facsimile or speech. They can also be used for slow scan visual services including closed circuit television, confravision and videostream—a videoconferencing service. KiloStream is available in various speeds including 2,400, 4,800 and 9,600 bits per second. KiloStream Plus combines the high data rates of MegaStream with the wide availability of Kilo-Stream. The service offers a 2MB/s path provided up to 31 channels are sited on the customers' premises, and individual circuits link a number of locations. For users requiring a large number of Kilo-Stream circuits over various routes KiloStream Plus is ideal. Mega-Stream is the highest capacity digital private circuit service available from BT. It is available nationally and can be used to link high-speed terminals, private branch exchanges, local and metropolitan area networks, visual services and mainframes; voice and data can be mixed. MegaStream is ideal for corporate networks.

Other Telecom services

15. System X. This is British Telecom's name for their computer controlled telephone exchanges linked by digital transmission and signalling systems. Older exchange equipment is scheduled to be progressively replaced by the new technology system over a number of years. With this system caller voice patterns are represented by on-off digital pulses. The system greatly improves the quality of transmission and calls are connected more quickly. The equipment is also cheaper to buy, install and maintain than older systems and takes up much less space.

Digital exchange systems, like System X, rely on the latest microchip technology. This means that exchanges no longer have moving parts prone to crossed lines, wrong numbers, and line noise as was the case with the older electro-mechanical exchanges and the more modern cross-bar and electronic read relay exchanges.

System X also facilitates integrated links between local and trunk exchanges, referred to as Integrated Digital Access (IDA). In addition to voice services IDA offers both circuit and packet switched data facilities which can be used for a wide variety of purposes, e.g. facsimile, electronic mail and slow-scan TV.

16. Packet switching. Packet switching is a technique whereby the terminal or computer in a data transmission system collects data into a block which is allocated an address. The block is sent to the local packet switching exchange which transmits it to its destination exchange. The communication lines between exchanges are only engaged when a packet is being transmitted. During lapses in transmission, lines are available to other users. If data is transmitted by the normal telephone network a charge is incurred for the length of time the line is used, even for the time when no data is being transmitted. Packet switching is designed to eliminate this. In the UK this applies where telephone calls or data transmissions on public switched telephone lines are charged on a time used basis.

17. Teletex. At the outset it is important not to confuse 'teletex' with 'teletext'. Teletex is the international text communication service embracing a set of internationally agreed standards, which ensures the interworking of terminals from any manufacturer on a number of different networks. Communication between various equipment cannot be achieved without standardisation. Teletex represents an automatic text transmission system thirty times faster than telex. Business correspondence, documents, data and messages can be transmitted between terminals which may be workstations or word processors in around ten seconds a page. Letters can be typed and sent automatically. Other work can continue while documents are transmitted or received. Copies of documents can be stored electronically or printed for filing in the normal office filing cabinets.

Digital PABX telephone exchange

18. General outline of PABX. Digital PABX telephone exchanges are an essential communication catalyst for the electronic office of the present and future. Digital voice and data communication systems provide the foundations for extending office automation.

The digital exchange translates voice analog signals into digital signals, which are the common language of computers and electronic equipment such as workstations, word processors and terminals in general. This technology will widen the horizons for developing automated offices as it makes it possible to access all electronic devices comprising the electronic office. This includes access to local area networks, mainframe computers, terminals, word processors, electronic mail stations, telexes, microcomputers and electronic printing equipment. The devices are connected to the wiring of the digital switchboard at no additional cost. PABX systems can also act as message switching centres for terminals and other devices. They also control the routeing of data or text from workstations.

19. ICL DNX–2000 digital PABX distributed network exchange. The DNX–2000 is a *D*istributed *N*etwork *EX*change which provides the means for integrating office communications as it can talk to and work with computers, word processors, telexes, electronic printing equipment and traditional telephones.

The system has bubble memory (which eliminates tape and disc) as the primary non-volatile storage medium. The exchange can be interlinked or used with other switching systems to provide integrated communications. It can handle 150 to 10,000 lines.

Features include discriminatory barring, automatic route selection, extension metering, automatic number identification and traffic analysis.

The DNX–2000 supports standard dial and MF telephones together with two special terminals—the DNX–50 and DNX–300. The DNX–50 is an electronic telephone providing display capability, flexible key assignment, hands free operation and an optional data port into the DNX–2000. Features include abbreviated dialling, dial by name, date and time display, numeric keypad for normal telephone operation and alphabetic keys for message generation. The DNX–300 dataphone can function as a console, maintenance position or a secretarial/executive extension. It has DNX–50 features plus electronic mail, diary, directory, full message switching capability and system statistics recovery. Other features include VDU, standard keyboard layout, fixed designation keys including dial keypad and fixed feature keys. It is built on distributed microprocessor architecture (*see* Fig. 8.2).

Terms used in data transmission

20. Serial transmission. With this type of transmission, each bit in a character is sent sequentially to the transmission line; by convention the least significant bit is usually sent first, viz.

$$0100011 \rightarrow$$

Speed of transmission is expressed in bits per second.

21. Parallel transmission. In a parallel transmission system, all the bits in a character are transmitted at the same time, viz.

Although it appears that seven signals have to be sent to the transmission lines at the same time, in practice special codes are used in order to limit the number of simultaneous signals which need to be

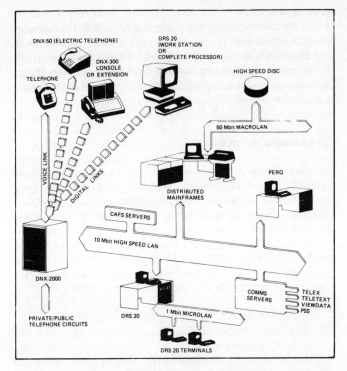

Figure 8.2 *ICL DNX-2000 digital PABX distributed network exchange.*
(Courtesy International Computers Limited)

transmitted, thereby reducing the technical problems which are introduced when more than one frequency is transmitted at once. Speed of transmission is expressed in characters per second in a parallel transmission system.

22. Frequency division multiplexing (FDM). With frequency division multiplexing a relatively wide band width (range of frequencies available for signalling) is divided into a number of smaller band widths, to provide more channels of communication.

23. Time division multiplexing (TDM). Time division multiplexing is a process whereby a channel which is capable of a relatively high information transfer rate (bits per second) is divided up into a number of time slots to provide a number of lower speed channels. For example, a line capable of carrying 2 400 bits per second could, by the use of TDM, theoretically be divided into four 600 bits per second channels, or a combination of different speed channels up to a maximum of 2,400 bits per second.

Transmission modes

24. Asynchronous transmission. With this mode of transmission each character is preceded by pulses, i.e. start and stop signals which serve to prepare the receiving mechanism for the reception of characters. The start bit triggers a timing mechanism in the receiving terminal which counts the succeeding bits of the character as a series of fixed time intervals. The stop signal resets the receiver ready for the next character. This mode of transmission may use start and stop signals between blocks of characters rather than individual characters and is used in slow-speed devices like teleprinters.

25. Synchronous transmission. This mode of transmission is used for high-speed digital transmission. The synchronisation of transmitting and receiving terminals is maintained by clocks which keep the devices in step with each other. Synchronisation takes place at the beginning of each transmission by means of special synchronisation characters which align the clock at each terminal. Transmissions are effected without gaps but if gaps occur in the data the transmitting terminal inserts idle bits.

26. Simplex transmission. The transmission of data in one direction only.

27. Duplex transmission. The transmission of data in both directions simultaneously.

28. Half-duplex transmission. The transmission of data in both directions, but not at the same time.

29. Polling. The process of establishing if any terminal in the communication network has a message to transmit. Polling is a continuous process requiring dedicated software and more complex terminals than would be required if using a multiplexor (*see* **4**). The mainframe computer polls each terminal several times each minute to service those with messages to transmit. Messages transmitted by the computer are received by all the terminals in the system but only the terminal to which the message applies displays or prints the message.

Services other than British Telecom

30. Mercury Communications. This is Britain's national and international communications organisation in competition with British Telecom. Mercury's national telecommunications network links together the principal business centres in England. International communications for voice, data and TV are provided by two satellite communication centres.

Progress test 8

1. What do you understand by the term 'data transmission'? (**1**)
2. What are the main purposes of using data transmission facilities? (**1**)
3. Define on-line data transmission. (**2**)
4. Define off-line data transmission. (**3**)
5. Explain the purpose of the following devices when used as part of a data transmission service: (*a*) modem; (*b*) multiplexor; (*c*) front-end processor. (**4–6**)
6. What is FAX? (**6**)
7. How is data encoded for transmission and error checking? (**7–9**)
8. What do you understand by the term Datel? (**10–13**)
9. Define the terms KiloStream and Megastream. (**14**)
10. What is System X? (**15**)
11. Explain what is meant by packet switching. (**16**)
12. Specify the meaning of the term Teletex. (**17**)
13. Outline the features of a Digital PABX telephone

exchange.   (**18, 19**)

    14. Define and contrast serial and parallel transmission.   (**21, 22**)

    15. Define the terms 'FDM' and 'TDM'.   (**23, 24**)

    16. Define the terms: (*a*) asynchronous transmission; (*b*) synchronous transmission; (*c*) simplex transmission; (*d*) duplex transmission; (*e*) half-duplex transmission; (*f*) polling.   (**25–30**)

Part three
Checks, controls, security and processing techniques

9

Checks, controls and privacy in computerised systems

Spectrum of control

1. Security measures. The extent to which security measures are applied depends upon a number of factors amongst which are:

 (*a*) confidentiality of the data;

 (*b*) the extent to which it may be subjected to unauthorised access;

 (*c*) the possibility of system failure;

 (*d*) the possibility of corrupting files;

 (*e*) the possibility of a disc file being stolen;

 (*f*) the nature of the system.

The term 'security' means ensuring that data is inaccessible to unauthorised personnel as opposed to ensuring the correctness of the data which is a matter of data validation. It also incorporates all file security measures relating to the 'DUMPING' of data from a master disc file to a magnetic tape file or another disc to safeguard against accidental erasure or corruption of the data or even theft of the master disc file. The security copy enables a file to be reconstructed by copying the data from the security disc or tape to the master disc (*see* **14**).

2. Security in on-line processing systems. Included in this category are such applications as: order processing, invoicing and sales ledger; purchase ledger, stock control and payroll, etc. To prevent unauthorised access to confidential files a password is provided to bona fide users of the applications. The password when input to the system is compared with that stored in the operational software. Access is barred if the password is incorrect. When entered, the password is not printed or displayed on the video screen for security reasons. Such applications usually have built-in enquiry programs to facilitate speedy information retrieval in response to queries. The data on the file is protected from being altered as amendments are not possible whilst the enquiry program is in use.

3. Databases. Some database systems are accessible by different application programs and are designed to prevent data being erased or altered accidentally by such programs. Alterations are only possible by the database software, i.e. the Database Management System (DBMS).

The ICL Viewdata system, for instance, has a number of built-in security measures. A user must enter a user name before access to information is possible. When information is confidential or of a restricted nature a password may be required. Access to some parts of the database can also be restricted to specified terminals. Each information owner must explicitly list those user names allowed to access his data. The list may include other information owners who can look at, but not amend, his part of the database.

Individual pages can also be restricted by giving them a list of user names. When a Bulletin user dials up the system and enters his user name the system checks this name against the parts of the database the user wishes to access. If the user name is on either the list of the information owner or the page list, access will be allowed.

4. Real-time systems. Real-time systems are designed to deal with dynamic situations in order to control a critical operation such as an airline seat reservation system which must be continually updated as events occur. Such systems accept random input at random time intervals and the status of files changes accordingly making it necessary to implement security measures. These take the form of dumping all relevant restart and audit information periodically, say every 2 to 3 minutes, to tape or disc. The dumped data can then be used to restart the system in the event of a malfunction.

Such operations are also provided with a second processor which is automatically switched into the real-time system in the event of the first machine ceasing to function for any reason.

5. Analysis of areas of control. If one views a large data processing department as a small business, which in effect it is, this will provide some indication of the range of checks and controls which need to be applied. A data processing department is a subsystem of a larger system which must be coordinated within the framework of corporate strategy and company policy. It can be seen then that even more checks and controls must be applied as the activities of a data processing department have a bearing on the efficiency and effectiveness of all, or nearly all, functions of a business.

The areas of control may be analysed very broadly within the following categories; they are purely arbitrary as they may be defined in different ways and referred to by different terms. If it is considered that a data processing department plays a major part in the operations of a business, then the relevant checks and controls must be applied to maximise its performance however they may be defined. The categories are:

- (a) organisational;
- (b) administrative;
- (c) environmental;
- (d) technological;
- (e) sociological;
- (f) procedural and operational;
- (g) development.

Types of control

6. Organisational controls. These may be summarised as follows.

(a) The data processing department in the larger organisation should function through a policy-formulating steering committee in order to ensure that only those projects are undertaken which will provide maximum benefit to the business as a corporate entity rather than merely maximising or optimising the performance of individual functions. This does not preclude the data processing manager gaining direct access to his immediate superior, the managing director for instance, as this is often essential during the course of day to day operations to resolve immediate problems.

(*b*) In addition to the remarks made in (*a*) above, the data processing manager should report to a higher authority than the functional level, as he himself is a functional manager. It is necessary for him to report to, and receive instructions from, a superior such as the managing director, so that overriding authority may be implemented in conflicting circumstances.

(*c*) The various activities of a data processing department should be organised to allow for the implementation of 'internal check' procedures to prevent collusion to perpetrate fraudulent conversion of data and master files regarding the transfer of funds to fictitious accounts, for instance. This course of action necessitates a separation of duties, as in the accounting function, but in this case instead of separating the cash handling from the cash recording it is necessary to separate systems development from systems operation. It also necessitates the independence of a data control section even though it is normally structured within the operations section under the control of the operations manager. The preparation of input should be shielded from the influence of operations staff as data must maintain the utmost integrity. There must also be independence of the computer file library, as in a large data processing complex chaos can occur if stringent controls are not applied to the movement of master files and program files. Strict control procedures are required to ensure 'purge' dates are adhered to, to avoid premature overwriting or prolonged storage.

7. Administrative controls.

(*a*) Access to data relating to business transactions should be restricted to functional and data preparation staff in the data processing department.

(*b*) Access to the computer room, if a centralised department, must be restricted to authorised personnel only (*see* **35**).

(*c*) Master files and programs must only be released from the library on the presentation of an authorisation slip and they must not be allowed to leave the data processing department unless by special authority for processing at a bureau in the event of a systems breakdown.

(*d*) Internal check procedures must be implemented as indicated above (*see* **6**(*c*)).

(*e*) Adequate security measures must be incorporated to prevent fraudulent entry of data to perpetrate fraud by the use of passwords and Datakeys (*see* **2**, **3** and **35**).

(*f*) Projects must be controlled to ensure they are implemented to time schedules as far as is possible (*see* **38** and **39**).

(*g*) Projects must be formally approved by management prior to systems development perhaps as a result of the deliberations of a steering committee.

(*h*) Budgeted levels of expenditure should be adhered to and controlled by means of a formal budgetary control system.

(*i*) Control of performance standards.

8. Environmental controls. Some computer installations require critically controlled conditions of temperature, power and humidity as well as the level of dust in the atmosphere. These factors must be continuously monitored to ensure trouble free operations. For example, dust in the atmosphere can corrupt magnetic files if it settles on the recording surfaces, and excessive heat can cause malfunctions in the hardware. This is not so critical as with the early mainframes but nevertheless must be controlled. Dust extracting mats and double doors as well as monitoring equipment achieve these requirements.

9. Technological controls. The controls to be applied in this area are mainly to ensure that the most suitable equipment is being used for all data processing activities. If an installation is still operating with punched card or paper tape input then it is certain that it is technologically obsolete and perhaps not so efficient as it could be using other methods of input, such as that achieved by the use of magnetic tape (standard reels or cassette tape) or magnetic discs (hard discs or floppies according to circumstances). Direct input methods requiring the use of workstations in the form of VDUs for order-entry systems may need to be installed to replace the older batch processing technique. Distributed processing using networks of minis or micros may be more suitable than the current centralised system using a second generation mainframe.

10. Sociological controls. With the continuing and expanding use of automation in the administrative environment it must not be overlooked that this, in effect, is a 'dehumanising' of tasks traditionally performed by people. We all know the consequences of this— REDUNDANCY. When developing computerised systems it is imperative that the 'human' aspect of operations is dealt with in the most humane way possible. People are not machines and need more than a little 'maintenance' to keep them motivated to their tasks. These tasks need restructuring in many instances as their former work is 'relegated' or 'farmed out' to a computer. This has the effect of 'deskilling' their work which can have a demoralising effect and needs careful control to avoid having staff with 'moronic' tendencies (*see* 1:**9–12**).

Procedural and operational controls

11. Summary of controls. The controls in this area embrace:

- (*a*) input controls;
- (*b*) hardware controls;
- (*c*) file security;
- (*d*) batch controls;
- (*e*) auditing and audit trails;
- (*f*) confidentiality of information;
- (*g*) software (program) checks:
  - (*i*) validation checks;
  - (*ii*) check digit verification.

12. Input controls. In batch processing applications in particular, source data is recorded on source documents by clerical staff and errors are often made. Such errors cannot be allowed to enter the computer system so it is necessary to correct obvious errors before releasing the documents to the batch control section of the data processing department (*see* **19**).

Checking would be concerned with detecting missing data fields or transposed digits. Assuming that data is to be recorded (encoded) on magnetic tape or disc to produce a transaction file, this will be done by an operator using a magnetic tape encoding machine or key-to-disc by means of a keying station. It will be necessary to verify the data in both instances and validate the data in the case of the key-to-disc system. In both instances it is advisable to utilise a different operator to avoid similar errors being made at both times, i.e. the initial recording and the verifying stages.

13. Hardware controls. Initially it is of paramount importance to ensure that all hardware is maintained regularly, perhaps by a maintenance contract, to ensure a minimum of down-time. It is necessary to 'check-out' the computer circuitry to ensure that all characters consist of the correct number of binary digits (bits) and this is accomplished during processing operations by parity checking (*see* 7:**7**, **8**). Check bits are automatically recorded on tape and disc during initial encoding and it is essential to detect data corrupted due to a parity failure otherwise the computer system will produce a high degree of error.

File security

14. Purpose of file security. The purpose of a file security system is to provide a basis for reconstituting master files containing important business information, as it is possible to overwrite or erase a file in error.

It is essential that file security precautions be incorporated in those electronic computer data processing systems which store master files on a magnetic media, to safeguard against the consequences of loss of data, errors or corrupted data.

Without such precautions, it would be necessary to reprocess data, in the event of loss or corruption, from the last run when the file was known to be correct.

The reprocessing of data for a number of previous runs is very disruptive to the work scheduled for the computer, and consequently has an adverse effect on the productivity of the electronic data processing (EDP) department. It is therefore imperative that the reprocessing of data is kept to a minimum.

15. The generation technique of file security. In respect of master files recorded on magnetic tape, the technique of file security applied is known as the 'generation' technique because files relating to two previous periods are retained transiently in addition to the current updated file and the current transaction file. The two previous period files plus the current file comprise three generations, which are referred to as Grandfather—Father—Son. The technique operates as follows.

(a) The first master file produced is referred to as the 'Son tape'.

(b) The 'Son tape' produced during the following updating run replaces the first 'Son tape', which becomes the 'Father tape'.

(c) The next updating run produces a new 'Son tape', the first 'Son tape' (at present the 'Father tape') becomes the 'Grandfather tape'. The previous 'Son tape' now becomes the new 'Father tape'.

(d) On the next updating run, the original 'Son tape' (now the 'Grandfather tape') is overwritten, and can in fact be used for producing the new 'Son tape' (see Fig. 9.1).

16. The dumping (copying) technique of file security. With regard to master files recorded on magnetic discs, the existing records are overwritten during updating, and consequently the previous records are destroyed.

File security in respect of disc files is often achieved by the technique of 'dumping', which involves copying the updated records from one disc to another disc or to magnetic tape. In the event of loss of data on one disc, the situation is resolved by using the records for further processing from the spare disc or the magnetic tape reel on which the records were 'dumped'.

The records are retained in this manner until the next dump is carried out and proved to be free of errors and corrupted data.

It is also possible to apply the 'generation' technique to disc files, by the retention of three generations of records either on one disc or on separate discs.

17. File safety and ensuring the confidentiality of information. The records retained for regeneration purposes are filed for safety away from the computer centre, in case of damage by fire, etc. Thus

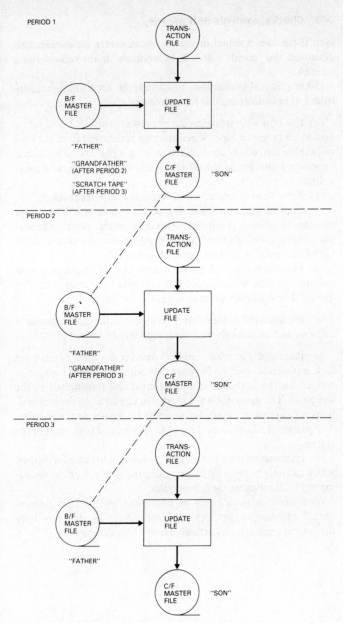

Figure 9.1 *Generation technique of file security.*

even if the files retained in the computer centre are damaged or destroyed the records will still be available in the remote filing location.

Other physical precautions which may be used to protect files from loss or damage include the following.

(*a*) Use of a write-permit ring to prevent overwriting of information on magnetic tape. When the ring is removed from the tape reel the file can only be read. When the ring is placed into position it depresses a plunger on the tape deck allowing the tape to be over-written.

(*b*) Prevention of unauthorised access to computer room.

(*c*) Implementation of suitable security measures to prevent sabotage if this is a possibility. This may require security guards patrolling regularly and perhaps the installation of alarms connected to the local police station to signal a break-in.

(*d*) File labels encoded on the header label of magnetic files to indicate the date when the information may be overwritten. The 'purge' date validation programs are used for this.

The confidentiality of information is largely achieved by means of software and includes the following aspects.

(*a*) Particularly in time sharing systems it is normal practice for each authorised user to be provided with a password which is entered on the keyboard of the terminal and transmitted to the computer. The password is not printed or displayed on the terminal, however, so that it cannot be observed by anyone in the vicinity. The password allows access to specific files related to the user of the system.

(*b*) Information on a file may be stored in a 'scrambled' format which can only be decoded by providing the system with the decoding key to unscramble the information.

(*c*) Specific terminals may be prohibited from receiving transmitted information by lock-out procedures. In this way only designated terminals will actually receive file information.

Data Protection Act

18. Data Protection Act 1984. With the wide use being made of electronic mail and databases the question of data privacy and integrity comes to the fore. This development has been recognised by the Data Protection Act 1984 which was approved by Parliament on 12 July 1984. The Act provides that all persons in control of personal data automatically processed on computers and all providers of bureau computer services to persons in control of such data should register with the Data Protection Registrar and comply with the Data Protection Principles.

The data protection principles apply where data users hold personal data and includes the following.

(*a*) The information to be contained in personal data shall be obtained and processed fairly and lawfully.

(*b*) Personal data shall be held only for one or more specified and lawful purposes.

(*c*) Personal data held for any purpose or purposes shall not be used or disclosed in any manner incompatible with that purpose or those purposes.

(*d*) Personal data held for any purpose or purposes shall be adequate, relevant and not excessive in relation to that purpose or those purposes.

(*e*) Personal data shall be accurate and, where necessary, kept up to date.

(*f*) Personal data held for any purpose or purposes shall not be kept for longer than is necessary for that purpose or purposes.

(*g*) An individual shall be entitled at reasonable intervals and without undue delay or expense to be informed by any data user whether he holds personal data of which that individual is the subject; and to access any such data held by a data user and where appropriate, to have such data corrected or erased.

Where data users hold personal data or where relevant services are provided by persons carrying on computer bureaux, appropriate security measures shall be taken against unauthorised access to, or alteration, disclosure or destruction of, personal data and against accidental loss or destruction of personal data.

Batch control

19. General considerations of batch control. It is one thing to process data, quite another to know that all the necessary data required for processing has been received, processed, errors signalled and corrections made. In order to control the flow of data in and out of the data processing system, it is normal practice to incorporate a data control section in the data processing organisation.

The data control section receives all incoming data for processing from internal operating departments or outlying branches. The data may already be batched when received in readiness for data preparation operations, unless the data is already in a form suitable for direct input to the computer. Each batch of data has a batch control slip attached, on which is recorded batch number, department or branch number, document count (number of documents in the batch) and other control totals if relevant such as hash or meaningful totals.

Each batch is recorded in a register in the control section for maintaining a record of the date when the batch was received. The batches may be vetted for correctness and completeness of data in general terms and then sent to the data preparation section for encoding on magnetic tape. Data are, of course, verified to ensure the accuracy of data preparation operations before being sent for processing. After processing, the batches of documents and the printed output from the computer are sent to the data control section, where they are entered in the register as a record that all batches have been processed or otherwise. It is then necessary to check for errors discovered during processing, as outlined below.

20. Errors correction routine. When the printed documents from the computer are received by the control section, they are checked for errors, signalled by an error diagnostic code or alternatively a separate error list is printed.

One of the first tasks undertaken by the control section is to compare the control totals with those generated by the computer, as it is possible that documents may have been overlooked during data preparation and not presented for processing and it is therefore essential that the fugitive documents are identified, traced and presented for processing.

After errors have been identified, it is necessary to extract the appropriate input document from the batch for correction. Corrected errors are then re-assembled in a batch with a batch control slip attached for re-processing. The new batch number is recorded on the print-out for cross-reference and control. The control of corrections is carried out in a similar manner to the control of original data.

Auditing computerised business systems

21. The approach to auditing computer applications. The work of both internal and external auditors is affected by the introduction of an electronic computer. While they need not be computer experts, they should be familiar with the mode of computer input, processing and output in order that they may conduct test checks with understanding. Auditors should also be familiar with computer programming so that they may recommend adequate controls to be built into the programs when they are being prepared. It is difficult and costly to amend programs once they have been completed, especially as they take a great deal of time to prepare initially.

An earlier approach was known as the 'Black Box' technique; the auditor extracted a sample of records and had them calculated manually. The results were then compared with the output from the computer and if there were no differences it was assumed that everything was satisfactory. In this respect, the 'Black Box' was the computer and in order to audit records it was not necessary for the auditor to know anything about how the computer processed the data or about the programming techniques.

The auditor may, however, assume wider duties in the present electronic data processing era. He must as before observe the principles of *internal check*, the separation of functions to prevent collusion and fraudulent intent. This includes the separation of data origination, control of input by means of 'batch totals', data preparation and processing, systems and programming.

Auditors should be consulted in an advisory capacity by system designers to establish the checks and controls which should be incorporated in the various applications under consideration.

Systems should be designed so that they are self-checking and self-correcting whenever possible. Auditors need to ensure that incorrect, i.e. invalid, data is rejected by the system before being subjected to processing operations. This is accomplished by in-built data validation checks such as range and limit checks; checks to ensure data is complete, of the correct type and for the correct period, etc.

22. System documentation. Systems documentation produced by the systems designer should pass through the audit department as a matter of routine so that auditors have the opportunity to assess the effectiveness of their recommendations and see that important checks and controls are incorporated and not overlooked. The documentation normally includes: the detailed description of the system (the system definition); decision tables which outline the conditions to be tested for and action to be taken; the flowcharts of the system structure and program flowcharts outlining the processing stages; a printout of the program coding, error-handling routines and test data to be used, etc.

The staffing of the system should also incorporate the principles of *internal check* whereby duties are separated so that collusion would be necessary to implement fraudulent practices such as collaboration between computer programmers and operators; data recording personnel and data conversion operators, etc.

23. Design philosophy. Auditors should determine the suitability of the design philosophy behind the processing tasks to be undertaken. This requires an assessment of the relative merits and demerits of batch processing versus on-line processing; centralised versus distributed processing and whether a database would best suit the needs of prospective systems integration projects rather than separate functional files.

24. System testing. It is essential for auditors to satisfy themselves that systems are suitable for their purpose and that they are achieving the objectives laid down in the systems specification. This is largely determined by running programs with test data representative of that to be actually processed. The results obtained are compared with pre-calculated values. Any differences are noted which form the basis for program modifications or even major restructuring of the system.

Trials should be incorporated to assess the accuracy with which transaction data is recorded on source documents prior to data conversion for input to the computer. Errors should be analysed to establish their nature and their cause. The effectiveness of the built-in validation checks are tested in this way.

25. Live operation. During the live operation of a project the role of an auditor is to ensure that the inputs are reconciled for both document number counts and values with predetermined control totals. This is for the purpose of assessing whether all the transactions are accounted for.

26. Audit trail. An audit trail is provided by means of a printout listing all the transactions processed during the run or period. In a sales ledger application this would include a list of all invoices, credit notes, remittances and journal adjustments. Details of VAT charges would also be listed. Some accounting packages facilitate the work of an auditor by printing out a system checklist indicating balances on the sales ledger and the corresponding balance in the debtor control account in the nominal ledger. The printout may also specify the number of the last invoice, credit note and similar details relating to the payroll and purchase ledger. Copies of source documents can also be stored for future reference.

27. Audit packages. Audit packages allow selected records to be printed from master files so that they can be subjected to further scrutiny to determine if all transaction details effecting the record are shown. By this means it is also possible to examine control parameters to ensure they accord with current needs. This applies to stock control levels in a stock control system and credit limits in a sales ledger system.

28. Data validation/error reports. Error reports containing details of invalid transactions are generated by data validation routines built into programs at strategic points. Many validation routines are included in the initial program to avoid processing errors in sub-sequent processing stages. Details of transactions may also be tested by applying spot checks taking random samples.

29. General aspects of system auditing. The optimum time for auditors to review the checks and controls incorporated in a computer/clerical system for the first time is immediately after the system specification has been completed. It is then possible to remedy any shortcomings or omissions before the system is implemented.

Other factors to consider are: preventing unauthorised access to the computer room and to information stored in files; assessing the adequacy of program amendment procedures and back-up arrangements in case of system failure; effectiveness of interfaces to other installations or in local area network activities; checking that computations have been correctly calculated on the basis of defined formulae; adequacy of audit trails and so on.

Software (program) checks—validation

30. Data validation. The objective of a data validation system is to detect errors at the earliest possible stage, before costly activities are performed on invalid data. It is therefore essential to ensure that source data is correctly recorded initially before data preparation takes place. Similarly, it is important to check the accuracy of data preparation operations before data is processed, and this is achieved by verification procedures.

When data is input for processing, it is subjected to a vetting procedure by means of an edit program which allows valid data to be written to the media to be used in subsequent processing—magnetic tape or disc.

Invalid data either may be written to another magnetic tape, or may be printed out on the line-printer as a special report, or errors may be indicated on the main report. The choice of method depends upon individual circumstances, and the manner in which the system is designed.

During the various stages of processing on the computer several types of check may be performed.

(*a*) Check to ensure that data are of the *correct type* in accordance with the program and master file.

(*b*) Check to ensure that data are for the *correct period*.

(*c*) Check to ensure that master files have the *correct generation indicator*.

(*d*) Check digit verification detects transposition errors when recording 'key' fields on source documents in respect of customer account codes, stock codes or expenditure codes, etc. (*see* **31–34**).

(*e*) Check to ensure that each character has the *correct number of bits*—parity check (hardware check) (*see* **13**).

(*f*) Check to ensure that records and transactions are in the *correct sequence and all are present*.

(*g*) Check to ensure that fields contain the *correct number and type of characters of the correct format*—format (or picture) check.

(*h*) Check to ensure that data *conforms to the minimum and maximum range of values*, for example, stock balances, gross wages and tax deductions, etc. As the range of specific items of data may be subject to fluctuation, the range limits may be input as parameters prior to a run instead of being incorporated in a program.

(*i*) In a nominal ledger computer application the validation of nominal ledger codes would be accomplished by reference to a nominal description file as an alternative to using check digits.

(*j*) In an order-entry system product codes would be validated by reference to a product file and customer account codes by reference to a customer file as an alternative to using check digits.

(*k*) Some errors may be detected by various types of check, e.g. a five-digit product code being used instead of a six-digit salesman code could be detected by a check on the type of transaction (*see* (*a*)). The difference in the number of digits could be detected by a field check (*see* (*g*)).

(*l*) An error in the quantity of raw material being recorded in tonnes instead of kilograms could or should be detected by visual inspection rather than a computer validation program. The unit of weight is normally pre-recorded on transaction data and weight designations are pre-defined in the program.

(*m*) Compatibility checks are used to ensure that two or more data items are compatible with other data items. For instance, discounts to customers may be calculated on the basis of order quantity but a discount may only apply if a customer's account balance is below a stated amount.

(*n*) Probability checks are used to avoid unnecessary rejection of data as data can on occasions exceed normal values in a range of purely random causes. If this arises with an acceptable frequency (probability) at a defined level of confidence (normally 95 per cent), then the data need not be rejected. This would tend to reduce the level of rejections and the time expended on investigating causes of divergences.

(*o*) Check to ensure 'hash' and other control totals agrees with those generated by the computer. (*See* Figs. 9.2 and 9.3.)

Check digit verification

31. Transposed digits. It is important to appreciate that the accuracy of output from data processing can only be as accurate as the input from which it is produced. Errors often occur in the initial recording and transcription of numerical data, such as stock numbers and account codes, frequently through transposition.

Check digit verification is a technique designed to test the accuracy (validity) of such numerical data before acceptance for processing. The data vet program performs check digit verification as part of the editing routine. Data is rejected as invalid when the check digit is any other number than the correct one. The data must then be re-encoded and represented for processing.

32. Check digit and modulus. A check digit is a number which is added to a series of numbers (in the form of a code number for stock or customer identification) for the purpose of producing a 'self-checking' number. Each check digit is derived mathematically, and bears a unique mathematical relationship to the number to which it is attached. The check digit is normally added in the low-order position.

Before indicating the way in which a check digit is calculated, it is necessary to understand what is meant by a 'modulus'. A modulus is the figure used to divide the number for which a check digit is required. Moduli in common use are 7, 10, 11 and 13.

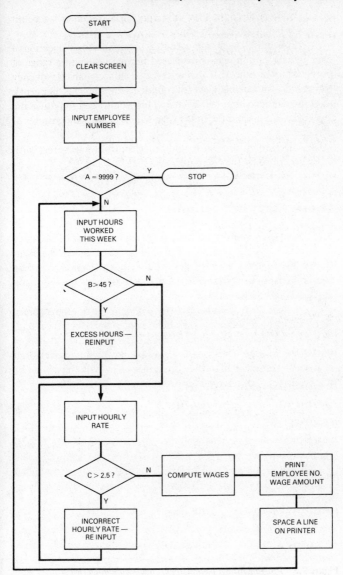

Figure 9.2 *Flowchart interactive processing: payroll application—validation checks.*

This program detects employee hours in excess of a stated
maximum and an hourly rate which does not conform to a specified
value.The routine could be built into a payroll system.

```
10 CLS
20 REM FILENAME IS WAGES
30 REM THIS PROGRAM DETECTS EXCESSIVE HOURS AND INCORRECT HOURLY RATE
40 LPRINT CHR$(27);"M";CHR$(27);"4";
50 LPRINT "This program detects employee hours in excess of a stated
60 LPRINT "maximum and an hourly rate which does not conform to a specified"
70 LPRINT "value.The routine could be built into a payroll system."
80 LPRINT
90 INPUT"Employee number?";A
100 IF A =9999 THEN 210
110 INPUT"Hours worked this week?";B
120 IF B> 45 THEN PRINT"Excess hours-reinput" ELSE 140
130 GOTO 110
140 INPUT"Hourly rate?";C
150 IF C> 2.5 THEN PRINT"Incorrect hourly rate-reinput" ELSE 170
160 GOTO 140
170 D=B*C
175 LPRINT"Employee number ";A," ";
180 LPRINT"Wage amount is ";CHR$(163);D
190 LPRINT
200 GOTO 90
210 END
Employee number  123           Wage amount is £ 112.5


Employee number  124           Wage amount is £ 40


Employee number  125           Wage amount is £ 45
```

Figure 9.3 *Program listing: payroll application—validation checks.*

33. Check digit calculation.

(*a*) Assume modulus 11 is selected for the purpose of calculating a check digit.

(*b*) Assume the number for which a check digit is required is 2323.

(*c*) Divide 2323 by 11 and note the remainder. Remainder is 2.

(*d*) Obtain the complement of the remainder and use as the check digit. 11 − 2 = 9 (complement = check digit).

(*e*) The number including its check digit now becomes 23239.

34. Calculation of a check digit using weights.
A weight is the value allocated to each digit of a number according to a specified pattern, to prevent acceptance of interchanged digits. A more refined method of obtaining a check digit is achieved by the use of weights.

(*a*) Assume the same number and modulus as in the above example, i.e. 2323 and 11 respectively.

(*b*) The selected series of weights are 5, 4, 3, 2.

(*c*) Multiply each digit of the number by its corresponding weight as follows:

		Weight	*Product*
Units digit	3	2	6
Tens digit	2	3	6
Hundreds digit	3	4	12
Thousands digit	2	5	10
		Sum of products	34

(*d*) Divide sum of products by modulus 11 and note the remainder. Remainder is 1.

(*e*) Obtain the complement of the remainder and use this as the check digit: 11 − 1 = 10 (assigned the letter **x**).

(*f*) The number including its check digit is 2323**x**.

A check may be applied to confirm that 10 or **x** is valid as follows:

Sum of the products	34
Add calculated check	10
	44

Divide by modulus 11 and note any remainder.
As there is no remainder, the check digit is valid.

Datakey and Smartcard

35. Datakey? A Datakey is an electronic memory circuit (EAROM) embedded in plastic and moulded to the shape of a key. It is a personal, portable information device which utilises alterable semiconductor memory. It is reusable and has an unlimited read/write life span.

Another device called a Keyceptacle Peripheral Subsystem is the interface between a Datakey and a higher level host system. It acts as the electronic liaison for the Datakey. The Keyceptacle access component incorporates the contact and routing circuitry which provides the physical exchange between the Datakey and the Keytroller electronic module. The Keytroller incorporates the intelligence for interchange between the Datakey and the host system. It consists of an encapsulated microcomputer with serial input/output communications. The firmware is the heart of the Keytroller (*see* Fig. 9.4).

36. An access controller interfaced with a user's equipment enables a Datakey to serve as a restrictive data filter assimilating and distributing information on an authorised basis. The Datakey can simultaneously record these transactions which effectively provides an additional method of monitoring a data security system.

Selective access can also be applied for personnel to gain access to buildings and data files, credit/debit systems as well as other applications. When personnel or customers are provided with a programmed Datakey, a perpetual, updatable record can be maintained for practically any information gathering purpose in a user's system.

As can be seen Datakey is a product that has an almost endless list

Figure 9.4 *(a) Datakey and Keytroller; (b) Close-up of Datakey.*
(Courtesy Data Card (UK) Limited)

of uses for applications including data capture, security system control, data input and data retrieval. Applications already using Datakey include shop floor data capture (where operator identity is an important factor); computer terminal security; software protection; physical access control systems; operator identity in photocopier systems; pre-payment in vending systems, as well as other applications in hotel accounting terminals and automatic test equipment.

In these particular applications the Datakey is used for a variety of purposes. In certain instances for a particular operation but in others carrying out a number of functions, e.g. identifying the operator to the host system, enabling specific accounts to be debited with the charge for the service, protecting the host system from unauthorised use and enabling any revised information to be written back to the Datakey.

37. Smartcard. A Smartcard may be defined as a credit card with an in-built microprocessor and memory. It offers more security than the normal credit card which has a magnetic strip on the reverse side. The microprocessor allows the card to be used for financial transactions and can store a bank balance. A Smartcard can also be used as a means of identification. The card is read when inserted into a reading device which transfers the details stored to a computer.

Systems development controls

Before developing computerised systems it is necessary, particularly in the larger installation, to obtain the relevant authority from the board of directors which may be based on recommendations of the data processing steering committee. The committee provides guidance to management on the basis of the results obtained from the conduct of a feasibility study, which indicates the points for and against a specific course of action. It is these factors which guide management in making decisions to pursue one course of action as opposed to another. Important factors which need to be subjected to some form of control or monitoring include those listed below.

38. Important factors to be controlled. The list which follows is meant to convey the important factors as a guideline for effective control of computerised projects, rather than being a complete list of all factors.

(*a*) Periodic reviews need to be undertaken to ensure that projects conform to laid down time schedules as far as is possible and that resources are not used excessively.

(*b*) It is necessary to assess the problems encountered during the course of investigations or design stages which were unforeseen during the preliminary survey.

(*c*) The highest degree of coordination must be sought between 'user' department staff and systems development staff to ensure a workable system is subsequently implemented.

(*d*) Design philosophy must be discussed before procuring expensive hardware and software. It is a matter of deciding the nature of processing facilities to suit the requirements of the system. Similarly it is pointless designing a real-time system which requires expensive hardware and systems support when all that is necessary is more frequent reporting cycles. This may apply to stock management situations. Of course, it is possible to implement on-line systems using terminals for direct entry of data, such as customer order details, without going to the extreme of making it a real-time system as on-line entry can be supported by effective batch processing systems at lower cost.

(e) Systems documentation must be prepared and maintained during the course of developing systems, to ensure it readily portrays the status of the system at any time. This is essential for continuity of development projects, as staff may leave and be replaced by personnel unaccustomed with the stage the system had reached and with the details of the system generally. Documentation should be developed on the basis of data processing and programming standards.

(f) Systems must be implemented with a minimum of disruption to current operations. Parallel running must continue until the computerised system proves to be adequate for its defined purpose and seen to be attaining projected levels of performance.

(g) Access to databases must be controlled by the use of passwords so that only authorised personnel can gain access to the system or to specific files.

(h) Effective fail-safe procedures must be implemented in the case of lengthy processing tasks or important operations such as the real-time control of a major or critical operation, e.g. airline seat reservation systems and stock management systems.

(i) Accounting records must be checked after being converted to magnetic file media to ensure that they contain correct information.

39. Critical path method for project control. Critical path analysis is a very useful technique for controlling computer development projects, whether for the initial implementation of a computer into an organisation, or for the development of complex systems for an existing computer.

The technique indicates the interrelationships of each activity including those which can be performed simultaneously and those which must be performed sequentially. 'Event times' are also computed, enabling the 'critical path' to be identified as it consists of those activities which form the 'longest route' through the network.

Any 'delay' on this path will delay project 'completion time' therefore it is imperative to be aware of which are the 'critical project activities' so that they may be constantly monitored. Activities with 'slack time' can be identified as this will enable 'resources', typically manpower, to be 'redeployed' to more critical activities if these are falling behind schedule.

The network must be continuously updated to enable planned times for systems analysis, document design, test runs, etc., to be compared with actual times achieved, so that appropriate action can be taken as circumstances decree.

It may be necessary to revise original time schedules (guesstimates) as more factual details come to light during the course of systems development, as unexpected complications may arise. In any event it is difficult to be precise in the time required for the various stages of a project.

Data processing standards and documentation

40. Purpose and objectives. The purpose and objectives of standards are for guiding staff in the general rules, conventions and code of practice relating to the development of systems. The project control system will be structured to be compatible with the various stages of development thereby providing a standard way of controlling all projects on the basis of a standardised schedule which should enable the highest possible level of project productivity to be achieved.

41. System and program documentation. System and program documentation standards outline the way in which systems should be structured and the manner in which they should be documented. This factor relates to the method employed and the style adopted for the construction of procedure charts, system flowcharts, data flow diagrams, data structure charts, system structure charts, decision tables and run charts. Standards also embrace programming methodology in respect of the use of standard coding sheets and the application of structured or modular techniques of program design.

42. Detailed design of system inputs, files and output. Documentation standards specify the way in which documents should be structured and compiled. Such documents contain details and specifications relating to the design of computer input which refers to the design of source documents and screen displays; the design of output from the computer either as a screen display or a printed report; and the structure of master files. The primary purpose of such standards is to adopt a uniform, effective method of documentation which enables systems to be designed in the most efficient way.

43. System continuity. The application of system and program documentation standards assists in attaining system continuity as it eliminates being dependent on system details which exist only in the mind of a system designer. It is imperative that all details of the current system and the proposed system should be committed to paper in its various forms, i.e. document layouts and specifications, as well as diagrammatically in the form of flowcharts, etc. This achieves continuity in the development of systems which is of extreme importance as it avoids disruption to the smooth development of a project.

44. Operations standards. The implementation of operations standards requires the compilation of a standards manual. Reference to the manual on points of procedure by operations personnel will ensure the adherence to laid-down standards. The standards should typically encompass details relating to the flow of work in respect of: handling procedures, batches of source documents when received from the user departments in respect of batch control and data conversion; security measures to be applied to the files after updating; work scheduling activities; archiving procedures; purging procedures in respect of retained files for security purposes; error control routines; output distribution routines and so on.

45. Performance standards. Performance in a data processing environment is essential and performance standards are required and should be implemented for the control of output in order to ensure scheduled completion times; input schedules should be prepared for controlling input to the system for ensuring it is received on time. This will prevent delays occurring and the build-up of work affecting other jobs in the queue. The cost of operations should be controlled to ensure operations are performed economically. This may be accomplished by the implementation of cost standards or budgets. Run timings should enable the time spent on different jobs to be effectively controlled and provide the means of compiling job schedules.

46. Standards officer. The implementation and effective adherence to standards should be under the control of a standards officer. The duties and responsibilities of such a person include advising management and staff, both in the data processing department and user departments as relevant to their activities in the data processing environment in the use of the various standards. The results attained and methodologies practised should be monitored to ensure they accord with the relevant standards. Staff suggestions for modifying established standards should be implemented if they provide the means of improving results and working practices. All modifications to existing standards and the application of new standards should be promulgated in a standards manual to ensure all details are fully up-to-date. The meaning and underlying philosophy of standards should be discussed with appropriate personnel.

47. Communication and coordination. The major benefit of standardisation relating to systems methodology and documentation is the provision of a medium for discussion. Discussions of system details are improved between designers and users, designers and programmers and designers and management. Such discussions enable misconceptions to be removed and system features to be more fully understood. When personnel from the different functions affected by systems development are able to communicate then many of the inherent problems are more easily dealt with. It is always good practice to compile a 'glossary of system terminology' which aids understanding of the language of system designers and terms used during discussions. The National Computing Centre has developed a comprehensive set of standards embracing systems documentation, programming and operating.

Progress test 9

1. The extent to which security measures are applied depends upon a number of factors. Discuss. (**1–4**)

2. Indicate the main areas of control in a data processing environment. (**5**)

3. Specify the nature of organisational control relevant to the data processing function. (**6**)

4. Specify the nature of administrative controls relevant to the data processing function. (**7**)

5. Outline the features of environmental and technological controls which should be incorporated into the data processing activity. (**8, 9**)

6. State the sociological factors which should be considered when developing computerised systems. (**10**)

7. (*a*) Describe the sequence of checks (human, hardware and software) involved in producing an accurate transaction file on magnetic tape from source data. (*b*) Describe what is meant by a check digit and illustrate how a modulus 11 check digit is calculated. (*C & G*) (**12, 13, 30–34**)

8. Specify the nature and purpose of input and hardware controls. (**12, 13**)

9. What precautions would you adopt to ensure the security and confidentiality of master files? (**14–17**)

10. Outline the main provisions of the Data Protection Act. (**18**)

11. Describe in detail the checks and controls that can be applied to input data before it is used to update a master file. Assume a batch processing system. (**19, 20, 30–34**)

12. What is an audit trail and why is it necessary? (**26, 27**)

13. List the typical checks applied to input data to ensure its integrity. (**30–34**)

14. Specify the nature of check digit verification. (**31–34**)

15. Define the nature and purpose of Datakey and Smartcard. (**35, 36**)

16. What are the important factors to be controlled when developing computer-based systems? (**38, 39**)

17. Describe briefly the role of critical path analysis in project control. (**39**)

18. Outline the nature and purpose of data processing standards. (**40–47**)

10

Processing techniques (1)— Batch processing

General outline of technique

1. **Definition of batch processing.** The technique of batch processing is very widely applied in clerical, mechanical and electronic data processing systems. It is concerned with processing batches of related data for a defined period of time as the basis for obtaining processing efficiency. Many businesses have high volume routine data processing requirements and have installed batch processing computer configurations to obtain the benefits of high-speed accurate data processing. The main features of a batch processing configuration are automatic input and output devices, which operate with a minimum of manual intervention under the control of a stored program after the devices have been loaded with transaction data and appropriate print-out stationery.

2. **Applications.** Batch processing operations relate to specific applications such as payroll, stock control, invoicing and sales ledger, purchases and purchase ledger and the nominal ledger, etc. Each application consists of a number of computer runs each of which is designed to accomplish a defined stage of processing in respect of each transaction.

3. **Stages of batch processing: job titles and tasks.** When a job is processed in a batch processing environment, it passes through many stages between data collection and job completion. The job titles of the personnel involved with data processing and the tasks they undertake are important.

(*a*) *Clerical staff—user department.* As transactions occur in the business relating to: goods sold to customers; units produced by specific employees in the factory; items received into the stores; items issued from the stores to production; transfer of personnel between departments; and other similar events, it is necessary to 'record' the relevant details on 'source' documents. These are the routine documents used by a business for recording routine trans-actions so that a record is available for accounting and data process-ing purposes. It is then necessary to 'batch' related documents in readiness for processing. Each batch has a 'control slip' attached on which are recorded various details (*see* 9:**19**). The batches are then sent to the 'data control' section.

(*b*) *Data control clerk.* The contents of batches are checked for obvious errors, either for immediate correction if they can be dealt with locally or for return to the originating department. The batches are then sent to the data preparation section (*see* 9:**20**).

(*c*) *Data preparation operator.* Data on the source documents is converted into 'machine sensible' media by relevant techniques and methods such as 'key-to-disc', 'key-to-diskette' or 'key-to-cassette' (*see* 4:**6–8**). The data is then verified to ensure there are no data conversion errors, as it is essential that errors do not enter the computer for processing otherwise GIGO ensues, i.e. garbage in, garbage out.

(*d*) *File and program librarian.* Issue the disc or tape files required for processing on the computer. These must be recorded in a register in order that a strict control can be maintained on their movements.

(*e*) *Computer operator.* The computer operator consults the run diagram and the system documentation in the manual, which pro-vides guidance on how the relevant computer 'runs' are to be set up. He then obtains the necessary master files and programs from the librarian. Each run is then set up and executed. When a run is completed the operator inspects the output and reports incon-sistencies to the operations manager to enable the relevant action to be taken. 'Control totals' provided with the input data are compared with the computer generated control totals and differences are investigated. This comparison indicates if any documents have been omitted from the run or whether any data has been corrupted.

Subsequent runs may require a changeover of stationery on the line printer or the insertion of new stationery with preprinted headings for payroll and invoices, etc. Programs, as well as master files when relevant for file updating must be loaded for each separate run.

Details of processing are automatically recorded on a 'log'. Messages from the operator to the operating system and responses from the operating system are displayed on the video display screen. The operator also acts upon messages displayed on the screen by the system. Typical runs include those for data validation, sorting data into a defined sequence, computing values, updating files, printing documents and reports and resorting of data for various analyses.

(*f*) *File and program librarian.* When files and programs are returned they are recorded in a register. Those which should have been returned but have not been remain outstanding in the register and this provides the means for 'chasing them up'. They have probably been left in the computer room and this carelessness must not be allowed to persist.

(*g*) *Data control clerk.* The output from the computer, i.e. printed documents, reports and analyses are recorded in the batch control register thereby maintaining control over the throughput of batches (*see* 9:**19**)

Stages of processing a factory payroll

The typical stages for processing a factory payroll are shown below.

4. Amendments to master file. It is essential to ensure that the payroll master file containing details of each employee in respect of earnings, tax and other deductions is up to date before current pay data is processed. Amendment data includes:

(*a*) details relating to new starters;

(*b*) details pertaining to leavers;

(*c*) amendments to National Insurance rates;

(*d*) tax code changes;

(*e*) changes of name (in respect of a female employee getting married);

(*f*) changes of address;

(*g*) changes of department;

(*h*) changes to rates of pay;

(*i*) changes to method of payment—cash to credit transfer direct to bank;

(*j*) additional deductions, i.e. wages advance or court orders, etc.

(*k*) changes to miscellaneous deductions, i.e. National Savings, repayment of loans, etc.

5. Collect current data. This relates to what may be defined as 'variable' data, i.e. pay details which can vary each pay period relating to:

(*a*) hours worked by each employee paid on hourly basis or, alternatively, variations from 'standard' working hours;

(*b*) number of units produced by each employee paid on the basis of 'payments by results' (PBR) schemes including 'bonus' schemes.

6. Conversions, computations and printouts.

(*a*) Convert data into machine sensible form.

(*b*) Compute gross wages:

(*i*) hourly earnings: hours worked × hourly rate;

(*ii*) piecework earnings; units produced × piece rate or terms of bonus scheme;

(*iii*) overtime premiums for evening or week-end work in excess of standard hours.

(*c*) Check computations and correct errors.

(*d*) Compute holiday credits.

(*e*) Compute cumulative tax to date and current tax to be deducted or refunded.

(*f*) Compute net pay, i.e. gross pay less tax to be deducted or plus tax to be refunded less (+ standard deductions + advance of wages + court orders + holiday credit + National Insurance deductions (employee)).

(*g*) Print payroll and pay advice notes including note and coin analysis.

(*h*) Print bank credit transfer slips for employees paid by this method.

7. Computer runs for payroll preparation. The amendments and current pay data will be converted into machine sensible form by an appropriate data preparation method such as 'key-to-disc', 'key-to-diskette' or 'key-to-cassette'. The data is then sent to the computer room for processing in batches. The payroll may be departmentalised in order to produce payrolls and payslips for each separate department. This is a convenient way of breaking the job into sections and it also facilitates audit trails and accounting routines as well as localising errors. Batch control totals are computed. The payroll may be structured into a series of runs as follows (*see* Fig. 10.1).

(*a*) *Run 1.* Payroll data is validated and a printed report is produced on the line printer or displayed on a video screen, indicating those details containing errors. Such errors need to be referred back to the originating department for correction. Correct or valid data is written in random order to a work file which may be on magnetic tape or disc.

(*b*) *Run 2.* This run is concerned with sorting employee pay data into employee number within department number to facilitate file reference and updating of the payroll master file in a subsequent run.

(*c*) *Run 3.* Gross wages are computed and recorded on a work file (either magnetic tape or disc).

(*d*) *Run 4.* This run is largely concerned with tax computations and calculating holiday credits, National Insurance deductions, fixed deductions and other deductions such as court orders. The payroll master file is referred to for various details of tax to date, National Insurance category, holiday credit to date and other related details. The master file is also updated to record taxable gross pay to date, total National Insurance contributions to date and tax to date, etc. Payrolls are also printed out in this run together with a note and coin analysis if relevant. Pay details are recorded on a work file for the next run.

(*e*) *Run 5.* The work file containing pay details is input and payslips and envelopes are printed out. These may be combined pay slips/envelopes containing a carbon insert to enable printing to take place inside the envelope maintaining confidentiality of pay details

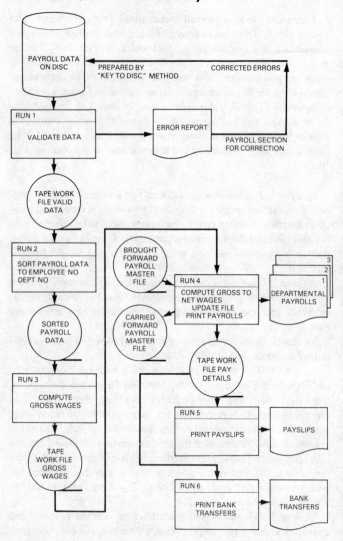

Figure 10.1 *Payroll run chart.*

as nothing is visible on the outside of the envelope.

(*f*) *Run 6.* When appropriate this run prints bank credit transfer slips for employees paid by this method.

Problems of dealing with random enquiries in batch processing environments

8. Off-line storage of master files. The off-line storage of master files creates problems in respect of random enquiries from user departments. To deal with such enquiries on an individual basis is not economically viable, as it would necessitate the setting up of runs specially for each enquiry which would be very disruptive. If enquiries are sufficiently numerous, however, it may be viable to schedule a special enquiry run to deal with batches of enquiries. In this case, access to appropriate records such as customer or supplier accounts can be facilitated by an enquiry package program. When an application is run daily then the details printed out may be adequate to deal with enquiries and this avoids the necessity of arranging a special run thereby saving important processing time. A 24-hour run-round time for dealing with enquiries may be suitable in most business instances but if this is inadequate an on-line enquiry system may be developed. In this instance, files must be stored on a direct access media such as discs, accessible by user departments by means of local enquiry terminals.

9. Absence of human-sensible records. The main problem of dealing with enquiries on a batch processing computer configuration is the absence of human-sensible records, as these are stored on magnetic media which are only machine-sensible. In clerical (manual) and mechanised systems access to records for enquiry purposes is facilitated by loose leaf records and ledger cards. All that is necessary to deal with an enquiry is to refer to the appropriate record in the file.

10. Reasons for increase in run time. This topic may be discussed on the basis of a question set by The Chartered Association of Certified Accountants in the December 1985 examination: Systems Analysis and Design.

A batch processing accounting system has been operating fairly satisfactorily for three years. Recently, however, there has been a significant increase in the time taken for the system to run on the mainframe, disc-based configuration. You have been asked to investigate the operation of the system in order to identify the cause of this apparent deterioration in performance.

Required:

(a) describe how you would undertake the investigation;
(b) discuss *four* possible causes of the increase in run time.

The investigation should be undertaken initially by discussing the situation with the data processing manager and the operations manager responsible for the day-to-day control of the computer room. They will be able to indicate the reasons for the increase in run time which may well be justified on the following grounds.

(a) *Accounting systems.* Some or all of the accounting systems may have undergone modifications during the three-year period to improve their performance or extended to provide additional reports and/or analyses. This may account for the increase in run time. Alternatively, or in addition to, these factors the volume of data for processing may have increased due to business growth reflected in a greater volume of invoices and statements of account or personnel on the payroll, for instance, which increases run time.

(b) *Job scheduling.* Many mainframe computers process several jobs concurrently in multiprogramming mode. A job description defines the various applications to be run together, the resources (input and output devices) required and the priority rating of each job. The scheduling factors, specified by the computer operations staff, provide the basis for the operating system to perform work scheduling activities automatically. *See* 20:**11–16**. If the computer operations staff do not schedule an optimum program mix then some systems are likely to incur an apparent increase in run time. The actual run time may, in fact, remain the same but the elapsed time is greater. The efficiency of processing should improve by the application of multiprogramming but unless the mix is right some jobs will require a lengthier processing time than if run separately. This is due to the interrupts which occur when switching between programs. For example, one program may have to wait for the printer which has been assigned to another program.

(c) *Inefficient staff.* Computer installations suffer from a high rate of labour turnover which means that data input staff and computer operators are frequently replaced. If inexperienced staff are employed then the time for changing over jobs on the computer may be extended which effectively increases run time.

(d) *Hardware malfunctions.* If any part of the computer hardware malfunctions excessively causing considerable time to be spent by the engineers in diagnostic testing then more down-time will effect the processing elapsed time, resulting in a delay. This will be interpreted as an increase in run time but is in reality an increase in idle time—the run still takes the same time but with delays between the various stages. Disc errors may also occur causing the disc system to attempt to overcome the error by a number of retries— this again will increase run time.

Progress test 10

1. Define the term batch processing indicating when it is most suitable for use. (**1**)

2. Briefly outline the nature of batch processing applications. (**2**)

3. When a job is processed in a data processing environment, it passes through many stages between data preparation and job completion. Give the job titles and describe the tasks undertaken by the personnel involved in processing such a job. (**3**) (*C & G*)

4. List the data elements which may need to be amended in a payroll application. (**4**)

5. Indicate the data to be processed and the main processing activities required to produce a factory payroll. (**5–7**)

6. Describe briefly a payroll system in a large manufacturing firm and give overall system flowcharts. (**4–7**) (*C & G*)

7. At 9.30 a.m. on Tuesday in a normal working week, the wages section of XYZ Ltd sends its transaction and amendment data to the computer department. At 4.00 p.m. (1600 hours) on Wednesday, the wages section receives paylists, payslips and other printed results back from the computer department. Give a detailed account of the activities which would typically take place in the computer department between the receipt of the payroll data and the despatch of results back to the wages section. (The following references provide

guidance on the solution to this type of question.) (**4–7**) (*ACA*)

8. What are the problems of dealing with random enquiries in batch processing applications? (**8, 9**)

9. What factors may cause an increase in run time? (**10**)

11
Processing techniques (2)— On-line systems

On-line processing concepts

1. **Definition of on-line processing.** The technique of processing data by computer by means of terminals connected to, and controlled by, a central processor. In this way, various departments in a company can be connected to the processor by cables. If operating companies are a number of miles away from the processor then they are linked by means of telegraph or telephone lines (*see* Fig. 11.1).

This type of processing provides multi-access to information files by terminal users and also enables them to update files with transaction data. Such systems are often used as a more efficient alternative to batch processing. In this case, instead of preparing data in a machine-sensible form for processing in batches at predefined periods of time, input of transaction data is effected by many terminals at random time intervals. The technique also embraces the use of microcomputers for transaction-driven processing (*see* 12:**11**).

2. **On-line applications.** Systems are being developed or are already in use for a wide range of applications in different types of industry including electricity and gas boards, banking, building societies, tour operators, retailing and stock exchanges, etc.

(*a*) *Electricity and gas boards.* By means of terminals situated in showrooms it is possible to inform prospective customers of the availability of appliances in response to their enquiries.

(*b*) *Banking.* It is possible to inform bank customers of the status

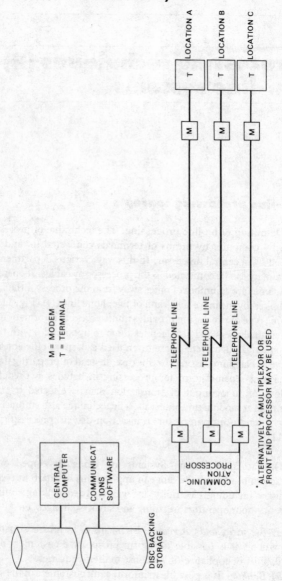

Figure 11.1 *On-line data transmission system.*

of their account by accessing the relevant file using an on-line terminal.

(c) *Building societies*. The use of terminals to enter details of clients' transactions in respect of savings, investments and mortgage repayments from branches to the central computer.

(d) *Tour operators*. Reservation offices accept telephone enquiries from travel agents regarding the availability of holidays in respect of clients' enquiries. By means of terminals the availability of the required holiday can be checked and booked immediately.

(e) *Stock exchanges*. Terminals located in major stock exchanges throughout the country and the offices of participating brokerage firms enable the speedy processing of share dealings.

(f) *Stock control*. Terminals located in warehouses provide the means for automatic re-ordering of stocks, updating of stock records, reservations, follow-up of outstanding orders and the printing of picking lists, etc.

(g) *Insurance companies*. On-line policy maintenance by means of terminals located in branch offices. *See* Figs. 11.2 and 11.3.

Building society on-line system—case study

3. **Background.** The systems were implemented over a two-year period and because of the high control and security requirement within the building society activity they were run extensively in parallel before being implemented. At the completion of this period it was then judged appropriate that a branch terminal system should be introduced to improve customer servicing at our 40 branch outlets.

The principal objectives in doing this were:

(a) to provide an efficient and speedy cash processing system;

(b) to make available to our customers as much information as possible;

(c) to provide a base for further services in the future.

In order to achieve these objectives it was recognised that the system chosen must be robust and should be state of the art technology in order to ensure that it would not become obsolete in the short term.

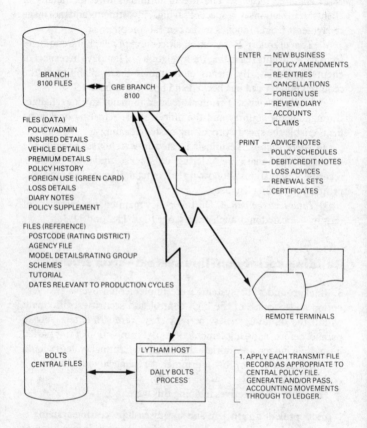

Figure 11.2 *On-line car insurance policy maintenance system: daily processing.*

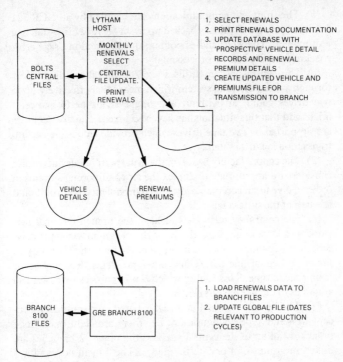

Figure 11.3 *On-line car insurance policy maintenance system: monthly processing.*

4. Hardware. A lengthy evaluation of alternative systems was undertaken and again it was decided to buy a package rather than developing a unique facility. We decided to enhance the central NCR system and to buy NCR branch processing equipment utilising the software package called BSIV. The details of this system configuration are as follows:

(*a*) The central processor is a NCR 8575 II diadic mainframe of 4 megabyte capacity. This comprises two 2 megabyte processors and whilst normally these run as an integrated system they are reconfigurable to single processor operation should either of the processors fail.

(*b*) The front end communications are handled by an NCR 721 front-end processor which is backed up by an NCR 621 free-standing multiplexor. The 721 handles polling, queuing and message error checking prior to central processing.

(*c*) The central system utilises six 200 megabyte disc drives through a disc switching system which means that effectively up to two drives could fail without affecting systems performance. I might add that this situation has never occurred. The disc facilities are supported by two tape drives which provide an on-line backup transaction logging system.

(*d*) The central facility has all of the usual peripherals but we also considered it appropriate to duplex the air conditioning systems in order to give us an acceptable level of environmental control should one half of the system fail.

(*e*) The central systems are linked to the branch terminal network via a Data Logic network management system which provides continual network diagnostic information and has the capability to predict potential line failure and other problems that may occur from time to time. This facility which is microprocessor-based also allows us to diagnose faults centrally.

(*f*) The branch terminal network is based on a multidrop concept in a star type configuration, i.e. there are eight main node branches linked to the central site and the other 32 branches are linked in groups of 4 or 5 to the nodes. The 8 main nodes plus 3 subsidiary nodes are backed up by autodial telephone lines which are activated should any one of the dedicated telephone lines fail. I should add here that all the branches in the network are connected by dedicated telephone lines running at 2 400 bps.

(*g*) Each branch has a branch processor varying in capacity from ¾ megabyte to 2 megabytes supporting from two to eight cashier terminals. Each two cashier terminals share a flat bed printer. The branch terminal system is capable of running in stand-alone mode should the communications linked to the central system fail. It is perhaps worth mentioning that we hold several spare terminals and keyboards and one or two printers so that we may occasionally replace equipment when it fails, ahead of the maintenance support that we have contracted for.

(*h*) The software package has approximately 60 different facilities for cash transaction processing, account set-up and information screen enquiries. All transactions are selected by function keys which minimise the number of key depressions required for each transaction process. The transactions are performed in real time, i.e. at the point that the central database has been updated the message to complete the transaction is transmitted to the branch. All relevant account information is checked against the central database prior to the performance of any transaction. Transactions are logged both centrally and at each branch and hence there is independent control information in both areas.

5. Benefits. The utilisation of real-time processing techniques means that the society's cash movement and holding position may be determined precisely at any time whilst the systems are in operation and this clearly benefits movement of funds and product performance information. The system has been implemented in our branches over a period of nine months, supported by intensive central training and on site branch support. Our customers have welcomed the additional service we are now able to offer as a result of technology and it has proved to be a most worthwhile application.

Insurance company on-line policy maintenance system: case study

6. System concepts. The system is based on the concept of distributed data processing being available to branch offices thus allowing branch staff to view, add, delete and amend policy information in an on-line, real-time mode. Each night any new or changed data is transmitted to head office for central policy file update on IBM mainframe equipment. Any resulting accounts transactions are passed through to the accounts system.

The central policy file is used for backup, statistical analysis, renewal selection and renewal printing—the volumes are too great to print locally on the equipment currently available (although amended and out of course renewal papers are generated at the branch as a by-product of those specific on-line transactions).

7. Processing. The computer renewal process is based on the pre-debit philosophy, and as such it generates debits for the central accounts system and certain time-related data changes to the central policy file (e.g. age of driver of insured may cause discount or load to become effective, or cease to be effective since the previous renewal). Various control prints and control procedures are built into the system at branch, class, file, record and policy level to ensure completeness of action and parity of data between branch and centre.

The on-line real-time aspects of the system were introduced at a pilot location in June 1981 and are now working successfully in all our UK locations (*see* Figs. 11.2 and 11.3).

Remote job entry and time sharing

8. Remote job entry. 'Remote job entry' or 'remote batch processing' is a technique which enables batch processing to be employed by remote operating units by sharing a centrally located computer. For this purpose the remote operating units are equipped with data transmission facilities for transmitting data in magnetic tape. The data is then processed at the central computer and the results may either be transmitted back to the remote operating units and printed on a local printer or they may be printed at the computer installation and despatched by post or messenger service to the remote units.

9. Time sharing. Time sharing is an on-line processing technique which enables many users to gain access to a centrally located computer by means of terminals. Users are geographically remote from the computer and from each other. Each user is also unaware that the computer is being accessed by anyone else, which creates the impression of having a computer for one's sole use. This is made possible by the computer continually switching between the various terminals at extremely high speed under the control of an operating system. These facilities may be provided either by an in-house installation or by a computer time sharing bureau.

10. Communications software. On-line terminal operations are controlled by communications software, which controls messages being transmitted by various terminals simultaneously. The software assembles and checks the messages before passing them to the computer, either for information retrieval requests or for file updating. For this purpose the communications software must communicate terminal requirements to the operating system so that it can call in the necessary programs from backing storage.

Communications software monitors communication lines and terminals for the detection of faults and requests retransmission of messages when errors are detected. It also modifies the priority of terminals as necessary. In addition, it facilitates the transmission of messages from the computer system to the individual terminals which may necessitate re-routing in the event of line or terminal faults being discovered.

Random file updating

11. Process of updating an on-line random file. The procedure relates to updating a random file stored on a floppy disc on an Apple 11e microcomputer. The activity mainly revolves around the need to open and close files which are an essential part of the file access and updating program.

(*a*) Operator loads the required program by keying in the program name, e.g. LOAD RANDOM 3

(*b*) The computer searches the disc file, locates the required program and transfers it (LOAD) to the internal memory ready for further processing

(*c*) The command prompt is then displayed to which the operator responds by keying in the command RUN, i.e. executes the file processing program

(*d*) The program then requests the filename to which the operator responds by keying in the name of the file to be processed

(*e*) The program then OPENs the relevant file and (in respect of the Apple 11e) READS record 0, for storing the number of records on the file

(*f*) The program then requests the number of records on the file

(*g*) The program then CLOSEs the file

(*h*) The program shown below then indicates that a message is printed on the screen:

THERE ARE N RECORDS IN THE FILE
WHICH RECORD DO YOU WANT TO READ?

(*i*) The operator keys in the number of the record to be updated(?)

(*j*) The program then displays a message:

READING RECORD(?)

(*k*) The program then reOPENs the file and READs in the required record

(*l*) The program then closes the file

(*m*) The program then displays a message:

QUANTITY TO ADD (or subtract) to which the operator responds by keying in the relevant quantity

Note: the program is simplified and only demonstrates the adding of a quantity to the quantity already in the record, i.e. the opening quantity or brought forward balance to use accounting terminology

(*n*) The program then adds the quantity and reOPENs the file and WRITEs the updated record to the file

(*o*) The program then CLOSEs the file

(*p*) A message is then displayed:

PRESS ANY KEY TO CONTINUE

(*q*) A further message is then displayed:

ANY MORE RECORDS TO BE READ?

to which the operator responds by keying in Y for Yes or N for No.

(*r*) If the response is Y then the program branches conditionally to the statement which causes a message to be displayed:

WHICH RECORD DO YOU WANT TO READ?

If the response is N then the program is terminated

Communicating with a computer—use of dialogue

12. Dialogue defined. At one time, only specially trained computer operators had the knowledge and expertise to communicate with a computer but this situation has now changed, particularly in respect of microcomputers, which are widely used for interactive processing of one type or another by non-specialists. These non-experts are financial managers performing investment analysis on clients' portfolios; accountants computing cash flows and management accountants using spreadsheets for budget preparation, etc.

The term dialogue is used to describe the language which allows people to converse with a computer for on-line conversational mode processing. An effective dialogue is important because many personnel formerly employed on tasks of a clerical nature are now using terminals or workstations linked to a computer. The use of an effective dialogue is important for such users as it is the principal means of interfacing personnel with the computer.

13. Natural language based. The aim of computerised systems is to simplify man/machine intercommunications by using natural language, i.e. English or other ethnic languages, to avoid the complexities of non-computer specialists having to learn computer languages. High-level languages such as BASIC go some way to achieving this objective. The computer translates natural language messages into machine code by means of interpreters or compilers. A notable example of this is a natural English language database query system known as INTELLECT marketed by Intellect Software International Ltd. *See* Volume 2. This software allows staff to ask the computer questions in plain everyday English which does not require any knowledge of programming whatsoever. This gives staff the confidence to use computers thereby providing a means of increasing administrative efficiency.

14. Oversimplification versus complexity. If a dialogue is oversimplified users may not be willing to use it because it belittles their intelligence. On the other hand, if the dialogue is difficult to understand this may have a dysfunctional effect. Dialogues need to be user-friendly, guiding the user through the routines by means of prompts or 'help' facilities which display explanations on the video screen or provide references to the system manual in response to the user hitting the 'help' key. Dialogues can be used at several levels and a particular class of computer user can select the one relevant to his/her level of experience.

15. Dialogue techniques. There are a number of dialogue techniques which can be used, including:

   (*a*) natural language based (*see* **13**);
   (*b*) menu selection;
   (*c*) use of keywords;
   (*d*) video screen form displays;
   (*e*) built-in dialogue within an interactive program.

16. Menu selection. Many business applications apply the menu technique for selecting different options specifying the various categories of processing which can be performed. These options can be selected in several ways two of which include:

(*a*) Location of a cursor adjacent to the required option. Selection is accomplished by depressing the ENTER or RETURN key.

(*b*) Selection of a specific code number or letter specifying available options.

17. Method of using a menu. The main stages concerned with using a menu for data entry and computations are:

(*a*) Select desired option: key in number or letter of option selected.

(*b*) Enter data: a message is displayed on the screen.

(*c*) Display data: the data is displayed on the screen.

(*d*) Compute as necessary: program performs appropriate calculations.

(*e*) Display required details: the results are displayed on the screen.

A menu for dealing with stock control records may be displayed on the screen as follows:

(*a*) initiate new record;

(*b*) display record;

(*c*) update a record;

(*d*) amend a record;

(*e*) print a record;

(*f*) display records below reorder level.

Return to menu. After dealing with a selection from the menu, and further selections are required, it is necessary to return to the menu for this purpose.

18. Key words. A dialogue may consist of key words which can be in abbreviated form which speeds up their entry to the computer. When using a word processing program, for instance, a series of options may be shown on the bottom of the screen, details of which are contained in the manual; but as an example of their use, if the S key is pressed, which is an abbreviation for SAVE, then the screen changes with the cursor located at SAVE DOCUMENT on the sub-menu. When the ENTER key is pressed the text is recorded on disc (saved). If it is required to clear text from the workspace then Z, an abbreviation for ZAP, attends to this.

19. Built-in dialogue within an interactive program. Many programs are designed to function conversationally for transaction processing requirements. Such programs generate messages on the screen some of which require a response from the user to input specific data and others ask the user if there are any more items to process to which the response is Y for Yes or N for No. Other programs, depending on their purpose, will generate messages such as 'Do you require to display another record?' or 'Do you require a printout?' to which the user response is Y or N. The program branches to the relevant routine according to the user response. A program designed to ensure that correct employee numbers were entered may generate the following dialogue (*see* figs 9.2 and 9.3):

INPUT EMPLOYEE NUMBER
The user responds by inputting the relevant reference number, i.e. the employee number. If the number does not fall within a stated range or fails a check-digit verification test due to transposed digits then a message would be displayed:

INVALID NUMBER–PLEASE REENTER
The user would then have to reenter the number which will not be accepted until it is correct.

INPUT HOURS WORKED AT NORMAL RATE
The user would then input the relevant details which would be rejected if the data did not conform to a defined limit for example:

DATA IN EXCESS OF ACCEPTED MAXIMUM LIMIT:
PLEASE REENTER
The user would then have to re-enter the hours worked.

Benefits provided by on-line systems

On-line systems provide a number of benefits all of which assist in improving administrative efficiency which is essential in the inflationary economy in which businesses operate. A number of benefits are outlined below.

20. Integration of clerical staff with the computer. A computer should not operate in isolation to the business as a whole but should be an integral element of the systems which support business operations. In this respect, on-line systems assist in harnessing the activities of clerical staff to the computer by the use of terminals. They then have access to the information they require for the efficient performance of their jobs in dealing with customer enquiries and order processing, etc.

21. Elimination of tedious tasks. Routine clerical tasks are replaced by terminal operations providing a greater degree of job interest. The benefits provided by this are a greater degree of operating efficiency and job satisfaction.

22. Reduction in paperwork. The volume of paperwork generated by normal clerical systems and batch processing systems is relatively high. On-line systems reduce the volume of printouts required for management reports as information may be displayed on terminal screens on demand. To reduce the volume of paperwork assists in stemming the tide of increasing administrative costs.

23. Improved accuracy. As terminal messages are checked for accuracy before being transmitted to the computer by data validation programs the quality of information in a system will increase as input errors are reduced. As a result information will be more reliable.

24. File updating improved. Master files are more easily updated by terminal keyboard with regard to transaction data, as special runs do not require to be set-up as in the case with batch processing applications.

25. Management information more readily available. Management information becomes more readily available by direct access facilities, which enables managers to obtain a greater degree of control of the operations for which they are responsible.

26. Improved customer service. Improvements in the level of customer service can be expected in those systems concerned with appliance sales, holiday bookings and account enquiries, etc.

27. Reduced data preparation costs. On-line systems dispense with the need to convert human-sensible data into machine-sensible data manually thereby eliminating encoding and verifying operations. This saves time and the costs associated with such operations. Data is input in a shorter time-scale as a result and processing as a whole becomes more cost effective.

Progress test 11

1. Define and give examples of on-line processing applications. (**1–9**)

2. Outline the purpose and nature of time sharing. (**9**)

3. On-line operations are controlled by communications software. Discuss. (**10**)

4. What are the main stages concerned with updating an on-line random file? (**11**)

5. What methods may be adopted for communicating with a computer? (**12–19**)

6. List the benefits provided by on-line systems. (**20–27**)

12
Processing techniques (3)—
Other processing techniques

Real-time processing

1. Real-time concept. Some businesses are dependent for efficient operation on up-to-date information being immediately available on request. This is particularly the case in respect of businesses with geographically dispersed operating units, such as airlines with dispersed booking offices and tour operators.

The term 'real-time' refers to the technique of updating files with transaction data immediately the event to which it relates occurs. This is in distinction to 'batch processing', which processes related data in batches at pre-defined periods of time.

A real-time computer system is communications-oriented, and provides for random enquiries from remote locations with instantaneous responses; because of this characteristic, this type of operation is referred to as on-line or 'conversational' processing.

Real-time processing is suitable when it is necessary to have the latest possible information in the following types of business operations:

(a) wholesale suppliers and manufacturers—availability of stocks;
(b) airlines—flight seat availability;
(c) steel making—yield optimisation;
(d) manufacturing—status of production orders.

It is important to appreciate that the use of a computer for real-time processing, although often a practical necessity, is not automatically implied. If, for instance, a perpetual inventory technique is applied to a clerical stock control system and all stock transactions recorded immediately they occur, rather than at defined periods of time then, in effect, it is a real-time system. This type of system, however, may have a slow 'response time' in the provision of management information and the updating process may be slow due to the volume of transactions. Therein lie some of the reasons why a computer is necessary, particularly as some types of business have dispersed operations such as airlines with dispersed booking offices.

Some computer systems are dedicated to real-time operations and others are designed to operate in both batch and real-time modes. *Note* that not all on-line systems are real-time systems.

2. Master files. In real-time systems, master files containing operating information are normally stored on magnetic disc and need to be permanently on-line to the processor for updating and retrieval requirements. Whereas with batch processing applications the master files are stored off-line between processing runs.

3. Output. Real-time systems display information on the screen of VDU terminals in a transitory manner, which contrasts with batch processing systems which have a predominance of print-outs. Even while information is being displayed on a VDU screen in response to a request for such information, its status can be seen to change as events occurring in other dispersed locations are updated on the information file, e.g. airline seat bookings.

4. Operating systems. An essential element of a real-time system is software in the form of an operating system which, in respect of a combined batch and real-time computer configuration, provides interrupt facilities to deal with real-time requirements. The interrupted batch program(s) is temporarily transferred to backing storage and the program required to deal with the real-time operation is called into the processor's memory. After the real-time operation has been dealt with the interrupted program is transferred back to internal storage from backing storage and processing is recommenced from a 'restart' point. All of which takes but a few seconds. (*See* Table 12A.)

5. Processing steps. Real-time processing processes each transaction or message through all relevant steps, whereas batch processing processes all transactions through specific steps before proceeding with other steps. The structure of processing steps is stipulated in the run sequence.

6. Dynamic nature of real-time systems. Real-time systems are dynamic as they accept random input at random time intervals and the status of files changes dynamically as a result. It is this characteristic which makes it difficult to audit or recover the system in the event of system failure. Both of these factors are provided for by means of periodic check points, say every two to three minutes, at which point all relevant restart and audit information are dumped to magnetic tape. The dumps can be used to restart the system.

Multiprogramming

7. Definition of multiprogramming. A small computer installation may process one program at a time and find that it is quite adequate for its processing load.

Eventually as more applications are transferred to the computer, it may be found that there is insufficient processing capacity operating on the present basis of one program at a time. Multiprogramming may then need to be considered whereby two or more programs can be processed concurrently. This enables overall processing time for all programs to be reduced even though the time required to process individual programs may be increased due to switching between programs. Such operations are controlled by the operating system but the computer operations staff are responsible for determining the program mix, that is the programs which are to be run together, and the order in which they are to be run. This is referred to as work scheduling and in a large installation it becomes a complex and time consuming task. (*See below.*)

8. Operating system. As the purpose of multiprogramming is to increase the utilisation of the computer system as a whole, there is a need to employ more powerful software in the form of an operating system incorporating automatic work scheduling features. A programmer may then specify scheduling factors in a 'job description' which allows the operating system to perform work scheduling activities automatically. A 'job description' specifies the name of the job, the peripherals (input and output devices) required, priorities, the streams of data to be input and output and the time programs take to run.

Table 12A Comparison of batch and real-time processing systems

Batch processing	Real-time processing
1. Routine high volume applications: —Invoicing —Payroll —Sales ledger updating —Stock ledger updating —Nominal ledger updating	1. Business control applications: —Steel making —Stock control —Airline operations and aircraft seat reservations
2. Data collected for a defined period of time and processed in batches	2. Random data input at random time intervals as events occur
3. No direct access to system by user departments	3. Direct access to system by user departments using terminals
4. Files only on-line during a processing run	4. Files permanently on-line
5. Magnetic tape files may be used for sequential access to records. Disc files may be used as an alternative to increase processing productivity by restricting access to records affected by current transactions— particularly useful means of storage for low hit-rate files	5. Direct access files only— usually fixed discs
6. Information on master files only as up to date as last updating run	6. Information on master files updated dynamically as events occur

Table 12A *Continued*

Batch processing	Real-time processing
7. Detailed documents, reports and transaction lists printed	7. Information normally displayed on a VDU screen as messages. As an alternative, messages may be printed on a teletype terminal
8. Audit trails facilitated by printing out lists of transactions applied during updating and by printing out file contents using an audit package	8. Audit trails not so well provided for as control is centred around the number of messages input rather than details of transactions
9. All transactions recorded on source documents which must be converted to machine-sensible input by costly and time consuming data preparation operations	9. Transaction details input directly by terminal keyboard, sometimes from source documents, sometimes not, depending upon the system. Absence of costly and time consuming data preparation operations
10. Information from computer files only accessible during a specially set-up run	10. Information permanently accessible on demand

9. Mode of operation. Multiprogramming operates in the following way—when processing is interrupted on one program, perhaps to attend to an input or output transfer, the processor switches to another program. This enables all parts of the system, the processor and input and output peripherals, to be operated concurrently thereby utilising the whole system more fully. When operating on one program at a time the processor or peripherals would be idle for a large proportion of the total processing time even though this would be reduced to some extent by buffering. Buffering enables the processor to execute another instruction while input or output is taking place rather than being idle while the transfer was completed. Even so, when processing one program at a time, basic peripherals are used for input and output such as disc drives and line printers which, being mechanical, are slow compared with the electronic speed of the processor and this causes imbalance in the system as a whole.

10. Off-lining. Multiprogramming employs the technique of 'off-lining' which requires the transfer of data to magnetic media for printing when the printer becomes available. In this way it is possible to process the payroll and prepare invoices by loading both programs into the main memory. While the line printer is printing an invoice line the processor switches to the payroll. Afterwards the processor reverts back to the invoice application. As the printer is being used for printing invoices, payroll data would be recorded on magnetic media for later conversion when the printer is available.

Transaction-driven processing

11. Nature of interactive processing. Transaction-driven processing is an interactive processing technique. The technique is interactive in the sense that the user and the computer communicate with each other in a conversational mode by means of a VDU with a keyboard. Transactions are dealt with completely on an individual basis through all the relevant processing operations before dealing with the next transaction. This is in distinction to batch processing which processes transactions in batches through each processing stage, i.e. validation, sorting, calculating, updating and printing, etc.

Transaction data is input either by a computer operator using a terminal or, alternatively, from remote points such as sales offices, warehouses, factory departments or accounts office according to the needs of a given application. Interactive processing allows files to be updated as transactions occur and enquiries to be dealt with on an immediate response basis.

Although on-line processing has already been outlined in Chap. 11 and interactive processing falls into this category, or may even be classified as real-time, the technique is outlined separately in this chapter to define the specific nature of on-line processing, as some on-line applications are not fully interactive. For instance, some on-line order entry systems only enter order details into the system via a terminal—the transactions are not fully dealt with as they occur but are stored on backing storage for subsequent batch processing.

Centralised processing

12. The computer as a centralised service in a single operating unit. When a business comprises only one factory or office as opposed to a group of factories or other business units, and a computer is implemented in the organisation, then the way in which it is used requires careful consideration. Sometimes the computer, under such circumstances, may be used only for processing routine accounting applications such as payroll, sales ledger, stock control and purchase ledger, etc.

To obtain the maximum benefit however, the computer should be used to aid management in problem-solving and decision-making by the use of quantitative application packages for linear programming, statistical stock control, production planning, network analysis and discounted cash flow, etc. When a computer is used for all the functions within the business it is a centralised facility in the form of a data processing and information system.

13. The computer as a centralised service in a group of operating units. When a business organisation is a widely dispersed conglomeration of various types of operating unit, including factories, warehouses and sales offices and a computer is in use, it is usually located at the head office of the group. In these circumstances the objective would be to provide the best possible service for the data processing and information needs of all functions and operating units in the group.

The benefits to be derived from a centralised service may be summarised as follows.

(a) Economy of capital expenditure due to the high cost of computers (in the 1960s and early 1970s) through having only one computer for use by the group instead of several located in the various units.

(b) If one large powerful computer is implemented, the resultant advantages are: increased speed of operation, storage capacity and processing capability.

(*c*) Economy in computer operating costs due to the centralisation of systems analysts, programmers, computer operators and other data processing staff as compared with the level of costs that would be incurred if each unit in the group had its own computer on a decentralised basis, i.e. avoiding the duplication of resources.

(*d*) Centralisation would also facilitate the standardisation of applications but this would depend upon the extent of diversity in the dispersed operations regarding payroll and invoicing structures, etc.

If the computer is also communications oriented, whereby all operating units are equipped with transmission terminals connected to the central computer, then basic data may be speedily transmitted for processing by remote job entry and the results transmitted back and printed on a local printer. This would reduce any time delay in receiving computer output through the post or messenger service. The possibility of an integrated management information system then becomes feasible, as data from dispersed units is speedily processed for local use and information becomes available at head office by means of the computer files for corporate planning.

Such a centralised computing service should be structured in the organisation at a level which enables the data processing manager to report to a higher level of management than the department level or functional level for which he is providing a service. This enables policy matters to be established at Board level, rather than at functional level, which establishes the use of the computer on a corporate strategic basis in order to optimise its use. If the data processing manager reports to the managing director, he is free from direct inter-functional conflict as problems are resolved at a higher level.

14. Trend towards distributed processing. The centralisation of data processing, as outlined in **12** and **13** above, was the trend of the 1960s, but the tendency of the late 1970s and early 1980s has been a reversal of this situation, largely due to the development of workstations, mini and microcomputers. These cost much less than mainframes, which makes it a viable proposition to install them in departments and branches on a distributed processing basis. This is the philosophy of providing computer power where it is most needed, instead of concentrating all processing in a single centralised computer system.

Progress test 12

1. What is meant by real-time processing? (**1**)
2. Outline the operating characteristics of real-time systems. (**2–6**)
3. Contrast batch and real-time processing systems. (Table 12A)
4. Define and explain the purpose and mode of operation of multiprogramming. (**7–10**)
5. Specify the nature of interactive and transaction-driven processing. (**11**)
6. Outline the concepts of centralised processing. (**12–14**)
7. Examine the reasons behind the trend in many organisations to move from centralised mainframe computing towards distributed data processing. (*ACCA*) (**12–14**)

13

Processing techniques (4)— Distributed processing networks and multi-user and multi-tasking systems

Local area networks

1. Distributed processing by network. Distributed processing is largely of two types: local area networks and close-coupled networks which are multi-processor systems. A local area network is often referred to as a LAN which in its simplest form is a 'cluster' of interconnected microcomputers forming a network or 'net'. A local area network is designed to serve a local establishment such as a factory and its administrative offices, providing a speedy and effective means of communication between the various sections and improving day-to-day efficiency. Networks may consist of interconnected workstations, intelligent terminals, microcomputers, wordprocessors and electronic mail facilities. LANs provide for the sharing of expensive hardware resources such as a high-speed printer and high-capacity hard disc storing programs, data files or a database which can be accessed by any authorised user of the network. Networks have different topologies, protocols, methods of data transmission and the type of cable used—which may be twisted-pair, coaxial or fibre-optic cable. (*See* 7 and Fig. 13.1.)

(*a*) *Twisted pair wires.* A transmission medium used in telephony which consists of a single wire with an earth return. The cable pairs are twisted to reduce the effect of 'crosstalk' with other pairs of

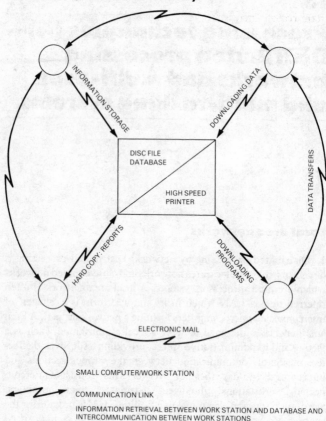

INFORMATION STORAGE

DOWNLOADING DATA

DISC FILE
DATABASE

HIGH SPEED
PRINTER

DATA TRANSFERS

HARD COPY: REPORTS

DOWNLOADING
PROGRAMS

ELECTRONIC MAIL

SMALL COMPUTER/WORK STATION

COMMUNICATION LINK

INFORMATION RETRIEVAL BETWEEN WORK STATION AND DATABASE AND
INTERCOMMUNICATION BETWEEN WORK STATIONS

Figure 13.1 *Outline structure of a local area network.*

wires. They are used for links between individual telephone
terminals and local exchanges. They have limited use for broadband
multiplexed channels because crosstalk can be excessive.

(b) *Co-axial cable.* A communication link consisting of an inner
central conductor, insulated from an outer conductor which functions
as a shield to reduce electrical interference and crosstalk. Several
tubes, as they are called, can be combined into a single bundle to

form a cable. There is a very low loss of energy when high frequencies are transmitted.

(c) *Optical fibre cable.* Optical fibre cable carries light pulses, not electric current, hence there are no electromagnetic fields to interfere with transmissions. The fibres are of very small diameter and they can be bundled to create cables in which each fibre may provide a broadband channel.

There exist over 50 different proprietory networks including Acorn's Econet; Ethernet of Rank Xerox; Corvus Omninet and IBM's PC-Net.

Two-way communication is possible between the various computers in the network for transferring data or messages electronically, i.e. electronic mail. The speed of transmission varies between one and twelve million bits per second. Ethernet transmits data at ten million bits per second which is much faster than the speed of telephone lines. Modems can link LANs to British Telecom's telephone system and to gateways to other networks which provides facilities for teleshopping, airline seat reservations, to Viewdata and other on-line information systems (*see* Figs. 13.1, 13.2, 13.3).

2. Network facilities. A variety of facilities are required to enable networks to function, they include a communication server for linking network users to a variety of communication devices by telephone line connections; a print server providing each network user with high-speed printing facilities and a file server which facilitates the storage of documents which can be retrieved and updated as necessary. An example of a simple network using the principle of shared resources is in the computer room of a college consisting of 15–20 microcomputers. Each of the micros is connected to a Corvus hard disc storing programs and files which can be directly accessed by any student from any computer in the computer room at any time. This avoids the cost of providing each micro with its own floppy disc drives.

3. Broadband and baseband networks. LANs can be either broadband or baseband. Broadband networks have a number of channels multiplexed together one of which serves as a high-speed data channel the other being available for other purposes such as video. Broad-

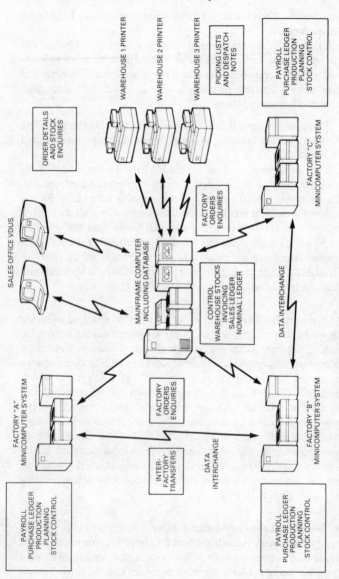

Figure 13.2 Outline of characteristics of a distributed processing network.

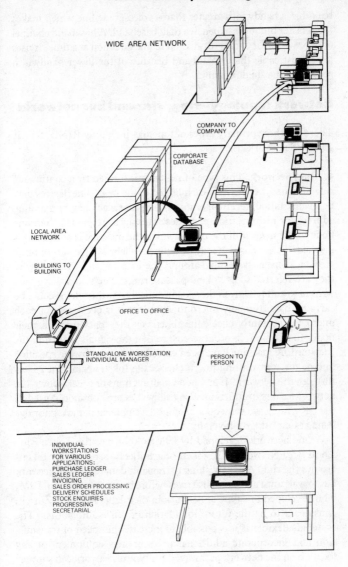

Figure 13.3 *Networks.*

band has a bandwidth greater than a voice-grade line which makes them faster but more expensive than baseband. A baseband channel only provides for data transmission in one direction at a time. It uses lower-cost cable than broadband because of the lower bandwidth required for a single channel.

Network topology—ring, star and bus networks

There are three primary types of topology including RING, STAR and BUS networks.

4. Ring network. This type of network is formed by a continuous ring of nodes, i.e. devices, each linked to the next. The devices may be a workstation, terminal or microcomputer, each having a unique address for identification purposes. Messages are passed from one node to the next until the one to which the message is addressed is reached. Tokens, which may be defined as labelled packets or units of data, constantly revolve around the loop or ring which is why they are referred to as 'token' passing rings. The tokens have data written to and read from them continuously. As the tokens could be carrying data from any micro to any other it is necessary for each micro to constantly check the tokens as they pass through their node. In addition, in order to ensure that the signals sent from the transmitting machine have been correctly received by the specified micro, the transmitting micro checks the token again as it passes through the network. If any node malfunctions or breaks down the network ceases to function. Ring networks are commonly used in the UK mainly as a consequence of the development of the Cambridge Ring at Cambridge University.

A ring network developed by IBM is known as the Token Ring Local Area Network. The token ring works by sending free tokens around the ring. A user wishing to transmit data round the network has to wait until a free token arrives before being able to do so. IBM, who developed this type of network in their laboratories in Zurich, consider it to be the future foundation of office automation. The system is flexible as it is possible to increase the speed of transmission and incorporate additional users or new equipment at any location on the network pathway. This type of network can support up to 260 terminals. Signal boosters are necessary for dispersed networks requiring a number of kilometres of cable. Speeds of 16MB/s (sixteen million bits per second) are possible which is a vast increase compared to the current four million bits per second. Moreover, tests are underway on prototype systems using fibre optic cables (replacing twisted pair copper cables) which it is expected will attain speeds of 100MB/s. IBM provide software for connecting a token ring network to PC Net, a lower performance network. It is also possible to connect mainframe computers on a token ring LAN either directly using a specially programmed PC or a Series 1 minicomputer. Links are also facilitated via other gateways. Because data is in labelled packets the network can carry traffic using IBM's Systems Network Architecture protocols and the internationally accepted Open Systems Interconnection (OSI) protocols (*see* Fig. 13.4).

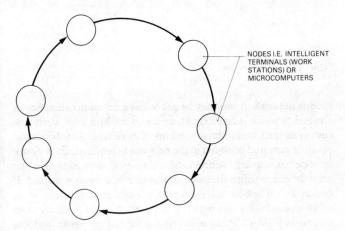

NODES I.E. INTELLIGENT TERMINALS (WORK STATIONS) OR MICROCOMPUTERS

Figure 13.4 *Ring network.*

5. Star network. Star networks have a central network controller or file server, usually a microcomputer controlling a disc drive, to which all nodes are connected. The network transmits data to specific nodes in accordance with the destination address. This type of network is used in time sharing systems whereby the central controller is a host computer to which all terminals are connected via modems (or acoustic couplers), multiplexors and telephone lines. If the central controller, whether a file server or central time sharing computer, breaks down the network ceases to function (*see* Fig. 13.5).

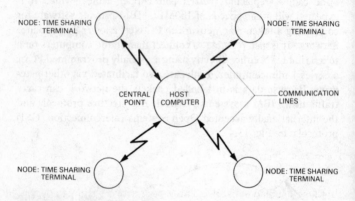

Figure 13.5 *Star network.*

6. Bus network. A bus may be defined as a communication line or channel to which is connected the various workstations, word processors or microcomputers by means of cable taps. Any device can easily be removed or added to the network as required. Each device or node has a specific address and messages are routed to all nodes until the one to which the communication is addressed is reached. If one or several devices fail, the network continues to function.

An example of a bus network is Ethernet which uses a system known as CSMA/CD, an abbreviation for Carrier Sense Multiple Access with Collision Detect. With this system, terminals listen to the carrier wave to detect if any other terminals are transmitting data. All terminals on the network can do this at any time because of the multiple access nature of the system. If two terminals listen simultaneously and both detect that no transmissions are occurring then both transmit data concurrently. Consequently both transmission signals collide. Both terminals detect this situation by the collision detect facilities and both wait a random period of time before retransmitting the data (*see* Fig. 13.6).

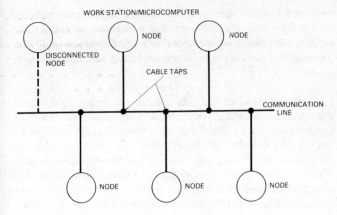

Figure 13.6 *Bus network.*

7. Close-coupled networks. This type of network is also known as a multi-processor system. Each terminal has its own processor for local processing needs. Communication takes place on a bus (electronic board) which has a file-serving processor alongside the application processors each of which is able to share any other's memory. The communication distances are very short which enables transmission speeds to be achieved in the region of one million characters per second which is much faster than local area networks using coaxial or twisted-pair cables. The central processor does not poll each user's processor for detecting data to be transmitted but is 'demand' activated or 'interrupt driven'. The protocol to handle data transmissions is less complex than that required for LANs and the complex protocols to deal with data collision and for ensuring the integrity of data are dispensed with.

Value-added network (VAN) and store and forward systems

8. Value-added network (VAN). This type of communication network provides additional services to the communication channels by third-party vendors under a government licence. The additional services include automatic error detection and correction as well as 'store and forward' message services, electronic mail and protocol conversions to access different computers and networks. The vendors can provide point-to-point or switched services on British Telecom and Mercury circuits provided they 'add value' to those circuits.

9. Store and forward. The term relates to the temporary storage of a message in a computer system for subsequent transmission to its destination at a later time. Store and forward techniques allow for routing over networks which are not always accessible. This will necessitate one or more computer-controlled exchanges or nodes which are able to store messages and release them for onward transmission when a transmission path is available. Messages for different time zones can be 'stored and forwarded' to the destination during normal daytime by this means.

Wide area networks

Whereas a local area network serves the requirements of an organisation for interdepartmental communications, a wide area network serves a wide geographic area and may in fact embrace a whole country or even the world. A wide area network usually takes the form of a packet switching network (*see* 8:**16**). However, a system known as Integrated Services Digital Network (ISDN), a single network able to carry and switch a wide variety of telecommunications services, is expected to evolve from an integrated digital network (IDN) which is a telephone network in which digital transmission systems are fully integrated with digital switching systems. Such systems are likely to incorporate most of the telecom services embracing speech and data transmission including electronic mail, facsimile document transmission (FAX), videotex such as Prestel, interactive videotex (on-line shopping), electronic funds transfer, inter-computer data transmission by packet switching and so on.

Multi-user systems

10. Multi-user systems. Multi-user computer systems allow several users to gain simultaneous access to a central computer by means of a terminal. The hardware costs of the computer are then shared by a number of users. This must be offset by the cost of the VDU and keyboard for each user. It is necessary to assess costs because it may be more economical to have multi-access to a large machine rather than each user having a separate machine. A more powerful computer system is required to service the needs of several users. When the peak processing period of several users coincides system degradation may occur resulting in slower response times. Some multi-user computers support sixteen terminals or more which allows them to access files and programs stored on hard discs and to print output on a high-speed printer.

11. Disadvantages of multi-user systems. A disadvantage of a multi-user system is that if the connecting cable is severed then the terminal becomes inoperative as it has no link with the computer. This is not the case with networks, however, because if a micro-computer becomes disconnected from the network it can continue processing but cannot communicate with other computers on the network. In such circumstances stand-alone computers and net-working computers have greater resilience than multi-user terminal systems. They do in fact become stand-alone systems in both cases.

12. Operating systems. Special multi-user operating systems are required to control terminal operations as only one user can access the system in any moment of time. Users must therefore suffer brief delay whilst awaiting their turn to access the system for the input or retrieving of data.

13. Record locking and unlocking. Multi-user systems require a hardware protection feature for preventing system crashes as a result of several users processing the same file concurrently. Record locking and unlocking facilities are also required to prevent a record being accessed by a user at the time it is being updated by another user. The first user of a file is allocated complete control to write to the file and other users are denied access until the file is closed. Some multi-user mini computers have partitioned memories which allow additional terminals to be added up to the capacity of the processor.

Multi-tasking systems

14. Multi-tasking defined. Multi-tasking is a technique which facilitates the running of two or more tasks concurrently with high-speed switching between them. Text and graphics can be transferred from one application to another by means of special software.

15. Microsoft windows. As an example of multi-tasking software Microsoft market a package called Windows which functions with existing applications. To run a program using the Windows software it is necessary to point to the appropriate file name with the mouse and double-click the button. A window is then opened for the particular application selected. The program's window can be closed when switching to a different task while the original task is being executed. Use of the software is controlled by a command-line substitute known as MS-DOS Executive. This shows a list of files in the current directory in a window and has a set of pull-down menus for copying files and cut and paste tasks. Windows can be moved around the screen and the size can be adjusted. An icon bar displays an icon for each program that is running or which is waiting the attention of the user. To view a background task its icon is moved from the icon bar towards the centre of the screen. This then reopens the application's window. The software needs to know details of a program before it can be executed, such as how much RAM it uses, the resources required and how the program writes to the screen, etc. These details are obtained from Program Information Files, known as PIF's. Each application requires a PIF. It is necessary to experiment according to the manual to find out these essential parameters.

16. Desk accessories. A number of desk accessories are supplied with Windows including a card file, notebook, calendar, calculator, clock and terminal emulator. To write one's own Windows-compatible applications a programmer's toolkit is required which is available from Microsoft. It enables the construction of pull-down menus, dialogue boxes, mouse support and application icons.

Progress test 13

1. Define the nature and purpose of distributed processing. (**1**)

2. Define the term 'local area network' and outline the range of structures and technologies used in different types of local area network. (*ACCA*) (**1–9**)

3. What is meant by broadband and baseband networks? (**3**)

4. There are three primary types of network topology. They are ring, star and bus. Outline the features of each of these. (**4–6**)

5. Define the terms: (*a*) close-coupled networks; (*b*) value-added networks (VAN); (*c*) store and forward systems. (**7–9**)

6. Define the nature and purpose of multi-user systems and wide area networks. (**10–16**)

7. What is the purpose of record locking and unlocking? (**13**)

8. Define multi-tasking. (**14**)

9. Specify the features of Microsoft windows. (**15**)

14

Computer bureaux and computing services

Computer bureaux

1. Definition of and factors to consider in selection of a bureau.
A computer service bureau is a company which operates a computer
to process work for other companies, particularly those which
cannot justify a computer of their own. A number of factors need to
be considered when choosing a computer bureau as it is necessary to
select one which is both reliable and efficient. The following factors
provide a reasonable assessment of a bureau's capability relative to
others:

- (a) reputation;
- (b) integrity;
- (c) efficiency;
- (d) competitiveness;
- (e) number of years established;
- (f) financial stability;
- (g) turnround time-reliability;
- (h) calibre of staff employed;
- (i) market standing;
- (j) approach to technological developments.

2. Types of computer bureaux. There are basically three types:

(a) *independent companies* specially formed for the provision of
computing services to clients;

(b) *computer manufacturers* with separately structured computer
bureaux;

(*c*) computer users with *spare capacity* who allow other firms to use their computer system either for standby facilities or for program testing prior to the installation of a similar computer system.

3. Services available from computer bureaux. In general, the range of services provided by computer bureaux is as follows.

(*a*) *Data preparation or conversion.* This service consists of the conversion of source data into a machine-sensible form for processing by computer. Conversion may be in the form of floppy disc, cassette tape, magnetic tape or optical characters. A bureau may be used for the initial conversion of master files when computerising systems.

(*b*) *Systems investigation and design.* This consists of the analysis of existing procedures and their conversion for processing by computer.

(*c*) *Program preparation and testing.* This service provides an addition to the service indicated in (*b*) above.

(*d*) *Hiring computer time.* Here the service to the client consists of processing the client's data using the programs supplied by the client. The hire charges usually vary according to the time of day the service is provided and the length of time the bureau's facilities are used.

(*e*) *Do-it-yourself service (DIY).* The provision of computing facilities to allow the clients' computer operators to process data with their own programs. The service is usually available during off-peak periods.

(*f*) *Time sharing.* Access to the bureau's computer by means of communication links, which in effect provides each user with computing facilities as if he had an in-house computer.

4. Reasons for using bureaux. Any particular company will of course have specific reasons for using a computer bureau, but in general the following reasons are common:

(*a*) to obtain valuable initial experience of processing by computer before deciding whether or not to install an in-house computer;

(*b*) to provide standby facilities, by arrangement, in case of breakdown of the in-house computer;

(*c*) to provide facilities for coping with peak data processing loads owing to insufficient capacity of the in-house computer;

(d) non-availability of finance for the installation of an in-house computer;

(e) space restrictions for accommodating a computer installation;

(f) to avoid the responsibility of operating an in-house computer;

(g) insufficient volume of work to justify the installation of a computer;

(h) to obtain the benefit of computer power at reasonable cost;

(i) to provide more information for management control;

(j) to test and prove programs to be run on a similar computer, when installed, to that used by a bureau;

(k) to obtain the skill and experience of bureau operating staff in the processing of data;

(l) recognition that a bureau is likely to have powerful, up-to-date equipment, made economical by processing a wide variety of work at high volumes;

(m) recognition that a bureau will be using, as far as possible, the most efficient techniques and software aids;

(n) to process jobs that cannot be processed economically by an in-house computer.

5. Disadvantages of using bureaux. One of the main disadvantages of using a bureau is the loss of control over the time taken to process data (turn-round time) suffered by an organisation, because of the competing requirements of other clients of the bureau.

In some instances, an organisation may be better served by an in-house computer but may be reluctant to take the plunge; as a result, no experience is gained directly in operating a computer installation. This may create indirect benefits to competitors, especially in the problem-solving applications for which a computer is so valuable. This means that competitors who use computers for their problem-solving needs probably generate optimum solutions, whereas a business without a computer may lose this advantage.

Computing services

Many computing services organisations originally started out as computer bureaux, providing data processing facilities to small businesses which could not justify the use of a computer. This has now changed to some extent due to technological developments which have already been discussed. Many bureaux have expanded the range of services they provide and may now be defined as computing service companies (*see* **6–10**).

6. Supply and installation of computing equipment. Some organisations now supply hardware including micro, mini and mainframe computers either to function as 'in-house' systems or as 'front-end' processors linked to other mainframes. They may also supply networked micros, intelligent terminals, multi-user and multi-processor systems.

7. Supply of software. In addition to providing software support with computing equipment as a complete package, some companies also function as software houses developing software packages for distribution through a dealer network or developing 'custom' (bespoke) software for individual companies to their specification.

8. Facilities management. This is an arrangement whereby a company transfers all or part of its data processing facility, including hardware and staff, to a contractor, i.e. a computing services organisation and then purchases back the processing requirements of the company. A specific level of service is guaranteed. Contracts vary according to specific needs of individual customers and may involve providing all operational and development staff to run an existing data processing installation or the transfer of the installation to the premises of the computer service company.

  Facilities management can provide an efficient service at less than the equivalent 'in-house' costs. It is useful when it is necessary to limit capital expenditure for upgrading or replacing an existing system.

9. Consultancy. Some companies will require the services of a consultant before embarking on the installation of computerised systems, and others will need advice on specific problems of a data processing nature. Consultancy services covering these needs are often provided by computing services organisations.

10. Turnkey services. Turnkey services may be defined as 'the supply and installation of a computer system in such a complete form that the user need only "turn a key" as it were to commence using the system'. Such a service is provided by external consultants. The user figuratively turns a key to gain access to the system for whatever purpose it is designed. This requires the initial identification of a client's needs, the selection of the most suitable hardware (computer system) and the relevant elements of software support. The service covers systems design, program coding, testing and debugging until the system is suitable for handing over to the client.

A business with very little data processing experience using sophisticated machines, or no computer specialists on the staff, would find this service of the utmost benefit as it would enable the changeover of systems to be accomplished by experts without too much involvement by management.

Progress test 14

1. Define the term computer bureau. (**1**)

2. (*a*) Describe the range of services offered by computer bureaux. (*b*) List the major features which should be considered when choosing a computer bureau. (**1, 3**) (*ACA*)

3. Specify the types of computer bureau available. (**2**)

4. List FOUR services offered by a typical computer bureau. (**3**) (*C & G*)

5. For what reasons would you consider using a computer bureau? (**4**)

6. What are the disadvantages of using a computer bureau? (**5**)

7. Many bureaux have expanded the range of services they provide and become in effect computer service organisations. What services would you expect them to provide? (**6–10**)

8. Define the following services: (*a*) facilities management; (*b*) turnkey services. (**8, 10**)

Part four
Development of computer systems

Development of Observation Systems

15
Framework for developing a computer system

Initial considerations

1. Data processing steering committee. A steering committee should be formulated with responsibility for appraising the viability of computer projects, to ensure they are cost effective and would be of benefit to the business as a whole, to optimise corporate performance rather than functional performance. Such a committee enables the data processing needs of the business as a whole to be coordinated with other functional activities within the framework of corporate plans.

Membership of a steering committee should consist of representatives of the various functions which will be affected by the installation of a computer into the business. The committee is likely to be chaired by the chief executive, which would enable him to have an overview of proposed computer projects and assess whether they accord with the future strategy and policy of the business. The interest of functions in a typical manufacturing business would probably be represented by the production controller, stock controller, chief accountant, sales manager, chief buyer and of course the data processing manager. The data processing manager is then in a position to be aware of company policy and can interpret its requirements more objectively before executing the needs of such policy.

2. Preliminary appraisal. A mainframe computer cannot be plugged in and away she goes, as it were— its successful implementation depends upon a number of factors. Management must make a decision on the basis of a feasibility study report either to implement or not to implement a computer. Whichever decision is made can have far reaching effects on the future efficiency of the business.

The correct decision is crucial because it is possible to make an incorrect decision in either of two instances. In the first instance management may decide not to implement a computer when they should or, in the second instance, to implement a computer when they should not. The consequences of failure to implement a computer when it is necessary is a reduction in administrative efficiency. On the other hand, the consequences of implementing a computer when it is not needed is chaos as systems will be disrupted, unnecessary costs will be incurred and organisational changes will be made needlessly.

3. Top management support. The time, effort and finance required for the initial implementation and development of computerised systems may deter the most enlightened managers unless the feasibility study report makes refusal difficult. This is a further pointer to the value of an accurate feasibility report. It is imperative for top management—the board of directors and functional managers—to show interest at the outset, otherwise projects will have little chance of success once a computer is installed.

Any dissension on the part of top management will filter through the organisation to the lower management levels and this in itself will detract from the successful implementation of systems. Departmental managers in charge of systems to be computerised will not, in all probability, provide the required level of support to systems staff which is so essential for the efficient operation of new systems. User departments need to participate in the design of systems with which they are concerned and for which they are responsible.

Education, training, communications and recruitment

4. Education and training programme. The reason for any lack of enthusiasm on the part of management may be ignorance of computers—or even fright—and this should be dispelled by means of a short induction course. Such a course may be conducted by internal systems staff if any are already employed in the organisation or, if they are not, selected managers and staff may attend a computer manufacturer's or college based computer appreciation course. The contents of a computer appreciation course may consist of the following:

(a) definition of a computer;

(b) the place of the computer in the organisation;

(c) duties of systems analysts and programmers;

(d) responsibilities of the data processing manager;

(e) outline of computer applications;

(f) benefits of using computers related to present systems if relevant;

(g) data preparation methods;

(h) processing techniques, batch, on-line, real-time and multi-programming, etc.;

(i) hands-on experience.

5. Communication. Before a large computer is implemented within the organisation the fact that this is under consideration should be communicated to all personnel, particularly those who are likely to be the most affected once a computer becomes operational. This course of action will dispel distorted rumours circulating within the organisation which could have a damaging effect on morale.

It is also necessary to communicate company policy with regard to possible redundancies when systems are transferred to the computer. Of particular importance are the arrangements to be made for retraining staff and possible redeployment.

In most companies it will be the responsibility of the managing director to formally communicate these factors and he should also stress the importance of obtaining the fullest cooperation of staff in the difficult transition period ahead, in respect of systems development and changeover.

6. Recruitment of effective data processing staff. A computer installation will only be as efficient as the personnel who manage, develop systems and program the computer. It is essential to obtain the services of an effective data processing manager who, first and foremost, should be a good manager. He should have a wide knowledge of business systems particularly of the business in which he is employed and due to this essential requirement he is often appointed from within the business. Former organisation and methods specialists and line managers have been appointed to the post of data processing manager on the basis of their knowledge of key systems in the organisation.

The data processing manager should have a considerable knowledge of computers, particularly of the model in use, or about to be implemented, but he need not be an expert in programming. He is responsible for interpreting and executing the policy of the steering committee, planning, organising, coordinating and controlling projects to ensure they achieve objectives.

Systems analysts should be recruited from within the organisation whenever possible to take advantage of their knowledge of the business which is of extreme importance for the development of computer systems. They must be aware of the needs of the operating functions and departments particularly the purpose and objectives of the systems they operate. This is the reason why O & M investigators often become systems analysts when a computer is implemented into a business.

A system analyst must have many talents and be capable of viewing the business as a total system and yet be able to analyse it into its constituent elements (sub-systems). He must be able to appreciate the interactions which occur between sub-systems and the effects computerisation is likely to have on them. He should design systems without unnecessary complexity as the simpler the design the more effective they are likely to be (*see* 16:**1–2**).

Programmers are required who are capable of writing simple, efficient programs. Unnecessary complexity in programs is likely to increase computer running time and produce documents and reports which are too complex for system needs. This situation requires a higher degree of coordination between programmers and systems analysts to ensure that ambiguity does not enter into programming as this will result in systems failing to meet their objectives.

Stages of systems design

7. **System life cycle.** The stages of system life cycle development

methodology are summarised below. A number of the stages are dealt with in greater depth within the various topic areas, particularly those relating to feasibility study, terms of reference, systems analysis and design. The stages are as follows.

(*a*) Define the problem.

(*b*) Management specify terms of reference.

(*c*) Conduct feasibility study:

(*i*) *Technical feasibility*. Demands on the system regarding terminal enquiries or volume of data to be processed by batch or on-line processing. Speed of system response required and the capability of hardware and software to meet these requirements.

(*ii*) *Economic feasibility*. Matters relating to cost/benefit appraisal.

(*d*) Present report to management with recommendations.

(*e*) Management decision to abort or continue with project.

(*f*) Plan the project.

(*g*) Carry out systems analysis.

(*i*) Fact finding (collect the facts including environment and functional analysis).

(*ii*) Verify the facts.

(*iii*) Record the facts.

(*iv*) Procedure analysis.

(*h*) System design.

(*i*) Design philosophy.

(1) Establish design objectives and constraints.

(2) Design alternative systems.

(*ii*) Design activities.

(1) Prepare procedure charts (for clerical activities), block diagrams and system flowcharts.

(2) Determine actions to be taken by means of decision tables.

(3) Design input documents and output documents and reports.

(4) Design file structures and layout.

(5) Develop the structure of computer runs by means of run charts.

(6) Evaluate run times.

(7) Design screen layouts for on-line terminal operations.

(8) Develop dialogue to be used by terminal/workstation operators.

(9) Develop fail-safe and restart procedures.

(10) Develop procedures for file security.

(11) Discuss with auditors and develop checks and controls to be incorporated.

(*i*) Prepare system specification (system definition).

(*i*) Details of the system including clerical and computer procedures, block diagrams, system flowcharts, decision tables and a narrative providing a general description of the system.

(*ii*) Input, output and file specifications and layouts.

(*iii*) Schedule of equipment required by the system including new equipment needs and alternative equipment proposals.

(*iv*) Nature and use of passwords.

(*j*) Present alternative proposals to management.

(*k*) Discuss proposals with management.

(*l*) Management decision—choice of proposals, if relevant.

(*m*) Prepare program specification: statement of program requirements including initialisation, parameters, processing stages, input and output requirements, test data and testing procedure to be applied, checks and controls to be incorporated, exception routines, conditions and actions to be provided for and arrangements for test runs.

(*n*) Programming.

(*i*) Program procedure charts (flowcharts).

(*ii*) Program coding sheets.

(*iii*) Prepare test data and testing procedures.

(*iv*) Prepare validation checks and other controls to be incorporated into the system.

(*v*) Compile source programs.

(*vi*) Debug programs.

(*o*) Convert files.

(*p*) System testing.

(*i*) Prepare precalculated results.

(*ii*) Test programs with test data by dry runs, i.e. desk checking.

(*iii*) Compare results with precalculated results.

(*iv*) Report to management and discuss the results obtained from system testing. Decide on future course of action.

(*v*) Make appropriate modifications to system or programs and recompile as necessary.

(*q*) Implementation.

(*i*) Plan system implementation.

(*ii*) Carry out parallel running of old and new system; implement direct changeover or pilot scheme as appropriate.

(*iii*) Prepare manuals for supporting department (users) and operation departments including data preparation and data control clerks.

(*r*) Evaluate results with expectations.

(*i*) Monitor system performance in coordination with user department.

(*ii*) Report to management to discuss the situation and decide on appropriate action.

(*iii*) Make relevant adjustments to the system.

(*s*) Maintain system.

(*i*) Develop, test and implement improvements.

(*ii*) Modify system to accord to changing circumstances.

(*iii*) Integrate related systems to improve processing efficiency.

It is important to appreciate that the 'system life cycle' approach to system design and development is the traditional approach but there are now a number of structured analysis and design methodologies currently available. One such methodology is that available from Michael Jackson Systems Limited. Michael Jackson has expanded his structured programming philosophy into the realms of structured systems design.

Note: Details relating to logical application modelling, data modelling, producing a 'first sketch' and prototyping are included in Volume 2.

8. Competing systems for scarce development resources. What strategy should be adopted when several systems are being considered for computerisation when there is a shortage of systems development staff? This is the theme of a question set by the Chartered Association of Certified Accountants in the December 1985 Systems Analysis and Design paper which is outlined below.

There are several manual procedures which are being considered for transfer to a computer in the organisation for which you work.

There is, however, a shortage of systems development staff, so only one of the proposed systems can be approved for development at this stage. You are required to do the following.

(a) Briefly describe *five* factors which you would use in selecting the one system to be developed.

(b) Identify *five* possible courses of action which may be taken to overcome the shortage of systems development staff and thus permit the more rapid implementation of the systems.

Before it is possible to draw positive conclusions from a diverse list of factors as a basis for selection it is advisable to prepare a summary of factors which could be used in selecting the one system to be developed as indicated below.

(a) Prepare a list of the important factors which will provide a basis for selecting one system for development.

(b) Award points to each factor from a maximum of ten for the purpose of indicating the relative weighting (importance) of the individual factors.

(c) Select the system with the highest points rating (score) for development.

The factors to include in the list are as follows.

(a) *Cost effectiveness.* If staff savings are a necessity then the system that reduces the staff by the greatest number will score the highest number of points. Alternatively the system which avoids increasing staff numbers by the highest number will score most points. An additional factor would be based on the reduction of total operating costs.

(b) *Operational efficiency.* The system which, if computerised, will achieve the highest level of operational efficiency will be the favourite contender. This may be assessed in terms of the number of days saved at the month end to produce statements of account; or the staff payroll; or month-end accounts. An additional factor might be achieving a greater degree of accuracy in the preparation of invoices. This has a bearing on customer satisfaction and the creation of a greater degree of goodwill. If the stock control system is a contender then it may be assessed on the value of the reduced level of stocks which will be possible due to improved stock management and control.

(*c*) *Development time and relative use of resources.* If time is of the essence to implement a computerised system then the system which will take the shortest time will score best. Alternatively, or in addition to the time factor, the system which utilises the lowest level of systems resources by way of systems analysts' time will score most points.

(*d*) *Simplicity.* The system which is the simplest to install may be looked upon in a favourable light as a system with few complications will achieve results as outlined in (*c*) above.

(*e*) *Company image.* The installation of a particular type of system may be a prestigious achievement for a company which may have a spin off by way of an increase in the level of goodwill. This may apply to an automated purchase order system which provides suppliers with a forward supply schedule and facilitates prompt payment of supplies.

(*f*) *Improved flow of management information.* Businesses must be controlled effectively to remain efficient or even to survive. A system which improves managerial performance by the provision of more timely information will tend to score well.

(*g*) *Improved problem solving and decision making.* Any system which will provide management with facts on which to base timely decisions or which provides the means of solving important strategic or tactical problems will tend to be favourably considered.

Five possible courses of action to overcome the shortage of systems development staff and permit the more rapid implementation of systems are as follows.

(*a*) Employ a systems house to develop the systems.

(*b*) Use program generators. *See* 20:**19–21**.

(*c*) Use application packages. *See* 20:**22–37**.

(*d*) Employ freelance systems and programming personnel (from advertisements in computer journals and magazines).

(*e*) Enlist the services of a recruitment agency to obtain trained staff.

(*f*) Employ the services of a personnel agency for hiring of temporary staff (similar to (*d*) above).

(*g*) Employ a training organisation for training suitable personnel on a short-duration external or in-plant course.

Two additional courses of action have been added to the number required by the question.

Feasibility study: objectives, costs and other factors

Important considerations concerned with conducting a feasibility study include the need to state the terms of reference and the boundaries of the study. It should also mention the structure of the team to conduct the study and the timescale for producing the report.

9. Objectives of study. At the outset it is important that objectives of the study should be clearly defined in order that the study team have a clear understanding of the requirements of the study. The objectives may be to determine if all or some of the following factors are feasible using a computer:

(a) reducing the number of staff in specific administrative functions because of cost;

(b) avoiding the need to increase clerical staff because the calibre of staff required is in short supply;

(c) improving the flow of information for management;

(d) providing problem solving facilities for management;

(e) improving cash flows by producing invoices and statements of account earlier;

(f) reducing the cost of processing each unit of data;

(g) streamlining accounting routines;

(h) providing the means for effective systems integration;

(i) improving the accuracy of information and data on business documents.

10. Choice of areas for improvement. In order to achieve the designated objectives it is necessary to select the areas of the business most likely to achieve them. Possible areas may be chosen on the following basis:

(a) those involving procedures which process a large volume of data, forms or documents;

(b) those involving procedures with a high proportion of repetitive operations;

(c) those involving procedures with a large number of clerical staff;

(d) those involving procedures which suffer from delays due to bottlenecks in processing perhaps due to insufficiently planned procedures, inadequate methods of processing or high-volume posting or calculating operations.

11. General considerations of a feasibility study. A number of important factors must be taken into account before any conclusions can be established and before the feasibility study report is presented to management. They include the following aspects:

(a) the alternative types of computer configuration available;

(b) the availability of standby facilities in case of breakdown of the computer;

(c) business trends and their likely impact on data processing commitments;

(d) the extent to which the organisation would need restructuring with the advent of a computer;

(e) the availability of experienced computer personnel, systems analysts and programmers, etc;

(f) the feasibility of using a computer bureau instead of installing an in-house computer;

(g) the feasibility of using several microcomputers instead of a mainframe computer;

(h) the incidence of redundancy in respect of clerical staff;

(i) the time necessary to develop computerised systems;

(j) the need for computer appreciation courses for management and staff.

12. Cost considerations of using a computer. Some of the elements of cost which must be considered by a management accountant, for instance, include:

(a) the cost of purchasing or renting a computer perhaps compared with the cost of using a computer bureau;

(b) the cost of developing computer systems;

(c) the cost of computer accommodation;

(d) the cost of recruiting and training computer staff;

(*e*) the manual cost of operating the computer system;
(*f*) the comparative costs of alternative methods of processing;
(*g*) the cost of writing off current equipment;
(*h*) the availability of finance to purchase a computer system;
(*i*) the cost of obtaining finance to purchase a computer system;
(*j*) the cost of converting master files to magnetic tape or disc.

13. Expected benefits of using a computer. The possible benefits are numerous if computers are planned and used effectively. *See* 1:**13**.

14. Feasibility study in an organisation possessing a computer. When a computer already exists in the organisation it is still necessary to conduct a feasibility study for any proposal to computerise a business system. The objectives and stages of feasibility study for a proposed system may be based on the following outline of action to be taken:

(*a*) define objectives of system to be studied;
(*b*) define objectives of the feasibility study (*see* **9**);
(*c*) collect facts relating to the current system, including types and volume of input, types and volume of output, frequency of processing, time for performing each main activity, number of staff employed on the system, type of files used, number of records in files, frequency of referring to files, frequency of updating files, file activity ratio ('hit rate'), problem areas and operating costs, etc;
(*d*) anticipated system development costs, including costs of file conversion;
(*e*) estimate run times;
(*f*) anticipate costs of computer operations;
(*g*) assess expected benefits;
(*h*) prepare feasibility study report;
(*i*) submit and discuss report with appropriate management;
(*j*) make decision to computerise and proceed with more detailed systems analysis if management consider proposals satisfactory; otherwise continue with existing system perhaps with minor modifications.

Systems analysis and duties of systems analyst

15. Systems analysis defined. Systems analysis is the term used to describe the process of collecting and analysing facts in respect of existing operations, procedures and systems in order to obtain a full appreciation of the situation prevailing so that an effective computerised system may be designed and implemented if proved feasible.

The difference between an organisation and methods investigation (a review of clerical procedures and methods) and a systems analysis project is one of objective rather than one of principle.

An O & M investigation sets out to improve the existing situation by the most suitable means, chosen from a number of possible alternatives. Systems analysis, however, has as its objective the design of an effective computerised procedure which will create benefits in excess of those possible by other means.

Systems analysis also embraces systems design, which is an activity concerned with the design of a computerised application based on the facts disclosed during the analysis stage. Both activities are carried out by the same person who is known as a *systems* analyst.

16. Duties of systems analyst. The duties may be summarised as follows.

(*a*) Collect, record and analyse details of existing procedures and systems.

(*b*) Develop ideas for a computerised system superior to the existing methods in use—improve system performance.

(*c*) Design system input, file and output requirements.

(*d*) Specify checks and controls to be incorporated in conjunction with audit staff.

(*e*) Define actions required to deal with various conditions arising in the system by means of decision tables.

(*f*) Specify the structure of computer runs.

(*g*) Specify the most appropriate processing technique for the prevailing circumstances.

(*h*) Estimate run timings.

(*i*) Prepare computer operating instructions.

(*j*) Define error messages to be incorporated in the system.

(k) Specify test data to be used for proving programs in conjunction with audit staff and programmers.

(l) Arrange for test runs in conjunction with programming staff.

(m) Document all aspects of the system in a system specification.

(n) Implement parallel operation of old and new system.

(o) Monitor results.

(p) Maintain system to accord to changing circumstances.

(q) Communicate with user department, systems staff and programmers as appropriate.

17. Systems analysis team. Some projects require a team of analysts, the size of which is dependent upon the complexity and type of system to be investigated. It is good policy to recruit suitable personnel from existing staff, as it is important that they should have a sound knowledge of the business which often takes many years to obtain in sufficient depth to analyse systems effectively.

The team should also include representatives from the various departments of the organisation that will be affected by the investigation. This approach ensures that personnel with an intimate knowledge of the systems being reviewed for computerisation have the opportunity to record facts which may otherwise be overlooked and which are important for the effective design of the computer system.

After the project is concluded the personnel on secondment go back to their department (unless recruited for systems work on a full-time basis due to their experience) and take an active part in the newly installed computerised system. By this means the best results are obtained, as personnel who have been brought into the picture are more likely to co-operate and accept the changes which have been implemented.

Collecting and recording facts

18. Interviewing. This technique collects facts by interviewing personnel connected with the system under investigation as it is considered that they possess vital information relating to the systems with which they are concerned. The interviewer should encourage the staff to give their point of view of how they consider the system may be improved and accordingly the interviewer should be prepared to listen rather than dominate the interview. He should possess sufficient tact, however, to steer any discussion in the desired direction.

There should be no mystery surrounding an interview and the purpose of conducting it should be stated as it must be appreciated that personnel become very apprehensive of pending changes. An interview should be concluded amicably and in such a manner that any further assistance will be forthcoming freely.

19. Questionnaire. A questionnaire may be used as an aid to interviewing as it has the advantage of containing pre-formulated questions, answers to which are essential for the development of the system under consideration. This approach avoids the possibility of overlooking important facts. Questions should be framed as simply as possible to avoid ambiguity, should be asked in a logical sequence, should not be too numerous and leading questions should not be asked. The answers obtained may be verified by interviews after the questionnaire has been completed or it may be used during the course of an interview.

20. Observation. This technique is used to obtain an overall visual impact of a systems environment. It takes into account details relating to the movement of personnel and forms, types of machines and equipment being used, the speed of operations, working conditions, idle time, numbers of staff, bottlenecks and delays, etc.

21. Inspection and examination. This entails the examination and inspection of documents regarding number of entries made, their general state, how they are filed and the effectiveness of the filing system. The state of machines and equipment will also be examined as will the general working conditions in the systems environment.

Recording techniques used in systems analysis

22. Procedure chart. A chart used for analysing the activities and their relationships within a defined procedure. It portrays the various activities in the procedure and by means of symbols indicates the type of activity performed. This type of chart is used in systems investigations to record the details of the existing procedures so that they may be subjected to further analysis. The symbols used in the construction of this type of chart are shown in Fig. 15.1. A typical procedure chart is illustrated in Fig. 15.2.

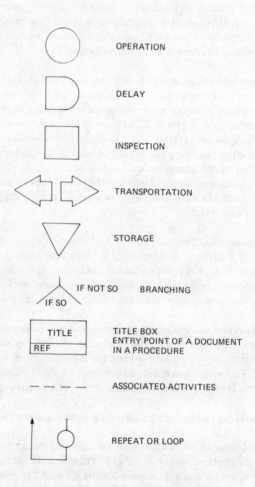

Figure 15.1 *Symbols for the construction of procedure charts.*

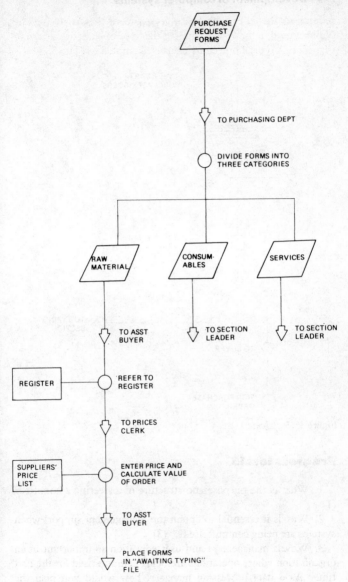

Figure 15.2 *Typical procedure chart.*

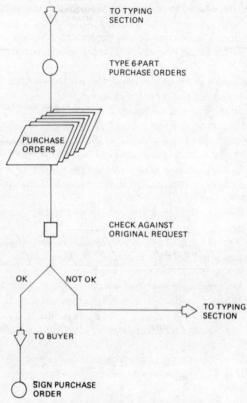

TO TYPING
SECTION

TYPE 6-PART
PURCHASE ORDERS

PURCHASE
ORDERS

CHECK AGAINST
ORIGINAL REQUEST

OK   NOT OK

TO TYPING
SECTION

TO BUYER

SIGN PURCHASE
ORDER

Figure 15.2 *(Contd.)*

Progress test 15

1. What is the purpose and structure of a steering committee?
(1)

2. Why is it essential to obtain top management support when systems are being computerised? (3)

3. Why is management and user education so important in an organisation whose operations are being computerised for the first time? As a data processing manager, how would you plan the

progressive education of the staff of the data processing department?   (**4**)

4. Before a large computer is implemented within an organisation the fact should be communicated to all relevant staff. Discuss. (**5**)

5. Why is it essential to recruit effective data processing staff for the operation of a computer installation?   (**6**)

6. List the stages of the life cycle of a systems project.   (**7**)

7. What additional work would the systems analyst have to do after passing specifications to the chief programmer and before the system becomes fully operational?   (**7** (*o*), (*p*), (*q*), (*r*), (*s*)) (*ACCA*)

8. Identify the stages in a system project when flowcharting or decision table techniques will be particularly useful. (**7** (*i*)) (*ACCA*)

9. How can the problem be overcome of systems competing for scarce development resources?   (**8**) (*ACCA*)

10. Why is it important to conduct a feasibility study either to implement a large computer initially or when contemplating the transfer of systems to an existing computer?   (**2**, **9–14**)

11. Describe fully the work carried out by a systems analyst during the investigation and analysis of a business system.   (**15**, **16**) (*ACCA*)

12. What are the principal duties of a systems analyst during the life of a systems project.   (**16**) (*ACCA*)

13. Why do some projects require a team of analysts?   (**17**)

14. Specify four ways of collecting facts during a systems investigation.   (**18–21**)

15. What is the purpose of a procedure chart?   (**22**)

16

Systems design and implementation

1. Objectives and essential considerations. The design of a computer-based system (and any other type of system) is a creative task which has as its objective the implementation of a system creating benefits and improvements superior to those achieved by other methods.

The system must therefore be designed so that basic business documents and reports are produced as effectively as possible in accordance with the needs of the business.

Provision should be made for automating decisions of a routine nature whenever possible, which may be incorporated in the program in the form of standard formulae, thereby assisting the various levels of management by freeing them from routine decision-making.

During the process of designing a system, it should be borne in mind that the system(s) under review should not be considered in isolation from other systems, as many systems are inter-related either by the need for basic information or by the output from one system being the input to other systems.

The processing requirements of the total system—the organisation—should be considered, even though it may be decided to design separate systems—'sub-systems'—initially. Even so, the separately designed systems should be planned in such a way that they may be developed with a minimum of amendment and disruption at a later date after gaining experience in the design and processing of separate applications.

2. Essentials for the effective design of systems. A well-designed system should take into account the following factors:

(*a*) production of the desired information, at the right time, in the right amount, with an acceptable level of accuracy and in the form required at an economical cost;

(*b*) incorporation of checks and controls which are capable of detecting and dealing with exceptional circumstances and errors;

(*c*) need to minimise the cost and the time spent on recording source data;

(*d*) need to minimise the cost and the time spent on data preparation;

(*e*) need to minimise the cost and the time spent on processing data;

(*f*) effective safeguards for the prevention of fraud;

(*g*) effective security measures in order to avoid loss of data stored in master files;

(*h*) efficient design of documents and reports;

(*i*) efficient design of computer runs;

(*j*) design of suitable coding systems to aid identification, comparison, sorting, verification and the elimination of ambiguity;

(*k*) policy matters and their effect on business systems;

(*l*) legal matters and their relationship with business systems;

(*m*) adequate handling of exceptions to normal situations.

While a system can be designed to process all possible variations or exceptions on a computer, this may create a considerable degree of complexity in programming and extend processing time to an unacceptable level. Consequently it may be more efficient to design clerical systems instead of computer systems to handle them. Refer to Volume 2 for further details.

Forms design

3. Principles for the effective design of forms. The design of forms is an activity concerned with designing the documents used for collecting source data relating to business transactions which is subsequently input to an information processing system. The documents or the printouts from an information processing system also have to be designed. Forms must be effectively designed whether they are for use in clerical systems or in combined clerical/computer systems. The following guidelines will indicate the primary factors to be taken into account during the form design process.

(*a*) The paper must be of the correct type and substance for its purpose. For example, a form may contain details of the operations and departments through which an item is to proceed during the course of manufacture. The document may be placed in the work bin containing parts which are covered in oil. Non-absorbent paper will be required.

(*b*) The colour of paper for distinguishing between individual copies in multi-copy sets.

(*c*) Colour of ink used for printing.

(*d*) Type faces, i.e. type font.

(*e*) Type size.

(*f*) Punching requirements for filing.

(*g*) Sprocket holes for feeding continuous stationery on a printer.

(*h*) Cut off or rounded corners.

(*i*) Direction of grain for ease of folding.

(*j*) Blanking requirements to obliterate information on specific copies of a document, e.g. blanking of prices on a despatch note forming part of a multi-part invoicing set.

(*k*) Simplicity of design.

(*l*) Entries should flow in a logical sequence.

(*m*) Data boxes should be adequate for the size of fields to be entered.

(*n*) How to combine related forms containing similar data for various sub-system requirements thereby reducing the number of separate forms.

(*o*) Consider the type of carbon paper required for entries onto copies, i.e. interleaved re-usable carbon paper, one-time carbon paper or 'no carbon required' (NCR) paper.

(*p*) Some forms may be designed for three-in-one applications to enable common entries to be made on several documents simultaneously thereby avoiding duplication of entries.

(*q*) Some applications may require printing on a carbon insert such as a pay advice sealed inside a pay envelope.

(*r*) Design should take into account speed and accuracy of entering data onto forms.

4. Form design question. The following question is part of a question set by the Association of Certified Accountants.

XYZ Ltd maintains its sales ledger system on a minicomputer. The sales ledger master file is held on magnetic disc. Accounts, which contain the usual standard data, are kept on a brought forward balance basis with the total balance analysed over current month, month 1, month 2, month 3 and month 4 and over. Visual display units are employed for the entry of transaction data and for the retrieval of data for answering enquiries. A variety of printed reports is produced on the line printer.

Draft, with TWO lines of sample entries, the Credit Limit Excess and Aged Balance report which is produced monthly for the Accounts Manager. Your answer should be in the format of a typical computer-produced line-printer report.

SOLUTION

A suggested layout for the report is shown in Fig. 16.1.

System specification

5. **Nature of a system specification.** A system specification is similar to any product specification whether it is a hi-fi unit, television set, refrigerator or radio. A specification provides the interface between systems analysis and system design.

6. **Contents of a system specification.** The specific details of a system specification are dependent upon the nature and complexity of the system but typically includes a number of sections which are summarised below.

(a) Introduction.
(b) System objectives.
(c) Systems description.
(d) Input specification.
(e) Output specification.
(f) File specification.
(g) Changeover.
(h) Equipment.
(i) Test data.
(j) Program specification.

(a)

TRANSACTION DATA:

1. INVOICES (SALES)
2. CREDIT NOTES (RETURNS)
3. CASH REMITTANCES, TRADERS CREDIT TRANSFERS, ETC.
4. CASH DISCOUNTS
5. ADJUSTMENTS (CORRECTIONS)

(b)

ACCOUNT NUMBER	ACCOUNT BALANCE	CREDIT LIMIT	CREDIT LIMIT EXCESS	CURRENT MONTH	AGED ACCOUNT BALANCE			
					1 MNTH	2 MNTH	3 MNTH	4 MNTH AND OVER
	£	£	£	£	£	£	£	£
12345	1000	800	200	500	200	300	–	–
12346	2000	1800	200	600	400	300	500	200

Figure 16.1 *Credit Limit Excess and Aged Balance Report.*

7. Introduction. This section includes details appertaining to the following.

(a) Name of the system.
(b) Glossary of terms used in the specification.
(c) Date of preparation.
(d) Statement of acceptance.
(e) Index to sections of the specification.
(f) System relationships.
(g) Details of amendments to original terms of reference.
(h) Departments involved with the system.
(i) Standards of performance.

8. System objectives. Expected benefits: tangible and intangible.

9. System description.

(a) Procedure charts and narrative relating to clerical systems.
(b) Data structure charts and data flow diagrams.
(c) System flowcharts and computer run charts.
(d) Decision tables.
(e) System structure charts.
(f) Coding system.
(g) Auditing procedures.

10. Input specification.

(a) Name of system.
(b) Name of document.
(c) Source and method of origination.
(d) Details of data elements.
(e) Frequency of preparation.
(f) Volume.
(g) Draft layout of document.
(h) Screen layouts.

11. Output specification.

(a) Name of system.
(b) Name of report.
(c) Number of print lines.

(d) Maximum size of fields.

(e) Destination of report.

(f) Draft layout of report.

(g) Screen layouts.

12. File specification.

(a) Name of system.

(b) Filename.

(c) File medium: tape reel, cassette, disc, floppy, fixed or exchangeable.

(d) File labels.

(e) Size of records.

(f) Record types.

(g) Number of reels/discs.

(h) Block size.

(i) Field names.

(j) File security, privacy and confidentiality; use of passwords.

13. System testing and changeover.

(a) Test programs with test data.

(b) Testing procedures: dry runs (desk checking).

(c) Pre-calculated results for comparison with results obtained from testing.

(d) Procedure for system modifications.

(e) Method of changeover: direct, parallel running or pilot.

(f) Changeover timing.

(*See* 15:7 (*p*)).

14. Equipment.

(a) Type of computer.

(b) Peripherals.

(c) Run timing.

(d) Computer utilisation.

(e) Terminal utilisation.

(f) Frequency of batch processing if relevant.

System modification requests

15. Pre-installation modifications. User department personnel when participating in the development of a computer-based system may request a modification to the potential design of the system for a number of reasons. The design may, for instance, create a number of previously unforeseen problems or fail to resolve existing ones. This situation may be discovered during prototyping, i.e. when running a model of the system in order to assess if it will achieve stipulated objectives. Such requests can be accepted after discussions have taken place between management, operating department (user) personnel and systems staff. This will necessitate a modification to the relevant systems documentation to ensure it accords to the system eventually implemented. A record of the modification should be promulgated, i.e. committed to a formal record indicating:

(*a*) authority for the request;
(*b*) date of request;
(*c*) system or sub-system in question;
(*d*) terms of reference indicating the reason for the request;
(*e*) agreed course of action.

It may be necessary to submit details of the modification to the audit department so that they can assess the adequacy, or otherwise, of the checks and controls incorporated, if relevant, and that it accords with accepted standards, principles and practice.

16. Post-implementation modifications. Post-implementation requests for modifications can be a more serious matter because it not only requires amendments to the design of the system but programs or parts of programs will need recoding, recompiling and retesting. This can be very costly, time-consuming and disruptive. Inferior system design should be avoided at all costs which is why defined checkpoints should be incorporated at various stages of development. A system will need updating due to technological and economic developments and the passage of time. Such modifications must be put on record in the manner outlined above. It is also necessary to maintain control of the implementation of the modification to ensure no unnecessary delay.

Benchmark tests

17. Benchmark tests defined. Benchmark tests are used to assess the performance of different computer systems for the selection of the system which best fits the requirements of the business's data processing commitment. The tests are applied to representative data and processing functions such as reading and writing records, sorting operations and multiplication, etc. The actual times obtained can be compared with manufacturers' published performance data for evaluating the various computer systems under consideration. Tests are conducted by benchmark programs which also provide valuable information in respect of the amount of internal storage used during processing.

18. Advantages of benchmark tests. These are summarised below:

(a) assists in selecting the most suitable computer system for businesses' data processing requirements;

(b) performance data is known in advance which assists in formulating job schedules (see 2:**44**).

Systems implementation, monitoring and maintenance

19. Systems implementation. Before a new computer system is implemented it may be necessary to conduct 'pilot' runs with test data to ensure that the system achieves its defined purpose and objectives. Programs must of necessity be subjected to trial runs with test data, consisting of both valid and invalid data for the purpose of ensuring that the program can contend with all possible eventualities. Corrections are then made either to the programs or to the system, which are then subjected to further trials. When the situation appears to be satisfactory 'parallel' running of the new system and the existing system can commence. The results produced by both systems can then be compared and any notable differences investigated and corrected. This is a 'fail-safe' procedure as it would have drastic consequences on the business if the old system was dispensed with before the new system had proved to be satisfactory. It is not unknown for 'bugs' to appear after parallel running has been dispensed with even after detailed trials have been conducted.

20. Monitoring performance. Computer systems must be monitored to detect any deviations from planned results and performance, so that suitable amendments can be effected and staff subjected to further training if necessary.

21. System maintenance. The term updating is sometimes referred to as maintenance in the context of ensuring that a system meets current requirements. Systems must be adjusted for the needs of change either for fundamental reasons, e.g. the introduction of VAT or for systems development in respect of integration or the introduction of on-line processing. When packages are used, amendments to programs may need to be effected perhaps for more efficient running of the relevant programs. This subject is more fully discussed in Volume 2.

Progress test 16

1. Indicate the objectives of systems design and the essential requirements for the effective design of systems. (**1, 2**)

2. Prepare a checklist for the guidance of systems analysts when designing forms for use in computer systems. (**3**) (*ACCA*)

3. Specify and describe briefly the contents of a system specification. (**5–14**)

4. Outline a procedure for dealing with requests for system modifications. (**15, 16**)

5. Indicate the nature and purpose of benchmark tests. (**17, 18**)

6. Outline the activities concerned with systems implementation, monitoring and maintenance. (**19–21**)

17
Flowcharting computer applications

Flowcharting techniques

1. Flowcharting. A technique adopted by system designers for representing the features and characteristics of a system diagrammatically to assist in the development of effective systems.

2. Flowchart symbols. A number of standard symbols are used in the construction of flowcharts. The symbols for the preparation of runcharts represent various types of hardware device and/or processing activity including input devices/type of input; action box specifying the nature of the computer activity; storage devices using disc and/or magnetic tape symbols which also indicate the nature of the files used in each run. (*See* Figs. 17.1 and 17.2.)

3. Block diagram. A block diagram, sometimes referred to as a 'system outline' or 'system function' diagram, is a low-level flowchart which portrays the whole of a system in simple terms. It indicates the inputs, files, processing and outputs independent of operation details. An example is provided in Fig. 17.3.

4. System flowchart. A pictorial or diagrammatic representation of a system prepared on the basis of flowchart symbols. The term is used in its widest sense to describe any type of diagram showing the functions, data flows and the sequence of events or activities in a

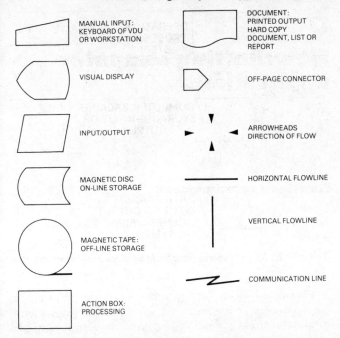

MANUAL INPUT:
KEYBOARD OF VDU
OR WORKSTATION

DOCUMENT:
PRINTED OUTPUT
HARD COPY
DOCUMENT, LIST OR
REPORT

VISUAL DISPLAY

OFF-PAGE CONNECTOR

INPUT/OUTPUT

ARROWHEADS
DIRECTION OF FLOW

MAGNETIC DISC
ON-LINE STORAGE

HORIZONTAL FLOWLINE

MAGNETIC TAPE:
OFF-LINE STORAGE

VERTICAL FLOWLINE

COMMUNICATION LINE

ACTION BOX:
PROCESSING

Figure 17.1 *Standard flowchart symbols for the construction of system
flowcharts and runcharts.*

system. Refer to Fig. 17.4. The chart portrays a columnar analysis
of the departments/functions concerned with a system indicating
the flow of documents into and out of the system together with an
indication of the processes performed on the inputs to produce the
outputs.

5. **Computer runchart.** Computer runcharts are a specific type of
flowchart for portraying the different elements of a system including
system inputs, processing operations and outputs from each run. A
runchart provides useful information to a computer operator as it
conveys the nature of the hardware devices required for each run by
means of appropriate symbols. Each run is shown separately with a
brief narrative specifying the activities performed and its relationship with other runs.

OPERATION
(PROCESSING
STEP)

COMPUTER BACKING
STORAGE – INPUT OR
OUTPUT

DATA TRANSFERS–
INPUT OR OUTPUT
(GENERALISED
SYMBOL)

Figure 17.2 *NCC flowchart symbols for the construction of computer run charts.*

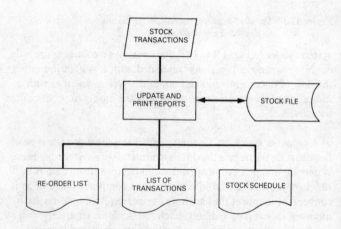

Figure 17.3 *Block diagram: stock control.*

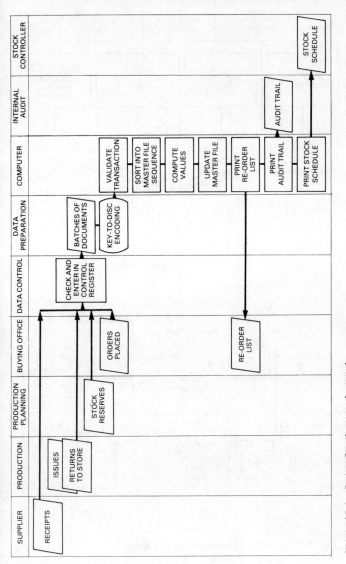

Figure 17.4 System flowchart: stock control.

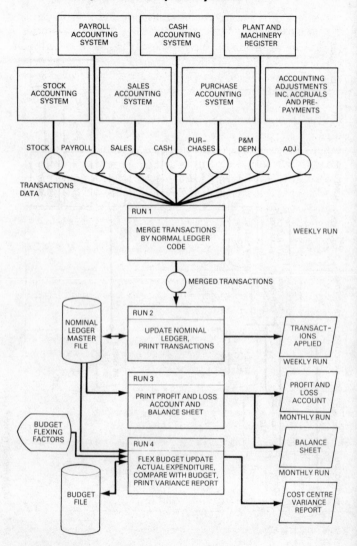

Figure 17.5 *Integrated nominal ledger flowchart.*

Figure 17.7 is constructed vertically progressing through the various tasks until the job is completed. Figure 17.6 is constructed on the basis of a columnar analysis showing inputs on the left and outputs on the right-hand side of the chart. Processes are shown by an action box and the movement of data in and out of files is shown under the 'master file' column heading.

6. Data flow diagram. Data flows are portrayed on this type of diagram pinpointing data origination points and destinations. Entities which send or receive messages from the system are diagrammatically represented by a 'terminal' symbol; activities or processes which alter the data structure are represented by an 'action box'; data storage is represented by the 'on-line storage' symbol as shown in Fig. 17.8. Each symbol is allocated a name which is used for cross reference to the system documentation.

7. System structure chart. This type of chart is primarily concerned with logical relationships rather than procedural details. They may be prepared on a modular basis as shown in the example contained in Fig. 17.9 which outlines the basic system structure in respect of printing a re-order list.

8. Computer procedure flowchart. This type of chart is mentioned so that its purpose can be indicated and how it differs from other types of chart. It is also known as a program flowchart whose function is to specify the processing steps required to be performed by a computer to accomplish a desired result. Program coding is done using the flowchart as a guide for ensuring that the logic of the problem is correctly coded. The flowchart specifies the setting and testing of counters, input routines, processing steps to be performed including computations and comparisons and the outputs to be produced (*see* Figs. 9.1 and 9.2). Refer also to 18:**6**.

Runs and routines

9. Computer run. A run is a unit of processing consisting of a number of operations applied to each transaction item within a batch. Each item is processed in accordance with a program which loops back to the next item after completing the processing on the

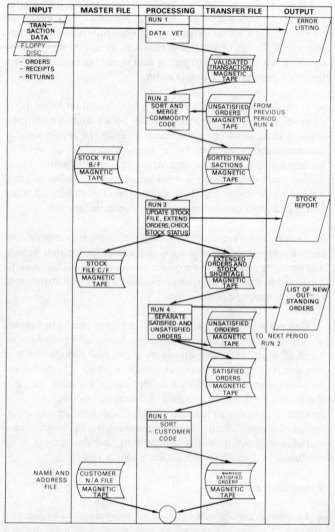

Figure 17.6 *Computer runchart—integrated stock control, sales invoicing and sales ledger system (using NCC symbols).*

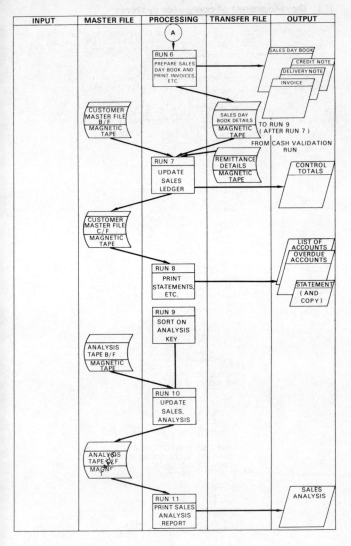

Figure 17.6 *(Contd.)*

NOTE: *the system illustrated assumes that complete processing is carried out once a month. In practice, certain parts of the processing may be performed daily, weekly or monthly.*

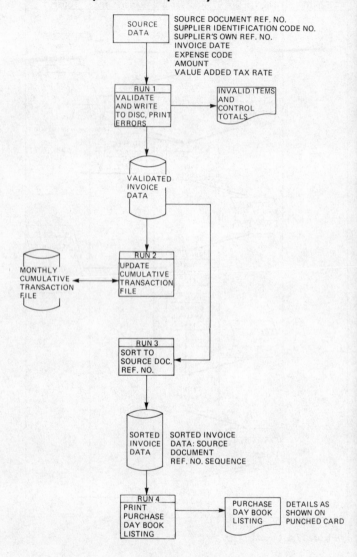

Figure 17.7   (a) Runchart: purchase accounting—daily routine.

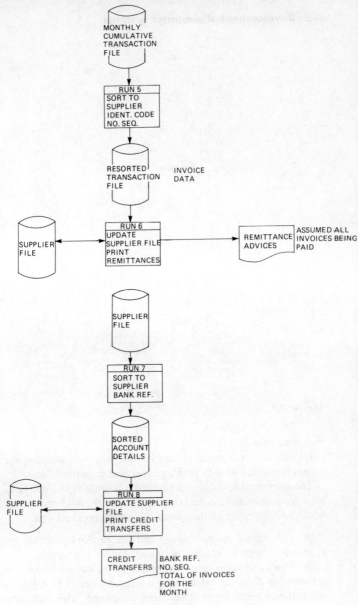

Figure 17.7 (b) *Runchart—monthly routine.*

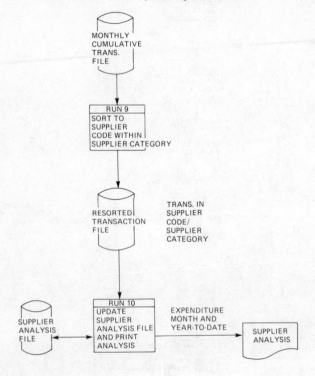

Figure 17.7 (b) (Contd.)

preceding item.

It is normal for each run to have its own program consisting of a series of instructions to be performed on each transaction item.

The number of operations performed in a single run should be as high as possible, and it is necessary to consider the following factors which have a bearing on the constituent elements of each run.

(a) The *size of internal storage* and the capacity available for storing the program, which may consist of many instructions.

(b) The *feasibility of segmenting programs* and storing the various segments in direct access backing storage devices to be called in when the previous segment has been completed. This technique

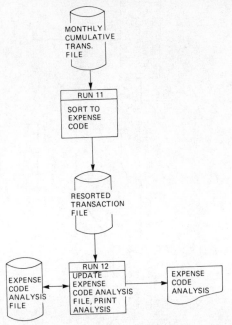

Figure 17.7 (*c*) *Runchart—computerised purchase accounting system.*

overcomes the non-availability of internal storage for storing the whole program.

(*c*) The *number of devices* (such as magnetic tape units or printers) required in a run should be no more than those which comprise the computer installation.

(*d*) The *complexity of the run* in respect of the number of different activities to be performed (such as calculating, printing and updating) within the run.

(*e*) The ability of the run to deal with *exceptions and errors* within the data being processed.

10. Processing routine. A routine may form all or part of an application consisting of a number of computer runs usually interconnected by the output from a preceding run forming the input to the succeeding run. For example, the output from a wages calculation

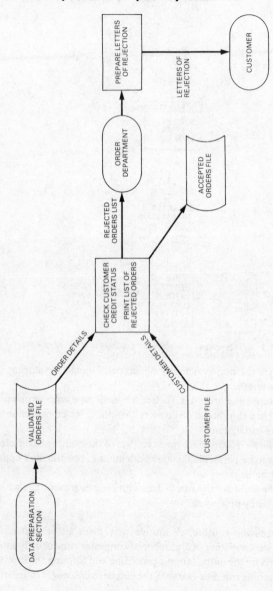

Figure 17.8 *Data flow diagram.*

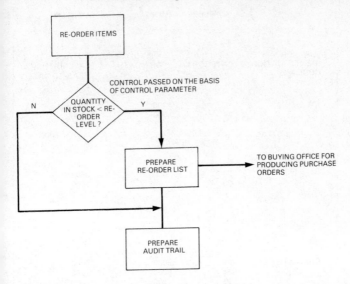

Figure 17.9 *System structure chart: print re-order list.*

routine includes the updating of the payroll master file which forms the input to the next run for printing payslips and pay envelopes.

Some routines consist of combinations of on-line and batch operations whereby data to be processed is input directly by the keyboard of a VDU. The data is validated by reference to specific master files before being stored on a work file ready for processing in batch mode.

Each stage of processing is controlled by a VDU operator who loads the appropriate program for performing relevant operations such as sorting, printing and updating.

In addition, specific segments or sections of a system have different processing frequencies, some segments being performed daily, weekly or monthly.

In other instances, routines are processed on an interactive transaction basis, dealing with each transaction individually through all relevant processing stages before dealing with the next transaction.

SUPPLIER ANALYSIS   MONTH ....

SUPPLIER IDENTIFICATION CODE NO.	SUPPLIER CATEGORY	EXPENDITURE FOR MONTH £		TOTAL EXPENDITURE YEAR TO DATE £	
123	10	100		1000	
	20	300		4000	
TOTAL			400		5000
125	10	200		1200	
	20	400		3600	
	30	—		1000	
TOTAL			600		5800
GRAND TOTAL	10	5000		10000	
	20	6000		12000	
	30	1200		3000	
	40	800		5000	
			13000		30000

Figure 17.10 *Suggested layout for monthly supplies analysis printout.*

Computer applications

11. Types of applications. There are many other computer applications, depending upon the nature of the business, for example, insurance, banking, tour operation, building societies, supermarkets, warehouses and so on. It is interesting to note that many organisations of a seemingly different nature have similar systems relating to payroll, purchasing, sales and stock control, etc.

It is also of interest to appreciate that seemingly different systems in different types of organisation have a great deal in common, for example: controlling the booking of rooms in a hotel chain, controlling the reservation of seats on aircraft, controlling banking transactions and the movement of commodities in a warehouse: all have one thing in common—the control of stocks of one type or another, i.e. rooms, seats, money and commodities.

12. Integrated nominal ledger application. Figure 17.5 illustrates the computer runs for an integrated nominal ledger system which may be performed by a nominal ledger package providing for the production of profit and loss statements, balance sheet and variance reports. The latter is achieved by incorporating budgetary control and budget flexing. Other forms of nominal ledger applications may not be so comprehensive and incorporate only sales and purchase transactions. Yet other applications may not produce profit and loss statements or balance sheets but restrict their output to accounts schedules or trial balance for the preparation of final accounts and balance sheets by normal accounting methods.

Run 1. Input is derived from data produced by the separate computer applications in respect of stocks, payroll, sales, purchases, plant and machinery including depreciations, accruals and pre-payments, accounting adjustments and cash. The data on the transaction files is deemed to have been validated in the relevant runs of the appropriate applications. The run is concerned with consolidating all nominal ledger data on relevant nominal ledger codes.

Run 2. The input to this run is the consolidated file from run one. This run is for the purpose of updating the nominal ledger master file and printing out a list of transactions applied for the purpose of providing an audit trail. The master file is stored on disc to facilitate direct access to relevant nominal ledger records.

Run 3. At the end of the month the nominal ledger master file is used for printing a profit and loss account and balance sheet.

Run 4. The nominal ledger master file records are input together with a budget file and budget flexing factors. The budget file is updated with actual expenditure for the period to obtain the cumulative expenditure to date for comparison with budgeted expenditure. This provides the basis for printing out a cost centre variance report.

Figure 17.6 outlines the structure of an integrated stock control, invoicing and sales ledger system.

CIMA questions and solutions

13. November 1979

G Manufacturing Limited has decided to computerise its purchase accounting system. It is expected that extensive expenditure analysis will ultimately be included but initially this aspect of the system will be restricted.

The computer configuration available comprises a medium sized central processor with punched card reader, line printer and two exchangeable disc drive units (each of 30 million characters). (Students should note that punched cards are not now applicable but this does not affect the logical requirements of the question.)

An outline of the new system is as follows:

Source document

A source document will be created clerically from purchase invoices passed for payment. The contents of this document will be

    source document reference number
    supplier identification code number
    supplier's own reference number
    invoice date

expense code   minimum × 1
amount   } occurs { average × 1.2
value added tax rate   maximum × 5

Output

This source data will be processed to produce these outputs.

(*i*) Purchase daybook, being a daily listing of all prime data input, in source document reference number sequence.

(*ii*) Remittance advices, containing supplier name and address and full details of invoices being paid in supplier identification code number sequence.

(*iii*) Credit transfers, containing payer and payee bank details and amount, in supplier bank reference number sequence.

(*iv*) Supplier analysis giving total expenditure for this month and this year to date per supplier, in supplier identification code number sequence within supplier category (note: suppliers are categorised according to the type of goods supplied, e.g. raw metal, stationery, lubricating oils).

(*v*) Expense code analysis giving total expenditure per each expense code.

It will be noted that (*i*) above will be produced daily, while (*ii*), (*iii*), (*iv*) and (*v*) will be produced at the month end.

Predicted volumes

Purchase invoices per day	200
Suppliers	2000
Expense codes	70

Any facts or figures not given may be assumed provided each assumption is clearly stated.

You are required to submit the following:

(*a*) computer system run flowchart(s) with brief narrative for the purchase accounting/expenditure analysis system;

(*b*) a description of the main files required;

(*c*) a suggested lay-out for print-out (*iv*) above, the monthly supplier analysis.

SOLUTION

Part (*a*). This part of the question required a runchart to be submitted for the system outlined. The runchart must obviously be based on the computer configuration available, which includes a card reader. This intimates that source data is to be punched into cards and subjected to batch processing operations. A runchart should be prepared (*see* Fig. 17.7).

Part (*b*). A description of the main files required is outlined below:

Supplier file. This will contain details as follows.

(*a*) Supplier identification code number.

(*b*) Name and address.

(*c*) Payee bank details.

(*d*) Invoice date and amount (each invoice).

Monthly cumulative transactions file. The details contained in this file are summarised below.

(a) Source document reference number.
(b) Supplier identification code number.
(c) Supplier reference number.
(d) Invoice date.
(e) Expense code.
(f) Amount.
(g) Value added tax rate.

Expense code analysis file. The details in this file are as follows.

(a) Expense code.
(b) Total expenditure for each expense code.

Supplier analysis file.

(a) Supplier identification code number.
(b) Supplier category.
(c) Total expenditure, for the month.
(d) Total expenditure, year to date.

Part (c). See Fig. 17.10.

Progress test 17

1. Define the nature and purpose of flowcharting. (**1, 2**)
2. Define and distinguish between the following charts and dia-grams: (a) block diagram; (b) system flowchart; (c) computer run-chart; (d) data flow diagram; (e) system structure chart. (**3–7**)
3. Define the nature of processing runs and routines. (**9, 10**)
4. Specify the nature of computer applications. (**11**)
5. Outline the characteristics of an integrated nominal ledger application. (**12**)
6. CIMA Question. (**13**)

18

Computer programming: principles and concepts

Program specification and documentation

1. **Designer–programmer interface.** A program specification is a formal directive from the system designer to the programmer specifying the requirements of the program to achieve the objectives of the system. The specification is an integral element of overall system documentation and provides an interface between the two stages of system development.

It specifies the name of the program for reference and retrieval purposes as well as the logical requirements of the system, i.e. what is to be achieved and the physical factors relating to how it is to be achieved. The specification must state who is responsible for the design of the system and the programmer who wrote the programs. It must indicate the data to be input for processing, the nature of the processing operations and the type of output required. The processing techniques to be applied such as batch, on-line, distributed (local area networks), centralised or transaction processing also require to be specified. The nature of the file media must also be specified, i.e. which files are to be on magnetic tape and which are to be on disc.

2. **Standards and guidelines.** The specification should also indicate that programming methodology and documentation should accord to programming standards. Refer to standards and documentation. In addition the specification should incorporate guidelines relating to priority interrupts, procedures for dealing with abnormal situations such as error conditions and when to abort

a program; error detection and correction procedures; utility programs to be employed; library subroutines to be incorporated and the use to be made of open and closed subroutines; dump and restart procedures, etc. It may also be appropriate to indicate the possibility of needing to apply program overlay techniques and backup requirements.

3. Program documentation. After programs have been prepared all the relevant documentation is held in the systems folder or manual which is referred to as a 'systems specification' because it contains all the details of the relevant system. The documentation includes low-level flowcharts indicating the broad characteristics of the system; decision tables outlining the logic of the system regarding the nature of the conditions to be provided for and the actions required to deal with them when they arise; program coding sheets of the source program prepared by the programmer together with the subsequent source program listing obtained from the compilation (or assembly) run; operating instructions for running the program specifying breakpoints in the program and stationery changeover needs, etc. In addition, the documentation contains input, output and file formats; data structure charts; charts consisting of sections relating to input, processing and output. The input and output sections are concerned with input, output and files whereas the processing section describes the processes necessary to convert inputs to outputs; program network diagrams are also included which illustrate interactions between data and the various processing operations.

4. Programming standards. If programs are produced within the framework of data processing standards this will aid the continuity of program development in the event of programmers leaving the company. New programmers will be in a position to assess the documentation as far as it has been developed and continue from that point on the basis of laid down standards relating to the construction of flowcharts, decision tables and coding, etc. Accordingly, they will attain an acceptable level of productivity and expertise much sooner than otherwise would be possible.

Standards have been developed by the National Computing Centre (NCC); the British Standards Institution (BSI); IBM and other major computer manufacturers; the International Organisation for Standardisation (ISO), the American National Standards Institute, Inc. (ANSI) and the European Computer Manufacturers' Association (ECMA). The BSI represent the UK in international organisations concerned with the preparation of international standards. Standards have been established for flowchart symbols and computer languages. The standards relate to file organisation methods, checkpoint/restart routines, job control programs, routines for label writing and checking on file media. Standardisation also includes the use of standard coding sheets and modular programming (*see* **16**).

Nature of computer programming

5. **Computer instructions.** Each operation performed by a computer (on transaction data relating to a specific application) is in accordance with a pre-defined instruction.

Each instruction defines a basic operation to be performed, identifies the address of the data to be processed, the location of the data affected by the operation and the input or output device to be used. The complete set of instructions necessary to process a job is known as a 'program'.

Instructions are of five basic types as follows.

(*a*) *Arithmetic/logic.* Add, subtract, multiply, divide, shift, round-off, collate and compare, etc.

(*b*) *Data transfer.* Read from input, read to output, read a character, read a word, read a block of data, print a line, transfer data to different locations in the memory, etc.

(*c*) *Conditional branch or jump.* The presence of specific conditions in the data being processed is established by a comparison of data factors or the testing of a counter which causes the computer to branch or jump to the next appropriate instruction (*see* Fig. 19.2).

(*d*) *Unconditional branch or jump and loop.* When it is necessary to execute an instruction which is not the next in sequence in the internal memory, this is achieved by an instruction known as an unconditional branch or jump. This provides the means of creating a loop in the program for executing a common sequence of instructions repeatedly to various units of data. A loop is terminated by a conditional branch after effecting a test (*see* Fig. 19.2).

(*e*) *Counter*. A counter is a memory location (unit of storage) used for the purpose of storing a control parameter for automatically controlling a processing sequence. A counter may be set with a specific number which is decremented by '1' after each event being controlled. The counter may then be tested to detect whether it reads '0', for instance. If a '0' is detected then a conditional branch is executed to a specific set of instructions. If the counter does not read '0' then a conditional branch is executed to a different set of instructions, perhaps to execute a further loop in the program (*see* Fig. 19.2).

6. Main stages of program preparation. A lot depends on the nature of the processing technique to be applied and the nature of the computer configuration to be used, as a different approach will be necessary for programming a system to run on a batch processing configuration from one to run on an interactive basis on a microcomputer. The stages outlined below apply in general.

(*a*) Define the nature of the problem by studying the system specification which contains details of the program specification.

(*b*) Decide on the type of language to use; assembly code (low-level language) or high-level language, which in the case of a mainframe computer may be COBOL, and in the case of a microcomputer BASIC.

(*c*) Determine sub-routine requirements, print format and layout, whether data is to be input via the keyboard of the console or microcomputer or within the program and the checks and controls to be incorporated etc.

(*d*) Prepare decision tables and program flowcharts as appropriate to the complexity of the problem.

(*e*) Determine programming strategy relating to the approach to developing programs, whether to adopt monolithic, modular or structured programming (*see* **15–17**).

(*f*) Specify breakpoints (*see* **7**).

(*g*) Code each statement (instruction) of the program in the relevant programming language. This stage produces the SOURCE program.

(*h*) If a microcomputer is being programmed the statements may be input via the keyboard. They will then be interpreted directly into machine code. For a batch processing configuration the 'source' program together with the assembler or compiler are then input to the processor for conversion into a machine code *object* program.

The process of assembling or compiling records the 'object' program on either magnetic tape or disc and prints out details of the source program including errors at the same time—this is known as a program listing. The programmer checks the list for errors and corrects them accordingly.

(*i*) The program is tested using test data as defined in the program specification. Any errors are noted and corrected.

(*j*) The program is stored on a suitable backing storage media for future use. For a mainframe computer this would be either magnetic disc or tape, for a microcomputer either floppy or Winchester disc or cassette tape.

7. Breakpoint. A programmer must determine the point in a program where it is necessary to insert a breakpoint when applicable. This is the point where a program is interrupted for a specific reason, perhaps for the operator to input a parameter or to change the type of stationery on the printer. For interactive processing by microcomputer it may be defined as the point in the program where a message is displayed on the screen asking the user to enter specific data to allow processing to continue.

Aids to programming: program generators

General features

The traditional method of preparing programs, first by the preparation of detailed program flowcharts from which programs are written using a specific programming language, is being superseded to some extent by program development software which either uses a 4th generation language (4GL); menus and prompts for guiding the user through all the stages of development; or structured programming techniques using interactive graphics. Fourth generation languages use a natural near English language several levels higher than a high-level programming language which makes it more understandable by non-computer specialists for developing their own application programs.

The traditional systems life cycle approach will be affected by this change of methodology as will the use of program flowcharting techniques which are likely to be replaced by structured programming techniques which develop structure diagrams automatically. See below.

System C

Program generators are software packages, like those marketed by System C Limited. The package may be used to develop traditional business applications such as payroll, accounts, invoicing and stock control. It can also be applied to the development of programs for applications where ready-made programs are unavailable. This type of package can also be usefully employed by experienced programmers as the Sycero programs are structured and documented in a manner which facilitates linking with other programs. By means of prompts and menus new records or files can be incorporated.

Building a program in 7 steps

Using Sycero, as an example of program builders or generators, the process of program building is very straightforward and can be accomplished in 7 steps.

(*a*) *Plan the system.* Define the elements of the system you want to create, the types of data to be input, the screen layouts for required displays and how many files are needed. Determine how the program is to handle the information.

(*b*) *Specify the system.* With the micro running proceed to select items from the main menu. By following the prompts proceed to define the types of files required and what items of information they will contain. The menu offers the following options:

    (*i*) system configuration;
   (*ii*) initialisation;
  (*iii*) system—file—field definition;
  (*iv*) screen definition;
   (*v*) screen processing;
  (*vi*) report definition;
 (*vii*) report processing;
(*viii*) program definition;
  (*ix*) generate a program;
   (*x*) create a 'live' data file;

    (*xi*) run a generated program;

    (*xii*) utilities;

    (*xiii*) end session.

(*c*) *Draw the screens*. Having specified where and how data is to be stored it is necessary to specify how the data is to be entered and displayed on the computer screen. On each screen type are descriptions of the items to be entered and the exact position on the screen where the item is to be displayed. Graphics facilities can be used to sketch in lines and boxes giving the system a professional finish.

(*d*) *Check the data*. It is prudent to incorporate a validation/verification procedure to detect when data has been entered incorrectly. Prompts indicate what needs to be input at any point such as stock number and also advises on the range of figures acceptable. Error messages can be displayed.

(*e*) *Define the program*. Define the program to operate on the data. There are certain standard operations which will almost always need to be carried out. Each system will require a file maintenance program to enter, amend and delete information. An enquiry program allows instant on-screen access to all data in any chosen form. Posting programs handle the logic of recording all transactions against a single item and updating files.

(*f*) *Produce the printout*. The system is now built and it is necessary to specify the printed output requirements—the report definition, i.e. the formatting. The system provides facilities for defining where on a printed page columns are to appear, how they look, what their headers are like and so on. Column totals can be generated, each page can be numbered and printouts can be stamped with the date and time.

(*g*) *Generate*. The Sycero software requires to know the name of the program. It then translates the data defined and specified into a computer program. The code produced is very lucid and structured.

Michael Jackson structured programming

Software known as Program Development Facility (PDF) provides for program development using structured programming methodology. It dispenses with the traditional program methodology of preparing detailed program flowcharts followed by program coding.

The PDF technique uses interactive graphics to develop structure diagrams known as 'hierarchy' charts which replace traditional program flowcharts. The structure diagrams are stored on disc and facilities are provided to modify them as necessary. The screen may be considered to be a window through which a diagram is viewed. A simple command generates pseudo-code (JSP structure text) and source code ready for compilation or preprocessing. Refer to program flowcharts (19:1–5) and system life cycle (15:7).

Low-level languages

8. Low-level language—machine code. At one time, in the early days of computers, all computer programs were written in machine code, i.e. an instruction (operation) code specific to a particular manufacturer's computer. Programs of instructions had to be written in a form that the computer could interpret and execute and accordingly this type of programming was classified as 'machine-oriented' as the instructions were in a form required by the computer but not in a form to assist the programmer to solve the problems under consideration, i.e. not 'problem-oriented'.

As computers operate by pulses of electricity representing data in binary code the instructions were written as a series of 0s and 1s in accordance with the 'bit' pattern of the instruction to be performed, e.g.

00101	00110	10100	00100	(binary)
5	6	20	4	(decimal)

The programmer was required to have a detailed knowledge of the computer with regard to core storage locations, registers and the function (operation) code, etc. He had to keep track of all core storage locations for data input, working areas, output assembly and the locations occupied by the program. However, the programmer's task is now made easier as these functions are performed automatically by software in the form of translation programs known as 'assemblers and compilers'.

As program instructions were written as a series of 0s and 1s far removed from basic English, it was classified as low-level language programming. However, not all computers used the same function or operation code, or indeed the same instruction format, which meant that a programmer probably had to learn a different function code and the operating details of another type of computer if he changed his job.

9. Low-level language—assembly code. To overcome these difficulties and to avoid the laborious task of writing programs in machine code, each computer manufacturer devised his own assembly code or assembly language. The advantage of an assembly language is that it enables a program to be written much more easily, at the same time allowing the same degree of flexibility that was available when writing programs in machine code. This means that programs can be prepared much more quickly than is possible with machine code, without the sacrifice of machine-running time when processing a job, which is not so with the high-level languages to be discussed later.

An assembly language enables program instructions to be written in mnemonic or symbolic code, that is in pseudo-code (a language which is not machine code). Programs written in this type of language are known as 'source' programs and they have to be translated into a machine code program by a programming aid (software) known as an 'assembler'. After assembling, the object program is input each time the job to which it relates is to be processed. The process of writing instructions in mnemonic or symbolic code is known as 'autocoding'.

Instead of writing 5 for 'add' and possibly 10 for 'compare', the programmer writes 'ADD' and 'COM' in accordance with the symbolic code for a particular computer. Also, instead of specifying actual storage addresses (internal memory locations) symbolic addresses are indicated in each instruction, i.e. OLDBAL, which is the symbolic address for 'old balance'.

An instruction in assembly language, for a single-address type computer, would take the form:

LDX   1   OLDBAL

This instruction means 'load the item of data named "OLDBAL" to accumulator 1'. The assembler automatically assigns a core store location to OLDBAL, which is indicated in the object program.

Assembly languages are still rather complex, and generally the number of instructions which have to be written are still the same as for machine code programming unless 'macro-coding' is used. Such a language is also biased towards the machine rather than the problem.

High-level languages

10. Portability of languages. Digital Research Inc. develop languages which allow the user to design applications programs, which can then be applied to various processors and operating systems allowing full portability from 8-bit to 16-bit or 32-bit environments: from microcomputer to mini or mainframe. Programming productivity has been enhanced by Digital Research as they provide the most important commercial programming languages in sophisticated compiler implementations which are portable. Some aspects of these programs are outlined in the following text.

11. High-level language defined. A high-level language is any problem-orientated programmer's language which allows statements to be written in a form with which the user is conversant, such as the use of mathematical equations for a mathematician and plain English-style statements for business applications. This is as distinct from machine-orientated languages which relate to a specific machine rather than the type of problem to be solved. Examples of high-level languages are outlined below.

(a) *Algol*. Algol is an acronym for *ALGO*rithmic *L*anguage which is a high-level problem oriented language for mathematical and scientific applications using algorithms. The language defines algorithms as a series of statements and declarations in the form of algebraic formulae and English words. Each operation is represented as a statement and each unit of data is known as a variable each of which is assigned a name by the programmer. An instruction or assignment statement of the form—$b: = a + c + 5.0$; effectively adds 5.0 to the numbers in the locations a and c and places the answer in location b. The statement consists of the name of a variable followed by: =, followed by any arithmetic expression whose answer is put into the left hand side variable.

(b) BASIC. A programming language widely used for time sharing applications and for programming mini- and microcomputers. It is a high-level language relatively simple to learn by non-computer specialists. The term BASIC is an acronym for *B*eginners *A*ll purpose *S*ymbolic *I*nstruction *C*ode. A simple program for adding two numbers and displaying the result on the screen of a terminal (such as a VDU) or microcomputer is outlined below:

```
10   INPUT A
20   INPUT B
30   C = A + B
40   PRINT C
50   END
```

For further details of BASIC refer to the M&E Handbook *Microcomputing* by the same author.

(*c*) CBASIC *Compiler*. This is the Digital Research Inc. industry standard commercial dialect of BASIC suitable for the business environment. CBASIC Compiler is a direct enhancement of CBASIC that is five to ten times faster in execution than most versions of BASIC. It is possible to write, test and combine separate modules for creating complete programs applying the modular, top-down approach (*see* **16, 21**). It includes facilities for graphics, expanded file processing techniques, supports multi-user operating systems and is compatible with CP/M Graphics.

(*d*) *Other versions of* BASIC. Microsoft BASIC which is very widely used; XBASIC which is a British engineering and mathematic orientated version with matrix-handling and XTal BASIC another British version which has a choice of screen or line-based editors.

(*e*) COBOL. This is an acronym for *CO*mmon *B*usiness *O*riented *L*anguage. It is a high-level programming language designed to assist the task of programmers by enabling them to write programs in a more simple form than is possible with assembly code. The language is largely used for mainframe computer applications. It is problem-oriented rather than machine-oriented as it is designed to assist the solving of business problems for such applications as stock control, payroll, sales and purchase ledger accounting.

COBOL consists of four divisions, these are:

- (*i*) identification division;
- (*ii*) environment division;
- (*iii*) data division;
- (*iv*) procedure division.

(*f*) CIS COBOL. This version of the language is that of Micro Focus Ltd. The CIS stands for *C*ompact, *I*nteractive and *S*tandard. It is a complete system for compiling, testing, debugging and executing standard COBOL programs. It has become the most widely favoured version of the ANSI 1974 COBOL language. It can be used for running existing mainframe and minicomputer programs on a microcomputer. A micro can also be used to develop COBOL software for larger computers.

(*g*) *Level II* COBOL. This version of the language is also attributable to Micro Focus Ltd. It provides the full facilities of mainframe COBOL on 8-bit or 16-bit microcomputers allowing the user to develop mainframe programs with the interactive facilities of a microcomputer. It allows portability of software between mainframe and microcomputers. Employs dynamic paging to allow implementation of programs greater than 64K on 8-bit microcomputers. Provides for interactive screen handling.

(*h*) *Pascal*. This is a high-level programming language which is highly structured, enabling programs to be written more efficiently without the problems of writing long programs using monolithic structure (*see* 15).

It executes programs quickly, much faster than interpretative languages like BASIC, but it is more complex and time consuming to learn initially. When preparing a program Pascal words are typed in boldface such as PROCEDURE, BEGIN, END, PROGRAM and WRITE. Modules consist of separate procedures each of which is an element of the main program. The main program 'calls' the procedures in the order they are to be executed.

(*i*) *Pascal/MT* +. This is a version of Pascal by Digital Research Inc. It provides speed and accuracy for developing microcomputer programs. It is a direct-compiling dialect of the full ISO standard Pascal—greatly enhanced and extended to maximise the inherent versatility and portability of the language. Pascal/MT + Native code compiler executes much faster than traditional p-code Pascal compilers. The programming system includes a compiler, a linker, run-time support library, disassembler and a symbolic program debugger. It is compatible with CP/M Graphics.

(*j*) *PL/1*. A powerful all-purpose language which rivals Fortran for scientific applications and COBOL for commercial applications. Digital Research Inc. have developed a version of the language for implementation on microcomputers. It is based on the ANSI Standard Subset G. It is easily transported from micro to mini to mainframe or from mainframe to mini to micro. The Digital Research Inc. PL/1 program development system includes an optimising native code compiler, an assembler, a linker, library manager, cross-reference generator and a comprehensive library of built-in functions. It supports CP/M Graphics.

(*k*) C. An advanced programming language built for coding power and speed of execution with a minimum of constraints. It allows skilled software developers to take full advantage of the inherent structure of the computer. C is ideal for applications which must achieve a high level of performance and for systems level programming. The Digital Research Inc. C programming development system includes a compiler, linker, run-time library containing a wide range of utilities which handles everything from transcendental functions to input-output.

(*l*) LOGO. A structured programming language which is becoming popular in the field of education as it is designed to allow very young children, in the four or five years' age group, to program a computer. The language was developed at the Massachusetts Institute of Technology in the late 1960s by a team led by Seymour Papert. LOGO takes the form of a 'turtle', i.e. a mechanical device or a triangle of light on the screen of a computer. Both forms provide the means for drawing lines either on a sheet of paper or on the screen (*see* 5:**23, 24**).

(*m*) *Fortran*. An acronym for *FOR*mula *TRAN*slation. It is a high-level language for scientific and mathematical use. The language was introduced by IBM in 1957 but has since developed into different forms. It has been replaced to some extent by BASIC and other high-level languages.

(*n*) *Lisp*. This language is designed to process data in the form of lists which is indicated by the name of the language, viz. *LIS*t *P*rocessing language. It is based on Algol.

(*o*) *Coral*. A high-level programming language for real-time applications developed by the Royal Radar Establishment at Malvern, England.

(*p*) *Forth*. A high-level programming language designed for small computers having the advantage of requiring a small amount of memory and being independent of a specific machine.

Diagnostic aids in a high-level language

12. Debugging aids. Many computers include a debugging aid in the BASIC which traces program statements during execution of the program. It may be used in either direct or indirect mode. Each line number of the program is printed on the screen as it is executed. The numbers appear in square brackets.

13. Typical error messages. In addition, diagnostic error messages are provided which indicate the nature of the program error. Typical error messages include:

NEXT without FOR
A variable in a NEXT statement does not match any executed unmatched FOR statement variable. See example in 11 (*b*).

FOR without NEXT
A FOR statement was met without a matching NEXT. See example in 11 (*b*).

Missing operand
An expression contains an operator with no operand following it. See example in 11 (*b*).

Out of data
A READ statement is performed when there are no DATA statements with unread data remaining in the program.

Return without GOSUB
A RETURN statement not having a previous unmatched GOSUB statement is met.

Undefined line
A nonexistent line is referenced in a GOTO, GOSUB, IF . . . THEN . . . ELSE, or DELETE statement.

Finding a fault in a program
Please note: to develop this fault finding explanation I have outlined below a simple program in order to illustrate what happens when the error tracing routine TRON is used with the Apricot F1 computer.

```
10   TRON
20   K=10
30   FOR J = 1 TO 2
40   L=K+10
50   PRINT J;K;L
60   K=K+10
70   NEXT J
80   END
```

When the program is executed the following appears on the screen:

```
[10][20][30][40][50] 1 10 20
[60][70][40][50] 2 20 30
[60][70][80]
ok
```

Note: The figures to the right of the square brackets are the results obtained from running the program.

If statement 30 is deleted from the program, when the program is executed the following details appear on the screen:

```
[10][20][40][50] 0 10 20
[60][70]
NEXT without FOR in 70
ok
```

If statement 70 is deleted from the program, the following details appear on the screen when the program is run:

```
[10][20][30]
FOR without NEXT in 30
```

If statement 30 is amended to read FOR J = 1 TO when the program is executed the screen displays the following details:

```
[10][20][30]
Missing operand in 30
```

Monolithic, modular and structured programming

14. Choice of language. High-level languages are not so efficient with regard to machine running time as those written in an assembly language. The reason for this is that a language such as COBOL or BASIC produces generalised sets of instructions from high-level statements which are required in more detail at the machine code compilation stage. Assembly codes on the other hand allow the programmer more flexibility in determining the series of instructions to achieve the desired results. It goes without saying that tasks may be processed in a number of ways, some of which are dependent more on the skill of the programmer than the language he is using.

15. Monolothic programming. The National Computing Centre publication *Program Design Methods* states that the term 'monolothic programming' relates to the largely undisciplined and non-formalised approach to the development of computer programs in which the programmer is allowed a completely free rein. Programs produced in this way reflect the programmer's own experience and personal interpretations.

16. Modular programming. This approach to programming adopts the technique of developing suites of related programs. The overall program is divided into modules, each of which is developed separately but on a coordinated basis. This enables the complete suite of programs to be prepared by a team of programmers if appropriate and programs become available more quickly as a result. It is also easier to debug programs and maintain them when they are constructed in this way. Modules include those for housekeeping, input, processing, output and the closing of files.

17. The nature of structured programming. Structured programming requires the development of a program as a series of independent sections designed to perform only one specified task. This enables program errors to be localised in one section only and assists in the maintenance of each section. Each section must have only one entry point and one exit point. There should not be any jumps to statements in other sections as this would violate the requirements of entry points and exits. The use of this form of programming is an attempt at standardising programming methodology. Structured programming includes such facilities as REPEAT . . . UNTIL and WHILE . . . WEND which are used to set up loops and complement the standard FOR . . . NEXT facility.

18. REPEAT–UNTIL. This facility allows repeated execution of a group of statements as a loop. A Boolean expression, C, is evaluated after each execution of the statements to establish whether

the loop should be terminated or repeated. The loop is repeated
until the expression, C, after the UNTIL is true e.g.

```
10   REPEAT
20   A = A + INT(RND(1)*6+1)
30   PRINT A
40   UNTIL A   = 30
50   END
```

The program computes random numbers and adds them together
until the total is 30. In this instance it would not be possible to know
the number of loops required which precludes the use of the FOR/
NEXT loop.

19. WHILE–WEND. A facility which allows a loop to be executed
as long as a logical expression, C, is true. This is the opposite of the
REPEAT–UNTIL facility which continues while the condition is
untrue.

20. IF–THEN ELSE. A statement which provides for branching
to a specified statement if the relation is true ELSE do as directed
otherwise. A simple program will make this clear:

```
10   CLS
20   INPUT A
30   IF A > 10 THEN PRINT "OUTSIDE RANGE OF VALUES" ELSE PRINT
     "NUMBER ACCEPTABLE"
40   FOR I = 1 TO 200:NEXT
50   GOTO 10
```

The program compares the value assigned to variable A to test if it is
greater than 10 and if it is to print a message 'Outside range of
values', ELSE print a message 'Number acceptable' when it is less
than or equal to 10.

Approach to program design

21. Top-down approach to program design. It now tends to be
standard practice to adopt a 'top-down' approach to program design
which requires a specific objective to be defined for a program. This
is then analysed into subsidiary functions in increasing levels of
detail. Each module should ideally consist of 50–100 instructions,
which simplifies the detection of errors and program testing.

22. Functional decomposition. This is a method for segregating a monolithic program into specific modules. The approach is to partition a list of program activities into separate functions on the basis of the frequency of processing, the type of input and output and processing activities.

A basic functional decomposition applicable to many programs would comprise the following elements.

(a) *Program set-up:*
  (i) data input;
  (ii) define constants;
  (iii) define work areas;
  (iv) open files;
  (v) define accumulators;
  (vi) define variables.
(b) *Inner loop:*
  (i) input data;
  (ii) compute;
  (iii) print/display output;
  (iv) update files.
(c) *Program termination:*
  (i) print control totals;
  (ii) close files.

Larger programs would subdivide the inner loop which converts a single level structure into a tree structure or a modular hierarchy.

23. Data-driven design. This is an alternative method for segregating a monolothic program into specific modules. This approach is based on the philosophy that the structure of a program should be determined by the structure of the data which it processes. The approach consists of a number of stages as follows.

(a) *Data stage.* This requires the preparation of a data structure diagram for each set of data to be processed (*see* Figs. 6.11 and 6.12).

(b) *Program stage.* The separate data structure diagrams are combined into a single program structure diagram based on the details indicated above in respect of program set-up, inner loop and program termination.

(c) *Operation stage.* The operations required to produce the output are defined and listed and each operation is structured in the program according to the logical requirements.

Table 18A Major differences between high- and low- level languages

Low-level language	High-level language
(a) Known as 'assembly, symbolic or mnemonic code'—operation codes are defined as mnemonics, e.g. LDA for load accumulator; operands are allocated labels or symbolic addresses, e.g. REC or ISS for receipts and issues.	(a) Uses expressions with which the user is conversant when problem solving without the aid of a computer. Various languages allow the use of normal scientific and mathematical notation in respect of Algol and Fortran, for instance. On the other hand COBOL allows the use of English style statements for business applications. Operation codes are referred to, depending upon the language, as 'keywords' such as LOAD, LIST and PRINT in the case of BASIC. Operands, known as variables in BASIC, are allocated identifying letters and sometimes a number such as A or A1 to represent specific operands. COBOL, as an example, allocates a name to operands such as RECIN for receipts into store and ISSIN for issues from store.
(b) Machine oriented as the language is specific to a particular manufacturer's computer.	(b) Problem oriented as high-level languages are not 'machine specific'.
(c) Object programs are 'assembled' by software known as an 'assembler' (see 20:42–5).	(c) Object programs are 'compiled' by software known as a 'compiler' or firmware known as an 'interpreter' depending upon the type of computer as mainframes normally compile and micros interpret (see 20:46–50).

Table 18A *Continued*

Low-level language	High-level language
(d) The translation from program code to object program in machine code is normally on a one for one basis where one machine code instruction is generated for each assembly code instruction.	(d) Translation from high-level language to object program in machine code is normally on the basis of many for one, i.e. many machine code instructions are generated for each high-level statement.

Table 18B Advantages and disadvantages of high- and low-level languages

Low-level language	High-level language
Advantages	*Disadvantages*
(a) Runs faster because it is machine specific (the features of a particular machine have been taken into account within the structure of the language).	(a) Runs slower due to the generality of the statements and the fact that they are portable between different machines providing a suitable compiler is available. Such languages are machine independent.
(b) Requires fewer instructions to accomplish the same result.	(b) Requires more storage overhead as programs require more instructions, due to their generality, to accomplish the same result.
Disadvantages	*Advantages*
(a) Programs take longer to code because of the more complex nature of the language.	(a) Programs can be written more quickly, in general, as the coding is easier to learn. Applications become operational much sooner.
(b) Lack of portability of programs between computers of different makes.	(b) Portability between computers of different types (*see* Disadvantages (a))
(c) Languages take longer to learn.	(c) Languages easier to learn.

Table 18B *Continued*

Low-level language	High-level language
Disadvantages	*Advantages*
(d) Programmers have to learn new languages when moving to installations using different machines with different low-level languages.	(d) Programmers can move to different installations using high-level languages without having to learn new languages.

Program dumps and restart procedures

24. Program dump. When programs are tested it is usual either to print out sections of the program from memory or to display them on a video screen for the purpose of tracing sequence errors which prevent the execution of the program. Sometimes when editing program errors on the screen of a micro they are not always effected in memory so it is advisable to print out the program or list it on the screen to verify whether the corrections have been implemented.

25. Dump and restart procedures. To avoid the consequences of hardware or software malfunctions a fail-safe procedure is adopted, particularly for lengthy or critical programs which are essential for the control of a real-time system. In such instances it is usual to implement checkpoint/restart routines. These provide for the periodic dumping of the contents of the internal memory which signifies the status of the system at that moment of time. Dumping is usually effected to disc or magnetic tape, thus enabling the system to be restarted from the point of the last dump without having recourse to the beginning of the program (which would be impossible to do in any event when controlling dynamic systems). It would however be possible to recommence from the beginning jobs running in batch mode, but this would hardly be a practical proposition.

Compile time and execution time errors

26. Compile time errors. When a source program is being compiled from a high-level language to a machine code object program, the compiler generates error diagnostics indicating the type of error in the various instructions—particularly syntax errors. Such errors must be corrected before progressing with program testing. Interactive compilers produce error diagnostics after every statement or instruction, whereas batch compilers list the errors at the completion of the compilation run.

27. Execution time errors. These may be defined in two different ways as follows.

(*a*) *Program error.* Microcomputers programmed in BASIC have interpreters, in ROM chips, for converting BASIC statements into machine code at execution time, i.e. at the time the program is run. It is only then that syntax and other types of error—logical errors—are signalled. This can be very frustrating as it can delay the running of the program. Errors should be detected and corrected during program testing prior to running the program on live data. The unexpected error may still arise at the most inopportune moment.

(*b*) *Data errors.* Data errors are detected when a program is run. These may be detected interactively when using a microcomputer, from validation checks built into the program. The computer automatically indicates if the incorrect type of data is being input, i.e. whether numeric data instead of alphabetic characters, or vice versa. When batch processing on a mainframe computer, the initial run is for validation purposes to detect errors before the data is subjected to processing (*see* 9:**30**).

Closed and open shop programming

28. Closed shop programming. This is a restriction whereby programmers are not allowed to test programs on the computer themselves but must allow the computer operations staff to do this on their behalf and provide the test results. The reason for this restriction is to curtail the use of the computer to the operations staff in order to minimise the time the computer occupies on program testing and to avoid disrupting routine processing schedules.

29. Open shop programming. This is a facility provided to programmers for program testing, which allows them to use the computer themselves, providing they are suitably experienced. This provides flexibility in program testing and does not rely on the good offices of operations staff to get the job done. If on-line programming facilities are available then there need not be any disruption to routine processing.

Closed and open subroutines

30. Open subroutine. An open subroutine is inserted into the main sequence of instructions, rather than transferring control to a subroutine, in a specific part of a program when it is required. When this definition is analysed the following considerations must be made. If it is a common subroutine then it will be repeated frequently throughout the program—this may apply when rounding values to one decimal place—which will increase the storage space required in the internal memory. On the other hand processing time may be saved by not having to branch to the subroutine each time it is required.

31. Closed subroutine. A closed subroutine is one which is inserted in the program once and is referred to when required by a GOSUB or CALL instruction. After execution of the subroutine, control is returned to a specific part of the program automatically. A 'stack' keeps control of subroutine operations and a branch back to the main routine is accomplished by a RETURN instruction, which automatically returns control to the instruction following the GOSUB instruction last executed.

32. Subroutine library. Subroutines can be stored in backing storage in a subroutine library, and can then be accessed by a CALL command when required for execution at a specific stage of processing the main program.

33. Link editing. The process of link editing can be applied for combining both external subroutines—those stored in a subroutine library on disc—and those specifically prepared for a particular application by the programmer. The input/output routines and other routines when combined form a complete suite of programs for a particular application. Consolidated programs can then be stored on disc ready for loading and execution at the appropriate time, i.e. run time.

Program maintenance

34. Volatile systems. Business systems are volatile as they are continuously being affected by external environmental influences of a random nature. Such influences may be due to changes in technology, competition or legislation. It is therefore necessary for business systems to be dynamic and respond to such influences appropriately.

35. Maintenance programmer. Programs are modified by a maintenance programmer who not only modifies them, for the reasons already indicated, but also keeps them up to date to accord with internal system changes for improving administrative efficiency. Systems may be integrated whereby separately structured systems are combined for improving their productivity.

In addition, programs may be modified to provide for changes in company policy. For example, changes in the payroll program to facilitate amendments to long service increments.

Progress test 18

1. What is the nature and purpose of a program specification? (**1–3**)

2. Specify the nature and purpose of programming standards. (**4**)

3. Indicate the nature of computer instructions.   (**5**)

4. Describe the stages in creating a working program in a high-level language.   (**6**)(*C & G*)

5. Describe the stages carried out by a programmer in the development of an application program.   (**6**)(*IDPM*)

6. List FOUR factors which are important in producing an efficient computer program.   (**6**(*a*)–(*f*))(*C & G*)

7. What is the purpose of a breakpoint in the context of programming?   (**7**)

8. Outline the nature of low- and high-level languages.   (**8–11**)

9. Specify the nature of diagnostic aids in a high-level lan-

guage. (**12, 13**)

10. Define the term 'monolothic' programming. (**15**)

11. (*a*) Describe the following program design techniques: (*i*) modular; (*ii*) structured. (*b*) Draw a comparison between these design techniques. (**16–20**)(*IDPM*)

12. What is meant by STRUCTURED PROGRAM? What advantages are claimed for structured programming? (**17**)(*C & G*)

13. Define the nature and purpose of the following approaches to program design: (*a*) top-down approach; (*b*) functional decomposition; (*c*) data-driven design. (**21–23**)

14. List the MAJOR differences between high-level and low-level languages. Explain, with the aid of examples, the advantages and disadvantages of BOTH types of language. (Tables 18A and 18B)

15. Explain the difference between compile time errors and execution time errors. Explain how a program dump may be used to rectify certain programming errors. Distinguish between a program dump and a dump used in dump-restart procedures. (**24–27**) (*C & G*)

16. Describe briefly the difference between closed shop and open shop programming. (**28, 29**)(*C & G*)

17. Distinguish between open and closed subroutines. (**30, 31**) (*C & G*)

18. What is a closed subroutine? What arrangements must be made to link it with the calling program? (**31–33**)(*C & G*)

19. State the importance of program maintenance. (**34, 35**)

19
Flowcharting and decision tables

Program flowcharts

1. Flowchart. Program flowcharts, sometimes referred to as computer procedure flowcharts, are often prepared as a preliminary to program coding to assist in determining the logical aspects of a problem and the correct sequence of statements required. Program flowcharts also show input operations, setting of counters, testing of counters, loops and branching, etc.

2. Flowchart symbols. By convention there exist a number of standardised symbols used for the draughting of flowcharts of all types (*see* Fig. 19.1). The symbols used for program flowcharts distinguish between an operation, i.e. a basic processing step, and a test including logical tests for establishing whether certain conditions exist in the data to be processed which determined the conditional branching requirements of a program.

Program flowcharting exercises

Questions relating to flowcharting problems arise quite frequently in examinations. The following are examples.

3. Program flowcharting exercise 1. This is a CIMA question which requires in the solution the setting and decrementing of a counter, program loops, conditional and unconditional branching.

Draw a program flowchart to read cards and accumulate the

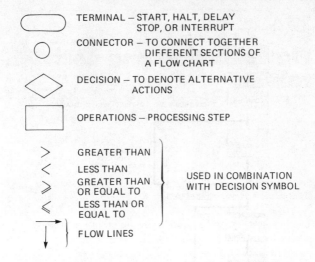

Figure 19.1 *Program flowchart symbols.*

quantities read into 10 fields in core, depending on the code in the card and print out the 10 totals, each on a separate line.

Card layout	Columns
Code	1–2 (range of 01–10)
Quantity	3–5 (max. 999, min. 001)

SOLUTION

Figure 19.2 provides the solution to this question.

4. Program flowcharting exercise 2. This is a question set by the Association of Certified Accountants. The solution necessitates testing for the end of a record and the end of a file; computing and accumulating values.

Data from a batch of customers' orders is held on magnetic tape and, for each customer, consists of: (*i*) customer account number; (*ii*) quantity of each product ordered; (*iii*) price per unit of product.

Where a customer orders more than one product, quantity and price are repeated for each item until all his requirements have

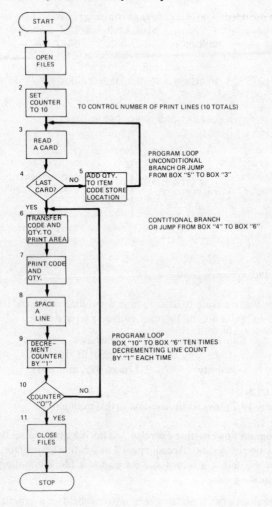

Figure 19.2 *Program flowcharting exercise 1.*

been included. The end of customer marker is '0' and the end of file marker is '–1'. You are required to draft a program flowchart to print out:

> (a) the value of each separate product sale on each order;
> (b) the total amount to be charged to each customer;
> (c) the total value of the entire batch or orders.

SOLUTION
Figure 19.3 provides the solution to this question.

5. Program flowcharting exercise 3. This is a CIMA question relating to file updating, necessitating the use of program switches.

Draw a program flowchart to update a stock master file held on a magnetic disc in item reference order. The input to update the master file includes receipts and issues and is held on magnetic tape which has been sorted by a previous program into the following sequence: (a) item reference; (b) receipts; (c) issues.

The control totals are the only items to be printed by this program.

SOLUTION
Figure 19.4 provides the solution to this question.

Decision tables

6. Use and construction of decision tables. Decision tables are used in the process of analysing the factors involved in a problem, which necessitates defining the conditions specific to the problem and the actions to be taken when the various conditions arise.

A computer program written for a specific application must provide for branching to appropriate parts of the program when specified conditions in data are discovered after testing.

A decision table enables the branching requirements of a program to be precisely specified.

Decision tables may be used to assist the preparation of a complicated flowchart to ensure that all conditions and actions have been catered for and that cause and effect relationships are clearly visible.

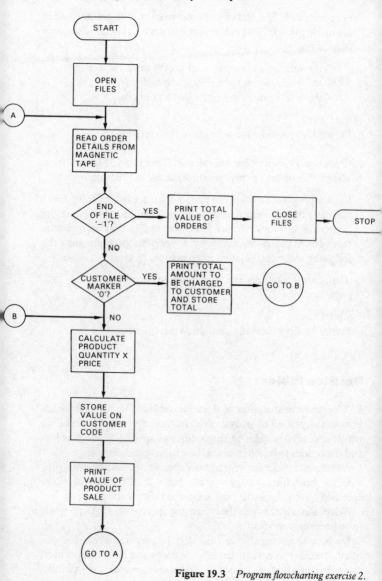

Figure 19.3 *Program flowcharting exercise 2.*

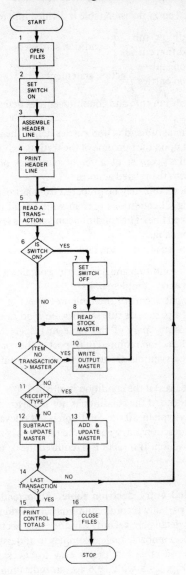

Figure 19.4 *Program flowcharting exercise 3.*

A limited entry decision table is divided into four parts:

(a) condition stub
(b) condition entries } condition statement
(c) action stub
(d) action entries } action statement

The condition stub and condition entries define the conditions to be tested.

The action stub and action entries define the actions to be taken dependent upon the outcome of the testing.

The 'rules' consist of a set of outcomes of conditions tests, together with the related actions.

A decision table may be prepared from a procedure narrative by underlining all conditions present with a solid line and all actions with a broken line. The conditions and actions are then recorded on the decision table.

The features of a decision table are as follows.

(a) Each condition and action stub contains a limited entry, that is to say an entry complete in itself.

(b) The entry part of the table in respect of the condition stub indicates if a particular rule satisfies the condition.

(c) The entry part of the table in respect of the action stub indicates the action required in respect of the condition entry.

(d) Three symbols are used in the condition entry part of the table.

 (i) Y (yes) if the condition is satisfied.
 (ii) N (no) if the condition is not satisfied.
 (iii) - (hyphen), if the condition is not relevant to the rule.

(e) In the action entry part of the table is **x** is recorded to signify a required action. If no action is required the column is left blank.

7. Extended entry decision table. An extended entry decision table only partially records conditions and actions in the stub. The remaining details are recorded in the entry sections. This type of table is more compact and less complex to understand than a limited entry decision table but is less easy to check for completeness. Compare Fig. 19.5 with 19.6 for an indication of the difference

	RULES			
	1	2	3	4
CONDITION STUB	CONDITION ENTRY			
SALES REGION CODE ⩾ £50	Y	Y	N	N
INVOICE AMOUNT ⩾ £1000	Y	N	Y	N
ACTION STUB	ACTION ENTRY			
DELIVERY CHARGES				
ADD £15 TO INVOICE TOTAL			X	
ADD £20 TO INVOICE TOTAL	X			
ADD £30 TO INVOICE TOTAL				X
ADD £40 TO INVOICE TOTAL		X		

SALES REGION CODE	⩾ 50	⩾ 50	< 50	< 50
INVOICE AMOUNT	⩾ 1000	< 1000	⩾ 1000	< 1000
DELIVERY CHARGES	£20	£40	£15	£30

Figure 19.6 *Extended entry decision table.*

between a limited entry and extended entry table.

8. When to prepare and use a decision table. A decision table may be used to assist the preparation of a program flowchart when the detailed logic involves a number of complex decisions. This ensures that all possible combinations and actions are met. The program flowchart is then prepared on the basis of one rule at a time working through the decision table. Decision tables may be used when programmer time is limited and the available software permits the direct input of decision tables.

Decision tables and program flowcharts

9. Decision table and flowchart exercise 1. This is a CIMA question.

Stockists Limited calculates discounts allowed to customers on the following basis:

Order quantity	% Normal discount
1–99	5
100–199	7
200–499	9
500 and over	10

These discounts apply only if the customer's account balance is below £500 and does not include any item older than three months. If the account is outside both of these limits, the above discounts are reduced by 2 per cent. If only one condition is violated, the discounts are reduced by 1 per cent. If a customer has been trading with Stockists Limited for over five years and conforms to both of the above credit checks then he is allowed an additional 1 per cent discount.

You are required to:

(a) construct a limited entry decision table illustrating the above situation; and

(b) draw a flowchart illustrating the above situation.

SOLUTION

The solution to this question is illustrated in Figs. 19.7 and 19.8.

10. Decision table and flowchart exercise 2. For additional practice in the preparation of decision tables and flowcharts the reader

CONDITION STUB	RULES											
	1	2	3	4	5	6	7	8	9	10	11	12
	CONDITION ENTRIES											
ORDER QUANTITY < 100	Y	Y	Y	Y								
ORDER QUANTITY < 200	–	–	–	–	Y	Y	Y	Y				
ORDER QUANTITY < 500	–	–	–	–	–	–	–	–	Y	Y	Y	Y
ACCOUNT BALANCE > £499	Y	Y	N	N	Y	Y	N	N	Y	Y	N	N
ANY ITEM OLDER THAN 3 MONTHS	Y	N	Y	N	Y	N	Y	N	Y	N	Y	N
TRADED FOR OVER 5 YEARS	–	–	–	Y	–	–	–	Y	–	–	–	Y
ACTION STUB	ACTION ENTRIES											
NORMAL DISCOUNT 5%	X	X	X	X								
NORMAL DISCOUNT 7%					X	X	X	X				
NORMAL DISCOUNT 9%									X	X	X	X
NORMAL DISCOUNT +1%				X				X				X
NORMAL DISCOUNT –1%		X	X			X	X			X	X	
NORMAL DISCOUNT –2%	X				X				X			

Figure 19.7 *Decision table and flowchart exercise 1: decision table.*

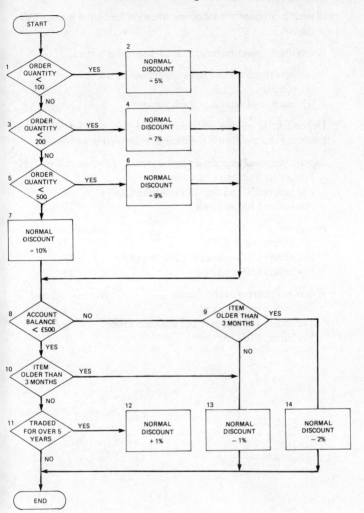

Figure 19.8 *Decision table and flowchart exercise 1: flowchart.*

may wish to attempt the following question set by the former IAS, now the AAT.

A soft drinks manufacturer sells to three sales outlets,

(a) supermarkets and large departmental stores
(b) retailers
(c) hotels and catering establishments.

Dependent upon the sales outlet and the value of sales, the following chart indicates the discounts allowed to customers.

Supermarkets and large departmental stores:	*Discount allowed %*
For orders less than £50	5
For orders £50 and over but less than £100	8
For orders £100 and over	10

Retailers:	*Discount allowed %*
For orders less than £50	3
For orders £50 and over but less than £100	7
For orders £100 and over	10

Hotels and catering establishments:	*Discount allowed %*
For orders less than £50	4
For orders £50 and over but less than £100	7½
For orders £100 and over	10

	1	2	3	4	5	6	7
CONDITION STUB	CONDITION ENTRY						
ORDER ⩾ £100	N	N	N	N	N	N	Y
RETAILER	Y	Y	N	N	N	N	—
HOTEL & CATERING	—	—	Y	Y	N	N	—
S & L	—	—	—	—	Y	Y	—
ORDER < £50	Y	N	Y	N	Y	N	—
ACTION STUB	ACTION ENTRY						
DISCOUNT							
3%	X						
4%			X				
5%					X		
7%		X					
7½%				X			
8%						X	
10%							X

Figure 19.9 *Decision table and flowchart exercise 2: decision table.*

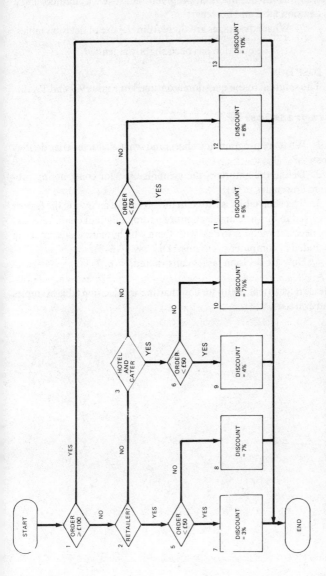

Figure 19.10 *Decision table and flowchart exercise 2: flowchart.*

(*a*) From the information given, construct a 'limited entry' decision table and flowchart.

(*b*) What advantages are there from the use of decision tables?

NOTE: The question has been slightly amended.

SOLUTION

The solution to the question is outlined in Figs. 19.9 and 19.10.

Progress test 19

1. What are program flowcharts and what characteristics do they possess? (**1**)

2. Define the nature of the symbols used for constructing program flowcharts. (**4**)

3. 'Decision tables are used in the process of analysing the factors involved in business applications regarding inherent conditions and the necessary actions to deal with them which, of necessity, must be included in computer programs.' Discuss. (**6–8**)

4. How are decision tables constructed? (**6, 7**)

Please refer to text (**3–10**) for flowcharting and decision table examples and exercises.

20
Software profile

The nature of software

1. **Definition**. Software is the term used to describe program support which enables computer hardware to operate effectively.

A computer system consists of both hardware and software, and it is only by the intelligent combination of both that the best results are obtained. Hardware is a collection of machines which can only perform tasks when directed to do so by the software.

Software enables a general-purpose computer configuration to be transformed into a special-purpose system for carrying out a unique series of tasks for a number of different applications.

In general, software consists of the programs used by a computer prepared either by the manufacturer or user, but, specifically, the term embraces the operating systems and application programs supplied by the computer manufacturer.

2. **Types of software**. The nature of software is as wide and as varied as the nature of the work performed by computers. Software includes programs for accounting, financial planning and control, managerial planning and control, communications, word processing and utility programs. To some extent the nature of the computer determines the tasks to be performed, which in turn determines the type of software required. A small home computer will have a need for games programs or home utilities such as money management, budgeting or letter writing programs. Small business and main-frame computers will necessitate the need for software relating to accounting matters in respect of payroll processing, stock control

and integrated accounting systems, etc. Most computers can utilise some form of word processing or database/records management software.

The types of software available for computers in general may be summarised as follows.

Table 20A   Spectrum of software

Nature of software	Type of software	Typical examples
System control	Operating system – general	Disc operating systems (DOS) UCSDp system CP/M UNIX DME/3 VME/K
	Operating system – networking	Designed to access local and networked resources (CP/Net)
Accounting packages	Application processing	Integrated accounting system General ledger Order processing Invoicing Payroll Stock control Sales ledger (sales accounting) Purchase ledger (purchase accounting) VAT records Business graphics
Managerial planning and control	Problem solving and optimising packages	Bill of materials (BOMP) Production control (OMAC) Project planning and control (PERT)

Table 20A *Continued*

Nature of software	Type of software	Typical examples
		Deployment of scarce resources (optimiser) Linear programming (LP) Simulation Priority decision system
Financial planning and strategy	Financial modelling packages	General financial planning (The financial director) Financial strategy (Busicalc) Financial planning by use of spreadsheet (Micro Plan, Supercalc) Integrated spreadsheet modelling, Graphics, WP, database and communications (Silicon office)
Communications	Communications software	Access to Prestel and private viewdata systems (Owltel) Teletype communications (Micro-Linkline) Downloading (Interlink)
Various applications	Word processing packages	Text processing (WORDPRO, WORDSTAR)
	Various	Letter writing Diary planner Mailing list

Table 20A   *Continued*

Nature of software	Type of software	Typical examples
	Database/data management systems	Card index Data and records management systems (many and varied) Natural language database query system Expert systems
System utility programs	Systems software aids	Editing Media conversion card or floppy disc to disc tape to disc Dumping files Job control language (JCL) Sorting/merging Report generators Housekeeping Debugging/trace routines Disassemblers Assemblers and compilers Program generators Expert systems builder
Sub-routines	Standard routines	PAYE routine for payroll processing Routines common to several programs
Home finance	Home management packages	Money management Budgeting
Games	Mainly for home computers	Many and varied
Miscellaneous	Programs for special purposes	Property management Civil engineering Builders

Table 20A *Continued*

Nature of software	Type of software	Typical examples
		Farm management
		Airline operations including seat reservation systems
		Hotel management and reservation systems
		Insurance
		Banking
		Building society administration
		Tour operators
		Electricity and gas boards, etc.

All computers whether mainframes, minis or micros, including those defined as 'home', 'personal' or 'business' computers require software. The degree to which software is used however, is dependent upon the processing power of the particular computer. Some computers operate on the basis of a standardised operating system which provides access to a wider range of software than would otherwise be possible. Other computers have large internal memories which is an essential prerequisite for the running of large, complex programs, and others have high resolution graphics facilities which widen the software horizons further.

No distinction is to be made between the various types of computer in relation to software apart from operating systems as it is considered appropriate to outline the general nature of software. Each job or application requires a set of instructions to accomplish the purpose and objectives of the system whether it is payroll processing, sales invoicing and sales ledger updating or stock control, etc. An essential element of software is the operating system.

Microcomputer operating systems

3. **Type of operating system.** Some microcomputers for home computing use cassette files which require a cassette-based operat-

ing system implementation. Disc-based microcomputers, however, function under the control of a disc operating system known as DOS. An operating system performs many important tasks which assists the activities of programmer and operator alike.

4. Booting. Some microcomputers have the operating system resident in ROM (read only memory) which is immediately available when the computer power is switched on. Others have the operating system stored on disc which has to be 'booted' into RAM by internally stored software. In such instances it is possible to use alternative operating systems such as MS-DOS instead of, or in addition to, CP/M which greatly enhances the number of applications packages available thereby providing a wider range of choice. A computer with the facility for interchanging operating systems is very versatile. Typical microcomputer operating systems include the following.

5. CP/M. CP/M is an abbreviation for Control Program for Microcomputers. It was developed by Digital Research Inc. and is their trade mark. It has a very large software base which means there are many software application packages designed to run under CP/M. One version is used for eight-bit home computers and another, CP/M sixteen-bit, is used for the later sixteen-bit computers. Concurrent CP/M-86 provides single-user multi-tasking facilities which allows the computer to process several programs simultaneously perhaps printing out one application whilst loading data for another and processing data on another. MP/M-86 is a multi-user system for sixteen-bit computers.

6. MS-DOS. An abbreviation for MicroSoft Disc Operating System. It has a large software base which means it is a popular system being used by various computers. This operating system is known as PC-DOS on the IBM PC. MS-DOS is an operating system designed for sixteen-bit computers which are usually business-orientated machines. MSX-DOS is used in the MSX eight-bit machines and Concurrent DOS is used for multi-tasking machines.

7. UNIX. This operating system was initially designed for minicomputers but is now being used on the more powerful models of microcomputers. It supports multi-tasking as well as multiple terminals connected to a single system. It is widely accepted as the main multi-user system available. Xenix is a multi-user system based on UNIX.

8. Apple DOS. This operating system is used on the Apple series of computers and is an eight-bit system. It has a large software base as many programs were written to run on Apple machines which are quite popular. It occupies relatively little memory compared with other operating systems as it is not so sophisticated.

9. BOS. BOS is an abbreviation for Business Orientated multi-user System linked to Microcobol. It has a limited software base which requires to be written in a specific version of Cobol.

10. Typical operating system commands. The commands listed below relate to MS-DOS but are representative of those used by other operating systems to a greater or lesser extent.

1. DIR	Lists the files in a directory with their size in bytes.
2. CLS	Clears the monitor/terminal screen.
3. TYPE	Displays the contents of a text file on the screen.
4. COPY	Copies one or more files to another disc.
5. DELETE	Deletes files from a disc.
6. DISKCOPY	Makes backup copies of contents of one disc to another.
7. DIR:SORT	Lists alphabetically sorted disc directory.
8. FIND	Searches for a specific string of text in a file.

Mainframe operating systems

Regarding the larger type of computer, the ICL 2950 has a choice of operating system, either the DME/3 (Direct Machine Environment) or VME/K (Virtual Machine Environment). The operating systems used by IBM's large processors are MVS/SP (Multiple Virtual Storage/System Product) and VM/SP (Virtual Machine/

System Product). It is now proposed to outline some of the features of MVS/SP.

11. MVS/SP (Multiple Virtual Storage/System Product). IBM provides two versions of MVS/SP. Version 1 is designed for IBM System/370, 4341, 303X and 3083/81 installations. Version 2 is an option for the IBM 3083/81 family and is designed to support installations with large networks, databases and applications. The systems resources manager is in control of all the work being processed. The resource usage of all operators is controlled and priority given according to the specifications agreed and set by the installation. Individual applications and transactions can be given order of priority. System resources—processor, input/output and storage can be balanced between testing and production work. MVS/SP schedules and priorities work automatically across multi-processors. If one processor becomes unavailable the other can continue processing without operator intervention. It prevents unauthorised access to data in main memory. The RACF (Resource Access Control Facility) provides protection of an installation's data. Access to any protected resources can be limited to authorised users. Personal passwords allow access to specific applications and information. Fast response times are provided to users of the TSO (Time Sharing Option) while handling other work. Job networking allows work, data and commands to be passed between central processors that may be remote from each other or connected in the same location. This allows for off-loading of work from one centre to another or the facility to send the job to the location of the data.

12. VM/SP (Virtual Machine/System Product). This system is supported on IBM System/370, 4300, 303X and 3083/81 processors. It is designed to enhance other IBM system control programs. With VM/SP each user appears to have his own dedicated computer, as all users have their own virtual machines.

13. Choice of operating system. Some manufacturers are offering a choice of operating system for their machines such as MSDOS, CP/M86 and Concurrent CP/M. It is possible to switch automatically between processors depending upon the specific application of those machines which are also providing both an 8-bit and 16-bit processor.

14. Typical tasks performed by an operating system.

(*a*) Execute and monitor input and output operations.

(*b*) Monitor the status of hardware devices.

(*c*) Monitor and process hardware interrupts.

(*d*) Format new discs.

(*e*) Maintain disc directories.

(*f*) Execute disc reading and writing operations.

(*g*) Diagnose disc errors.

(*h*) Execute disc commands relating to the deletion, copying, renaming and dumping of files.

(*i*) Report on the status of disc usage and bytes available.

(*j*) Control file read-only protection.

(*k*) Provide work area in internal memory for programs.

(*l*) Provide for loading programs, chaining between programs and passing parameters.

(*m*) Receive, interpret and execute commands from the operator.

(*n*) Provision of facilities for inputting and editing commands.

(*o*) Assigning logical input/output devices to the various input/output ports.

(*p*) Provision of batch processing of commands.

(*q*) Implement the use of passwords.

(*r*) Provision of debugging aids.

Job Control Language (JCL)

15. Purpose of JCL. The purpose of JCL is to control the running of jobs on a computer. Often on a large computer several jobs are run concurrently in multiprogramming mode. The JCL enables the names of jobs, the files to be used, the peripherals required, priorities of the various jobs and interrupt procedures to be specified. It enables a computer operator to communicate with the operating system by means of the console for the purpose of controlling the processing of the various jobs.

16. Job control language. Job control commands are written in a job control language. In batch processing applications the job commands are usually predefined and input with a source or object program with the relevant data, or are stored in a 'command file'. Special symbols distinguish commands from program instructions. Examples of job control commands are listed in Table 20B below.

Table 20B   Job control commands

Mainframe computers	BASIC for use with microcomputers	Timesharing systems
Compile	Run	Login
Execute	Load	Logout
Delete	Save	EOJ (End of Job)
Start	Verify	
Sort	Clr	
Dump	List	
Edit	New	

The BASIC commands may be defined as follows:

(a) Run—the computer executes the program resident within the internal memory.

(b) Load—the computer loads a program from backing storage into the internal memory.

(c) Save—records a program stored in the internal memory to cassette or disc backing storage.

(d) Verify—ensures that a program has been 'saved' correctly.

(e) Clr—clears the screen.

(f) List—lists a program stored in internal memory on the screen.

(g) New—clears the internal memory of program and variables ready for a new program.

Utility programs

17. Utility programs defined. Utility programs are also referred to as 'service' or 'general-purpose' programs, as they are used for applications in general regardless of the nature of specific application programs. All processing activities require the support of utility programs, particularly when processing data in batch mode. This type of processing requires operations of a routine nature such as 'sort/merge' for the purpose of arranging transactions into the sequence of the master file to which they relate prior to file updating; the conversion of data from one media to another, e.g. the conversion of data in floppy discs to magnetic tape or high speed discs after being validated. This arrangement enables data to be processed faster; copying of files for security purposes usually applies only to disc files which are copied to magnetic tape; reorganising disc files periodically to eliminate overflow conditions on the tracks; house-keeping routines including such tasks as the writing of header labels on magnetic tape files, the blocking and deblocking of records and zeroing memory locations to ensure garbage is eliminated; and input/output routines and so on.

18. Examples of utility programs. In addition, other utilities include 'toolkit' which is a program for enhancing the BASIC language by additional commands, such as TRACE, AUTO and RENUMBER, all of which assist the tasks of programming and debugging of programs. Toolkits are loaded either from backing storage or they reside on a chip. 'Trace' is a software facility which enables programs to be checked for the detection of errors. Each step in a program is monitored by the software and displayed on the video screen while the program is running. A 'disassembler' is software which converts machine code into assembly code, i.e. mnemonic code. It enables machine code programs to be stepped through one instruction at a time for editing purposes. 'Report program generators' such as NCR's PICO (Parameter Input/COBOL Output) allows programmers to custom-design report programs by simply entering report parameters through a video display terminal. PICO generates the report from the program with or without user code identification. The parameters permit data access from up to ten data files providing versatile report design.

Other facilities allow programmers to develop programs from remote terminals on-line to a computer. This allows programs to be created, modified, tested and debugged interactively without interrupting routine processing, as both can run concurrently.

A software tool, known as Visual Information Processor (VIP), allows software companies to write programs with a common user interface. It is written in the systems language—C and has a collection of link utilities which allows the software companies to adapt their programs to run on different machines. Programs that use VIP have many of the benefits associated with Apple's Lisa.

Sub-routines consist of instructions to perform tasks common to many different applications, an example being the PAYE routine which affects all payroll programs. This is called into the main program when the relevant stage of processing is reached. Whether the main program is a software package or an internally developed program, the PAYE routine would be obtained from the computer manufacturer. Its use avoids the necessity of writing the routine for every installation running the payroll application. In other instances, entirely different programs require a similar sub-routine for performing a common series of instructions; this may relate to statistical computations or the printing of column headings at the top of each page of a report, etc. They are stored in a library until required, when they are called into the internal memory. This subject is discussed further in the chapter relating to programming (*see* 18:**30**–**31**).

Program generator

19. General features. Program generators are software packages which allow non-computer specialists to develop their own application programs. The task is made easier than writing the program with a normal high-level programming language such as BASIC. This is mainly due to the software generating the equivalent of several BASIC statements. One such program generator or program builder is marketed by System C Limited.

The package may be used to develop traditional business applications such as payroll, accounts, invoicing and stock control. It can also be applied to the development of programs for applications where ready-made programs are unavailable. This type of package can also be usefully employed by experienced programmers as the Sycero programs are structured and documented in a manner which facilitates linking with other programs.

20. Building a program in 7 steps. Using Sycero, as an example of program builders or generators, the process of program building is very straightforward and can be accomplished in 7 steps.

(*a*) *Plan the system.* Define the elements of the system you want to create, the types of data to be input, the screen layouts for required displays and how many files are needed. Determine how

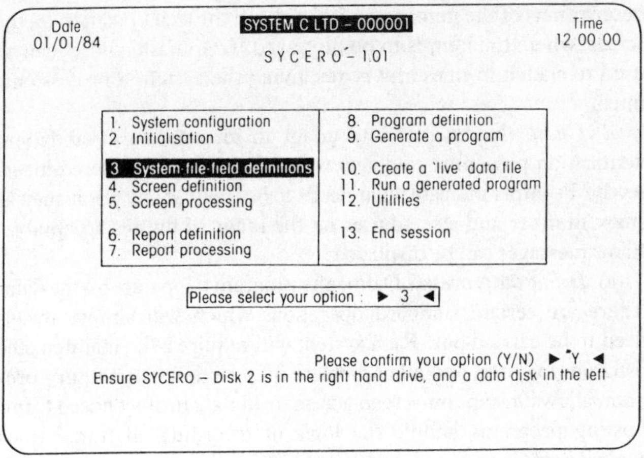

Figure 20.1 *Menu display: program generator.*

the program is to handle the information.

(*b*) *Specify the system.* With the micro running proceed to select items from the main menu. By following the prompts, define the types of files required and what items of information they will contain. The menu offers the following options.

  (*i*) system configuration;
  (*ii*) initialisation;
  (*iii*) system-file-field definition;
  (*iv*) screen definition;
  (*v*) screen processing;
  (*vi*) report definition;
  (*vii*) report processing;
  (*viii*) program definition;
  (*ix*) generate a program;
  (*x*) create a 'live' data file;
  (*xi*) run a generated program;
  (*xii*) utilities;
  (*xiii*) end session.

(*c*) *Draw the screens.* Having specified where and how data is to be stored it is necessary to specify how the data is to be entered and displayed on the screen of the computer. On each screen type in descriptions of the items to be entered and the exact position on the screen where the item is to be displayed. Graphics facilities can be used to sketch in lines and boxes giving the system a professional finish.

(d) *Check the data.* It is prudent to incorporate a validation/verification procedure to detect when data has been entered incorrectly. Prompts indicate what needs to be input at any point such as stock number and also advises on the range of figures acceptable. Error messages can be displayed.

(e) *Define the program.* Define the program to operate on the data. There are certain standard operations which will almost always need to be carried out. Each system will require a file maintenance program to enter, amend and delete information. An enquiry program allows instant on-screen access to all data in any chosen form. Posting programs handle the logic of recording all transactions against a single item and updating files.

(f) *Produce the printout.* The system is now built and it is necessary to specify the printed output requirements, i.e. the Report Definition, i.e. the formatting. The system provides facilities for defining where on a printed page columns are to appear, how they look, what their headers are like and so on. Column totals can be generated, each page can be numbered and printouts can be stamped with the date and time.

(g) *Generate.* The Sycero software requires to know the name of the program. It then translates the data defined and specified into a computer program. The code produced is very lucid and structured.

21. General aspects of report generators. The NCC Microsystems Centre lists in the region of 40 packages in its software directory. These range in price from approximately £85 for a micro-oriented package to run on micros like the Apple, to £2,500 for a mini-based package. The price of program generator packages is also related to the operating system, to some extent, and a package for the Unix multi-user system costs in the region of £2,000. For MSDOS the cost is in the region of £400–£750.

Application packages

22. International Directory of Software. This is a publication by Computing Publications Ltd which assists the selection of software packages. It describes 5 100 software products under 107 categories and 24 industry groupings. The publication also provides Quarterly Bulletins. The products contained in the directory include Accounting, Administration and Banking, Communications, CAD/CAM, Data Management, Development Aids, Distribution, Insurance, Microprocessor Systems, Modelling and Statistics, Production and Utilities.

23. Source of packages. Packages are available from a number of sources depending upon the type of computer. Programs for microcomputers, for instance, are available from mail order sources as advertised in computer magazines; or over the counter from retail shops and stores. Packages are also available from dealers in microcomputers, who provide hardware and software, and directly from the computer manufacturer in some instances.

Software for the larger computer, i.e. mainframes, is available from a number of sources including the manufacturer of the hardware who also develops the software, from specialist organisations known as software houses, and from private organisations who have developed programs for their own use which they make available to other users for an appropriate fee. Packages are also available from a number of computer bureaux who have expanded their activities.

24. Cost of software. Sometimes a minimum of software is supplied free of charge when the hardware is purchased, this is referred to as being 'bundled' and would include the operating system, utilities and applications software. Other software has to be purchased as required on an 'unbundled' basis, it is charged separately.

Microcomputer manufacturers often have a sales promotion policy of providing extensive software with the machine at no extra cost, in order to generate sales of the hardware. This is dependent upon the economic circumstances which prevail at the time and whether a new model is to be launched or new software is becoming available, etc.

25. Package defined. Packages are pre-written computer programs which are widely used for common applications in order to avoid unnecessary duplication of similar programs by many users. It is a means of rationalising programming effort but this does not imply that the same type of package is not available from more than one source. They are sometimes provided to suit the needs of different models of computer and sometimes in competition. The need to shop around is no less than with competing sources of supply of other commodities and products.

A package consists of a suite of programs, sometimes on the same storage media, for the different routines required to achieve the purpose of the specific application. It consists of documentation in the form of a program/systems manual, containing details of how to set up the program and run it on the computer. The package also includes the relevant media on which the program is stored. This is usually tape or disc.

26. Package compatibility. Whether a package is suitable for a particular model of computer depends upon a number of factors. Packages for a specific make of computer are designed to run on the model with a defined memory capacity, therefore packages will not run on machines with less than the specified memory capacity. Compatibility also depends on the operating system being used (i.e. whether it is standard, such as the MS/DOS operating system). Standard operating systems have a wide range of packages available which can run on any machine using that particular operating system, regardless of the make of machine.

When manufacturers of the larger mainframe computers launch a new model they normally provide for a migration path from one machine to another by making software compatible for the older model and the later model.

In other instances packages are designed to be run on disc based systems and others on cassette or magnetic tape (large reels) based systems. Once again the type of operating system is important because disc operating systems vary, i.e. some discs are soft-sectored and others hard-sectored (*see* 6:**32**).

In other instances a package may be compatible with the system but incompatible with regard to the hardware, so it is important initially to choose a computer that can accomplish system requirements on specific hardware. Dialectical variation in a programming language such as BASIC is also a determining factor, as many machines have their own versions of the language and programs will run only on machines using a specific version.

Credit card-type microchip

27. RAM and ROM card. A credit card-type microchip called Astron is marketed by Cumana. It is a high capacity RAM and ROM card which is being developed to have a storage capacity of one Mbyte.

28. Alternative to floppy disc. It is envisaged as an alternative to floppy disc for the storage of programs. It is likely to be adopted by software houses because of the degree of protection it offers against copying. The card's memory also aids the protection of software because of its capability of storing in-built encryption facilities. *Note:* integrated packages are discussed in Volume 2.

Outline of accounting packages

As an example of the facilities offered by accounting packages, the details outlined below are based on the packages available from MPSL who distribute BOS (Business Operating Software).

29. Sales ledger. This provides facilities to maintain customer accounts from the entry of invoices, credit notes, payments and journals through to credit checking, production of statements and cash forecasting. Both balance forward and open item accounting are available.

30. Invoicing. This provides facilities to produce invoices and credit notes and sales analyses by customer, product, territory and salesman. Invoicing automatically maintains stock records and sales ledger accounts. The invoicing package requires the sales ledger package.

31. Inventory control. This provides facilities to maintain stock records, to record and control stock issues and receipts, to check reorder levels and lead times and to provide total financial management of stock.

32. Purchase ledger. This provides facilities to maintain all aspects of a company's purchase ledger; from the logging of transactions and the approval of payments, through to the calculation of discounts, scheduling of payments, printing of cheques and credit transfers and the maintenance of supplier details.

33. Nominal ledger. This provides facilities to maintain all aspects of a company's accounts. The package accepts input directly or from the sales ledger package, purchase ledger or fixed assets package and produces profit and loss statements, trial balances, balance sheets and detailed schedules by company, department and account type.

34. Payroll. This provides facilities to produce payslips, credit transfers and management reports for a company payroll. The package fulfils all Inland Revenue requirements for the calculation of tax deductions, contracted-in and contracted-out National Insurance and covers SSAP reporting (UK).

35. Order processing. This handles all aspects of multi-warehouse sales order processing: back orders, forward orders, regular orders, picking lists, delivery notes and invoices. Order details per product and per client can be displayed on demand. This package requires the sales ledger package and operates in conjunction with the inventory control package and microsafes.

36. Fixed assets. This maintains a complete register of the fixed assets of a company or group of companies, and automatically calculates depreciation either by historical cost or current cost conventions. Current cost accounting conforms to SSAP 16(UK).

37. Menu driven packages. Many package programs, especially for microcomputers, function on an interactive basis allowing the user to select the required option. In a stock control package the user can select the code for the required option from the 'menu' displayed on the screen (*see* Fig. 20.2). The various codes provide for item creation, item change, item deletion, stock enquiry, stock posting, printing of a stock list or reorder list, etc. A return to the menu is achieved by pressing a defined key indicated by the program. A different option can then be selected. This interactive mode enables newly created records containing errors to be corrected by keying in the code for 'item change', followed by the key field of the item to be corrected.

STOCK CONTROL MENU

(1) NEW ITEM
(2) PRINT ITEM DETAILS
(3) DELETE ITEM
(4) STOCK MOVEMENTS
(5) DISPLAY ITEM DETAILS
(6) PRINT MINIMUM STOCK REPORT
(7) PRINT FULL STOCK LIST

ENTER SELECTION

Figure 20.2 *Screen display: stock control menu.*

Electronic card index and electronic diary

38. Electronic card index. With the advance of technology into the office it is foreseeable that the normal office cabinet will tend to be less frequently used and will perhaps disappear completely in the not too distant future. The reason for this is the prevalence of databases and smaller versions of databases called electronic card index systems. With the aid of a microcomputer and a software package, records can be created and stored electronically on cassette or disc. One such system allows for up to ten lines per card and up to 255 cards. Records can contain one to twenty-five cards. The records can be searched, browsed through and printed. Facilities are also provided for calculations on any two fields. A mailing list can also be printed.

39. Electronic diary. Some microcomputers have diary software available to assist the business executive in keeping track electronically of his appointments. The software has facilities which enable details of appointments to be input, sorted, browsed through on the video screen and edited. Data can also be stored in backing storage. One can immediately have the day's appointments to hand by displaying the contents of the diary file each morning.

Arguments for and against the use of packages

40. Arguments for the use of packages. These are summarised as follows.

(a) Programmers are able to concentrate their efforts on applications for which no suitable packages exist due to the special nature of a particular task.

(b) It is unnecessary to employ specialist programmers, particularly when using microcomputers, as packages are available for most requirements.

(c) Applications can be up and running (operational) much more quickly than would be the case when developing one's own computer systems, including the writing of programs.

(d) Expertise is 'built-in' when using packages which, in effect, deskills the use of computers, particularly the use of micros.

41. Arguments against the use of packages. These may be summarised as follows.

(a) Package programs may take longer to run than specially written programs, but this depends on the relative skill of programmers and whether machine code is used rather than high-level languages. Compiled programs usually take longer to run because they contain more instructions than machine code requires to achieve a specific task.

(*b*) It may be necessary to modify a package, as it may not be compatible with system requirements in all instances and this fact will increase the cost of the package.

(*c*) Purchased programs may cost more than internally written programs but this is dependent upon the expected volume of sales of the package since the larger the sales volume the lower the cost to the ultimate user, as the development costs are spread over a greater volume of sales.

Assembler

42. Definition. This is a program which translates a 'source' program, written in an assembly or programming language, into a machine code 'object' program.

The translation process is performed by the computer itself, and this is known as 'automatic programming'.

43. Purpose. The purpose of such a procedure is to simplify and speed up the task of programming by enabling the programmer to write programs in a language much simplified compared with that used for writing programs in machine code. Therefore, instead of writing a program which is immediately compatible to the computer, a program is written which is more compatible to the programmer for solving the problem and the computer is used for the conversion of the program to one which it can interpret and execute.

44. Translation. The assembler translates symbolic or mnemonic function codes into the equivalent machine codes and symbolic addresses into actual internal store locations. Each mnemonic instruction is normally converted into a machine code instruction on a one-for-one basis, but it is possible to use the technique of 'macro-coding', which enables a complete sub-routine to be incorporated into the object program by means of writing a single 'macro-instruction'. Once again, the objective is to simplify the task of programming.

45. Object program. The term object program is used to define the program which is generated by the translation process and which is then used for processing the data of a specific application. The term source program is self-explanatory, as it is the original program written for processing the data of a specific application but which is not directly usable by the computer.

After translation, the object program is retained either in magnetic tape or magnetic disc. In addition, a print-out is produced by the line-printer of both the source and the object program instructions, for comparison and error checking. It is also possible to have a print-out of diagnostics as an aid to error checking.

Compiler

46. Definition. This is a program which translates a source program, written in a high-level language, into a machine code object program.

A compiler performs the task of assembling the object program, but is generally more complex than an assembler because each source program instruction in a high-level language such as COBOL generates a number of machine code instructions, i.e. a macro-instruction generates a number of micro-instructions.

As a result of the increased complexity, the compiler is larger in terms of the translation instructions it contains, and this produces a problem of internal storage capacity, as a large amount of storage is required, to accommodate the compiler during the compilation run. It is sometimes necessary to compile a program on a computer which is different to that on which the compiled program will be run on account of this factor. As a matter of interest, this is the reason for stating the source computer and object computer in a COBOL program.

47. Purpose. Compiling is performed for similar reasons as for assembling—to reduce the complexity and time involved in writing programs.

48. Storage requirements. To give some idea of the storage required for both assembling and compiling, it must be appreciated that during translation the internal memory must hold the source program, the compiler or assembler and the resulting object program.

Interpreter

49. General features. Interpreters are usually used by personal or small business computers, whereas mainframes utilise compilers. Interpreters and compilers are translation programs which, in respect of small computers, convert statements written in BASIC into machine code. When the command 'run' is keyed in, each statement in the program is interpreted and if any statement does not conform to the rules or grammar (known as syntax) of the language then a syntax error is displayed on the screen. This can be a disadvantage as it slows down the execution of the program until the errors are removed. In addition, each statement is interpreted each time the program is executed and this also tends to slow down its execution.

50. Switch to compilers. Many small computers now have compilers available, which means it is only necessary to translate the program once, during the compilation run, and the compiled program is then stored on tape or disc backing storage until the relevant application is to be run. As each statement does not have to be translated at 'run time' the program runs faster than an interpreted program. An interpreter is more 'firmware' than 'software' as it is stored on a ROM (read only memory) chip which is part of the electronics of the computer.

Modelling packages and spreadsheets

51. General characteristics of a modelling package. A suite of application programs designed to provide for the needs of business, i.e. financial and corporate planning, including cash flow and balance sheet projections, etc. A package in general consists of a model-building language, model-running language, report generator, What-if? facilities, and a statistical sub-system for data analysis. The language used to describe the model is usually straightforward and easily learned by non-computer specialists, which allows models to be constructed and run on a computer by accountants, corporate planners and managers.

52. Spreadsheets. In addition to the more usual application packages there are business modelling packages available such as Supercalc. It allows the user to create a spreadsheet or electronic worksheet on which to define the problem. A spreadsheet is an alternative technique which allows the computer to be used for what may be called pencil and paper calculations for preparing budgets and profit forecasts, etc. It allows recomputations to be made on all relevant data very speedily in response to changes to specific variables such as selling price, volume or overheads. The 'what if' facilities allow budgets to be computed very quickly and amendments made in the simplest possible manner automatically. The underlying principle of the spreadsheet is that the video screen operates as a highly flexible window. The window 'rolls' automatically so as to display the area around the current cursor position. The screen can be segregated into smaller windows if necessary. The worksheet is viewed through the window. The window and spreadsheet do not physically exist as they are simulated by controlling the display on the screen. The spreadsheet is divided into a grid of small rectangles known as cells. The cells contain numeric data, text or formulae and each cell can be identified by co-ordinates (*see* Fig. 20.3). *Note:* The subject of spreadsheets is expanded upon in Volume 2.

Word processing

53. Characteristics of word processing. Word processing is primarily concerned with the normal typing requirements of a business as distinct from the reports produced by data processing systems. Whereas data processing is concerned with processing data in the most efficient manner, word processing is concerned with processing words in the most efficient manner.

The term word processing is currently used as a more fashionable or sophisticated name for automatic typing which was first used by IBM. Word processors may be called jet-age typewriters, but that is only part of the story as word processing equipment has electronic

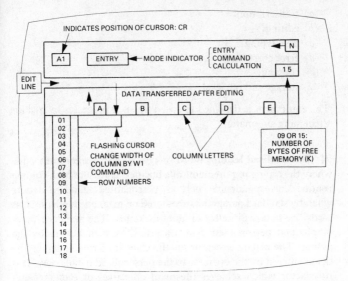

Figure 20.3 *Spreadsheet: main features of screen image.*

intelligence which generally consists of a processing unit supported by a separate memory. It is mainly this intelligence which distinguishes the word processor from the older automatic typewriter.

The technique is meant to provide increased cost effectiveness in respect of the typing requirements of a business. Technological developments are such that it is difficult for the prospective user of word processing equipment to keep pace with the changes taking place. It is this factor which makes the choice of suitable equipment very difficult, especially when this is linked to the need to learn how to use it in the most effective manner. There are many different makes and models on the market which have different characteristics and capabilities.

Word processing equipment should not be implemented without first conducting a feasibility study as it involves a change of method and necessitates the use of capital intensive equipment instead of typists. The method or technique of word processing is primarily for accomplishing the following office functions:

(*a*) transcription;
(*b*) editing;
(*c*) final typing;
(*d*) error correction;
(*e*) copying;
(*f*) storage and retrieval.

The equipment is designed to speed up such processes by making them more automatic.

54. Personalised letters. Word processors are of significant value where the typing requirements of a business consist of high volume routine correspondence such as personalised standard letters whereby standard paragraphs are stored on magnetic media such as cards, cassettes, diskettes or mini-diskettes. The standard paragraphs and personalised details are indicated on a form by the author. The machine then prints the standard letter, reducing the detail entered by the operator to the personalised details only. It is this factor which achieves the main objectives of economy and efficiency because standard paragraphs are not constantly retyped at the speed of the typist but at the automatic speed of the machine, which can be in the region of 920 words a minute. With conventional typing the speed of a typist is greatly reduced by the need to make corrections and to completely retype text, as well as paper handling, interruptions and fatigue. A possible speed in the region of fifty to seventy words a minute is reduced to ten to fifteen words a minute by these factors. Extensive retyping also increases stationery costs, and produces additional wear on typewriter ribbons and the typewriter.

Lengthy reports or high quality text which usually require extensive editing and revision can be processed to advantage on word processing equipment as the correction of errors is simplified because to erase an error it is only necessary to backspace and retype the character, since characters are stored magnetically in the same way as in a computer system. This feature also enables words to be added to, or inserted on, any line on the magnetic media without having to repeat the remainder of the line. Word processing equipment offers no advantage in respect of short one-off letters or memos.

55. Benefits. The main benefits of word processing systems may be summarised as follows:

(a) increased volume of output;
(b) higher level of quality;
(c) increased speed of output;
(d) higher level of productivity;
(e) reduced level of fatigue;
(f) lower level of costs.

Progress test 20

1. What is software? (**1**)
2. What types of software are used in computer operations? (**2** and Table 20A)
3. Define the nature and function of an operating system. (**3–14**)
4. (a) What is the purpose of a job control language (JCL)? (b) List FOUR commands in any JCL with which you are familiar and state how and when they are used. (**15, 16**)
5. Explain what is meant by the term UTILITY PROGRAM. Give examples of THREE frequently used utility programs. (**17, 18**)
6. Define what is meant by a program generator and specify its purpose. (**19–21**)
7. Indicate the sources of packages, stating the cost factors which must be considered. (**22–24**)
8. Outline the nature of typical accounting and other business packages. (**29–37**)
9. Define the terms: (a) electronic card index; (b) electronic diary. (**38, 39**)
10. Give the arguments for and against the use of a pre-written computer applications package as the solution to a business problem. Use an example to illustrate your arguments. (**40, 41**) (C & G)
11. Specify the nature and purpose of an assembler. (**42–45**)
12. Distinguish between the mode of operation of a compiler and that of an interpreter. (**46–50**) (C & G)

13. Outline the general characteristics of a modelling package. (**51**)

14. Specify the features and uses of spreadsheet packages. (**51**)

Appendix
Examination technique

Examination questions in respect of data processing and management information systems are often descriptive and aim to test the candidates' knowledge of how well-defined principles are applied to business situations or problems.

The subject is very wide and practical, candidates should always take care to demonstrate fully the wider implications of what may appear to be very narrow questions.

The examination candidate is recommended to observe the following points.

1. Read each question thoroughly before attempting an answer, in order to avoid any initial misunderstanding of the requirements of the question. A good answer to the wrong question does not score marks.

2. Allocate sufficient time to answer each question. It is fatal to omit an answer to a question through spending too much time on other questions. It is much better to have a fairly complete answer on all the questions rather than no answer at all on some of them.

3. Having determined the requirements of each question, the first one to be attempted should be selected. It is good practice before committing yourself to the answer paper to jot down main headings or topics to be covered on a scrap pad. By this means, initial thoughts may be clarified and the full scope of the question appreciated.

4. The answer may then be written on the answer paper, observing the following points.

(a) Write legibly to enable the examiner to interpret your answer easily.

(*b*) Show a good command of English, sentence structure and grammar.

(*c*) Outline the answer on the basis of topic or subject headings sub-analysed as appropriate as follows:

(*a*)
   (*i*)
   (*ii*)
(*b*)
(*c*)
   (*i*)
   (*ii*)
   (*iii*)

By this means the examiner can easily assess the points being made and can more readily appreciate their relevance and award marks accordingly.

(*d*) Keep to the subject and be as concise as possible without unnecessary padding—you either know the subject or you do not. Make sure you do before sitting the examination, even if only to save examination fees.

5. Allow sufficient time to read the answers before handing in the paper so that corrections can be effected.

6. Answer questions from your own experience whenever possible, as this shows the examiner that you are conversant with the subject in question.

7. Some answers require the presentation of a flowchart or other recording technique, and it is important to use drawing aids in their construction, i.e. charting symbol templates, coins (for circles), and a rule (for straight lines). Neatness of presentation is very important if maximum marks are to be gained. It is also essential to determine the type of flowchart required, e.g. procedure chart, system flowchart (runchart) or program flowchart.

Index

M&E Handbooks

Law

'A' Level Law/B Jones
Basic Law/L B Curzon
Cases in Banking Law/P A Gheerbrant, D Palfreman
Cases in Company Law/M C Oliver
Cases in Contract Law/W T Major
Commercial and Industrial Law/A R Ruff
Company Law/M C Oliver
Constitutional and Administrative Law/I N Stevens
Consumer Law/M J Leder
Conveyancing Law/P H Kenny, C Bevan
Criminal Law/L B Curzon
English Legal History/L B Curzon
Equity and Trusts/L B Curzon
Family Law/P J Pace
General Principles of English Law/P W D Redmond, J Price, I N Stevens
Jurisprudence/L B Curzon
Labour Law/M Wright, C J Carr
Land Law/L B Curzon
Landlord and Tenant/J M Male
Law of Banking/D Palfreman
Law of Evidence/L B Curzon
Law of Torts/J G M Tyas
Law of Trusts/L B Curzon
Meetings: Their Law and Practice/L Hall, P Lawton, E Rigby
Mercantile Law/P W D Redmond, R G Lawson
Private International Law/A W Scott
Public International Law/D H Ott
Sale of Goods/W T Major
The Law of Contract/W T Major
Town and Country Planning Law/A M Williams

Accounting and Finance

Auditing/L R Howard
Basic Accounting/J O Magee
Basic Book-keeping/J O Magee
Capital Gains Tax/V Di Palma
Company Accounts/J O Magee
Company Secretarial Practice/L Hall, G M Thom
Cost and Management Accounting – Vols 1 & 2/W M Harper
Elements of Banking/D P Whiting
Elements of Finance for Managers/B K R Watts
Elements of Insurance/D S Hansell
Finance of Foreign Trade/D P Whiting
Intermediate Accounts/L W J Owler
Investment: A Practical Approach/D Kerridge
Partnership Accounts/J O Magee
Practice of Banking/E P Doyle, J E Kelly
Principles of Accounts/E F Castle, N P Owens
Taxation/H Toch

Humanities and Science

Biology Advanced Level/P T Marshall
British Government and Politics/F Randall
Chemistry for 'O' Level/G Usher
Economic Geography/H Robinson
English for Professional Examinations/J R L McIntyre
European History 1789–1914/C A Leeds
Geology/A W R Potter, H Robinson
Introduction to Ecology/J C Emberlin
Land Surveying/R J P Wilson
Modern Economic History/E Seddon
Political Studies/C A Leeds
Sociology 'O' Level/F Randall
Twentieth Century History 1900–45/C A Leeds
World History: 1900 to the Present Day/C A Leeds

Business and Management

Advanced Economics/G L Thirkettle
Advertising/F Jefkins
Applied Economics/E Seddon, J D S Appleton
Basic Economics/G L Thirkettle
Business Administration/L Hall
Business and Financial Management/B K R Watts
Business Organisation/R R Pitfield
Business Mathematics/L W T Stafford
Business Systems/R G Anderson
Business Typewriting/S F Parks
Computer Science/J K Atkin
Data Processing Vol 1: Principles and Practice/R G Anderson
Data Processing Vol 2: Information Systems and Technology/R G Anderson
Economics for 'O' Level/L B Curzon
Elements of Commerce/C O'Connor
Human Resources Management/H T Graham
Industrial Administration/J C Denyer, J Batty
International Marketing/L S Walsh
Management, Planning and Control/R G Anderson
Management – Theory and Principles/T Proctor
Managerial Economics/J R Davies, S Hughes
Marketing/G B Giles
Marketing Overseas/A West
Marketing Research/T Proctor, M A Stone
Mathematics for Economists/L W T Stafford
Microcomputing/R G Anderson
Modern Commercial Knowledge/L W T Stafford
Modern Marketing/F Jefkins
Office Administration/J C Denyer, A L Mugridge
Operational Research/W M Harper, H C Lim
Organisation and Methods/R G Anderson
Production Management/H A Harding
Public Administration/M Barber, R Stacey
Public Relations/F Jefkins
Purchasing/C K Lysons
Sales and Sales Management/P Allen
Statistics/W M Harper
Stores Management/R J Carter